The Changing Dimensions of Security: India's Security Policy Options

The Changing Dimensions of Security: India's Security Policy Options

Editor

Dr SURESH R.

Associate Professor & Hon. Director
V K Krishna Menon Study Centre for International Relations,
Department of Political Science,
University of Kerala,
Kariavattom Campus, Thiruvananthapuram,
Kerala State

Vij Books India Pvt Ltd
New Delhi (India)

Published by

Vij Books India Pvt Ltd
(Publishers, Distributors & Importers)
2/19, Ansari Road
Delhi – 110 002
Phones: 91-11-43596460, 91-11-47340674
Fax: 91-11-47340674
e-mail: vijbooks@rediffmail.com
we b: www.vijbooks.com

Copyright © 2015, Suresh R.

First Published : 2015

ISBN: 978-93-84464-80-6

All rights reserved.

No part of this book may be reproduced, stored in a retrieval system, transmitted or utilized in any form or by any means, electronic, mechanical, photocopying, recording or otherwise, without the prior permission of the copyright owner. Application for such permission should be addressed to the publisher.

The views expressed in this book are those of the contributors in their personal capacity. These do not have any official endorsement.

CONTENTS

Contributors	vii
Introduction	1

PART – I. The Changing Dimensions of Security- A Theoretical Perspective

1. India's Strategic Thinking and Policy Options   24
   Professor Mohanan Bhaskaran Pillai

2. Insecurity and the Search for Security: A Biological Perspective   39
   Dr S. Sathis Chandran

3. Examining India's National Security Semantics: A Theoretical Consideration   49
   Dr Nanda Kishor M S

4. Theorizing the Sino-Indian Ties in the Emerging Global Order   65
   Dr Harish K. Thakur

PART – II. India's Security Concerns in the Emerging Global Order

5. The Defence Aspect of India's National Security   81
   Professor B Vivekanandan

6. Nuclear South Asia: Strategic and Security Dimensions   88
   Dr C. Vinodan

7. Indo-US Nuclear Deal and India's Nuclear Policy   120
   Mr Rajesh Kuniyil

8. Sino-Indian Relations in the Era of Globalization — 142
Dr Devender Sharma & Dr Ved Prakash Sharma

9. Pakistan's Afghan Policy in Post 2014 Scenario: Options for India — 152
Dr Sudhir Singh

PART – III. Maritime Security of India: The Challenges and Options

10. Challenges and Options for a Maritime India in the 21st Century — 169
Commodore R S Vasan

11. Terror on High Seas — 184
Dr Vibhuti Singh Shekhawat

12. Emerging Maritime Threats and Challenges in India's Marine Domain: Post 26/11 — 190
Dr Mukund Narvekar

13. Post 26/11 Terrorist Threats in India – Is National Counter Terrorism Centre alone the Solution? — 228
Mr. Unnikrishnan G

PART – IV. Human Security in India: The Challenges and Policy Options

14. India's Security Challenges and Policy Options: A Human Security Perspective — 239
Dr Suresh R

15. The Changing Dimensions of Security and Emerging Nontraditional Threats in South Asia: A Human Security Perspective — 254
Mrs. Rakhee Viswambharan

Index — 267

Contributors

1. **Dr. Mohanan Bhaskaran Pillai**, Professor & Coordinator, UGC Special Assistance Programme Department of Politics & International Studies, Pondicherry University.

2. **Dr. S. Sathis Chandran**, environmentalist.

3. **Dr. Nanda Kishor M S**, Assistant Professor, Department of Geopolitics and International Relations, Manipal University, and Post-Doctoral Fellow (Erasmus Mundus), Leiden Institute of Area Studies, Leiden University, Netherlands.

4. **Dr. Harish K. Thakur,** Associate Professor, Department of Political Science, Govt. College, Sunni, Himachal Pradesh University, Shimla.

5. **Professor B Vivekanandan**, Former Chairman, Centre for European and American Studies, Jawaharlal Nehru University, New Delhi.

6. **Dr. C. Vinodan**, Assistant Professor & Chair Centre for Strategic and Security Studies, School of International Relations and Politics, Mahatma Gandhi University, Kottayam, Kerala.

7. **Mr. Rajesh Kuniyil**, Deputy Director, ICSSR Research Project, School of International Relations and Politics, Mahatma Gandhi University, Kottayam, Kerala.

8. **Dr. Devender Sharma & Dr. Ved Prakash Sharma**, Research Associates, Department of Political Science, Himachal Pradesh University, Shimla.

9. **Dr. Sudhir Singh**, Faculty, Department of Political Science, Dayal Singh College, University of Delhi.

10. **Commodore R S Vasan,** Head, Strategy and Security Studies, Center for Asia Studies, Chennai & Director, Chennai Centre of

China Studies.

11. **Dr. Vibhuti Singh Shekhawat**, Associate Professor & Head, Department of Humanities and Social Sciences, Malaviya National Institute of Technology, Jaipur, Rajasthan.

12. **Dr. Mukund Narvekar**, Assistant Professor, Department of Political Science, Goa University, Goa.

13. **Mr. Unnikrishnan G,** Senior Research Fellow UGC, Department of Political Science, University of Kerala, Thiruvananthapuram, Kerala.

14. **Dr. Suresh R**, Associate Professor, Department of Political Science, University of Kerala, Thiruvananthapuram, Kerala.

15. **Mrs. Rakhee Viswambharan**, Assistant Professor & Head, Department of Political Science, Sree Narayana College, (University of Kerala) Chempazhanthy, Thiruvananthapuram, Kerala.

Introduction

With the end of the cold war, the concept of security has come under analysis from scholars of international relations and other discipline. In the classical formulation, security is about how nation states use force to manage threats to their territorial integrity, their autonomy, and their domestic political order, primarily from other nation states. This classical national security formulation has been criticized on various grounds. A nation may be secure but does not mean that all people living in that nation are secure. The social economic and political orders prevalent in that nation have an implication on the security of the people.

The debates on security is centered mainly on the assumptions about what security is, what is being secured, the causes of insecurity, and how best to address insecurity. International relations theorists and policy experts have varying perspectives on these questions, which have evolved and have had changing levels of acceptance over time. Realists and neo-realists emphasise the nation state as the central referent of security, both as the lens through which security is understood, as well as the tool by which security is best maintained. Liberal theorists recognize a wider set of values embedded in the concept of the state and state security, in the methods and means to address insecurity, and the actors involved. The critical constructivist scholars understand that the interests and identities of nation states are themselves constructed by the distribution of ideas and interests within the state-based system and this shapes a state's security interests and how these are conceived, and in turn impacts upon the actions necessary to ensure security. Thus there are divergent views with regard to concept of security, whose security, that is whether the security of the nation or people, the causes of insecurity, and how to ensure security.

The Westphalia state system had made nation states as the basic unit in the international system. And nation states are sovereign and independent. Each nation decides their internal and external policies. The prime responsibility of a nation state is to promote and protect its national interests. The national interests of nation states are mainly to ensure peace, security and prosperity within its territories. However they differ with regard to the means adopted to achieve these national interests. Some nations employ aggressive means and some peaceful methods. And foreign policy of a nation is the means to achieve their respective national interests. Therefore, though the national interests are similar nations frame divergent foreign policy, which in turn is conditioned by the interplay of internal and external factors. Thus, the foreign policy changes in accordance with the transformations in the internal and external conditions so also the security policy.

Independent India took the initiative to a nonaligned foreign policy rooted on the Indian tradition of faith in nonviolence. However, the cold war politics of super power rivalry and competitions along with an unfriendly atmosphere in the South Asian region prompted India to fall in the lines of power politics as propounded by the realist. The ensuing armament, arms race and competitions prompted India to keep its nuclear weapon option open and also involve in a 'civilian cum military alliances' with the former Soviet Union. At that period the international politics was purely based on power politics and India and likeminded nations had only limited policy options to ensure security of the nation from external threat.

However, the end of cold war and the ongoing globalization process along with the proliferation of nontraditional threat to security of the nations led to accelerated pace of multilateralism in international relations. Though the great powers are not ready to accept the new developments, the post-cold war events such as threat from non-state actors to the security of nation, the global economic slowdown, and global climate change compelled even the most militarily powerful nation to seek multilateral approach to address these trans-border menaces.

The ideological confrontations during the cold war led to armament, arms race between the capitalist bloc and communist bloc nations. During the cold war period military security was the dominant security concern of nation states as the threat to security of nations emanates solely from rival nation states. However, in the changed context of international power structure and the advent of nontraditional threat to the security of nations along with the ongoing economic integration at the global level and greater interaction of people across the world transcending artificial territorial boundaries compelled the nation states to evolve a common strategy to address emerging security concerns.

The global movements towards democratization and protection and promotion of human rights supported by ICT once again brought individuals rights and security into focal point. It appears that even if nations are secure people living there may not be secure. The civil wars taken place in some nation states to protect the rights of multiethnic groups or the demand for right to self-determinations of people are examples of such a situation. In this context security means people's security and international efforts are required to ensure people's security from any threat emanates from within or outside the nation states. Thus human security assumes great significance in the post-cold war era of profoundly interdependent global system.

The initiative taken by the new government at the federal level towards good neighbourhood and better relation with great powers along with focusing more on human security issues appears to be policies in the right direction. The shift from a land centric security paradigm to maritime security and coastal security are also visible in recent times. The initiative towards coastal security with the active involvement of coastal dwellers, in fact promotes human security. There is a blurred boundary between national security and human security in the case of coastal security. Any initiative to improve the living condition of the coastal folk would ultimately lead to better people-security agency relations and consequently better national security. In the emerging coastal security initiatives the coastal people were considered as the eye and ears of security agencies involved in coastal security.

Thus when it comes to security policies the internal and external factors are significant. The internal security challenges posed by various extremist organizations within India with external support can also better addressed through our focus on human security issues especially the poverty alleviation and reduction of unemployment. The good neighbourhood and a better relation with external powers are very important for India to address its own internal human security issues.

However, when it comes to implementation of policies one of the major hurdle before political executive in India is the Colonial trained permanent executive or bureaucracy. They have been trained to maintain *status quo*. Therefore, any major change initiated by political executive with regard to foreign policy or security policy will be resisted or delayed by the bureaucracy. Mere policy statements without commensurate action are of no use in both domestic as well as external sphere. A change in the mindset of the permanent executive is *sine qua non* for any major shift in policy decisions and subsequent implementation.

Another major hurdle is the propaganda unleashed by certain paid 'strategic thinkers' and 'think tanks'. They at times precipitate a minor border skirmish to the level of war like situation through the use of modern media. They also at times act as agent of arms race. It would be very difficult for the political executive to convince the citizens about the real situation, when there is collusion between these agencies and the permanent executive. Since national security is such an important concern of the nation no democratically elected government dare to take a strong radical stand ignoring the public opinion. Thus though there is marked change in security situation at the regional and global scenario there is no commensurate change in the security policy. This book is an attempt to examine the changing dimension of security and the policy options.

In a well-structured article entitled 'India's Strategic Thinking and Policy Options' Professor Mohanan Bhaskaran Pillai traced the evolution of India's strategic thinking and analyzed it lucidly. He maintained that India's security environment is very much complex with its internal and external dimensions. He had pointed out that the two most important security issues before India are jihadi ideology with its various shades and utter poverty of teeming millions. The attempt has been to identify the most suitable policy options to tackle these two and other security concerns of India. Such an enquiry, he pointed out that, has naturally taken us to the strategic culture of India and the grand strategy/doctrine originated from the platform of the country's strategic culture. He further maintained that extensive studies have been undertaken by foreign and Indian scholars to delineate the nature of India's strategic culture. However many Indian scholars have pointed out that India do not have an explicitly stated security doctrine and it is a major drawback in framing policies for addressing complex security issues. He had concluded that a quick

Introduction

overview of the foreign and strategic behaviour of India shows that the recurring theme in India's policy behaviour is strategic autonomy.

Dr S. Sathis Chandran, the well-known environmentalist in his insightful article on 'Insecurity and the Search for Security: A Biological Perspective' pointed out that the primary motivation of life has always been search for security. In other words this can be stated as striving to guarantee individual survival safeguarding resources for the present and for the future expansion of the species which includes producing enough progeny. The story of evolution of life has been episode after episode of confronting challenges and continuing beyond crises. The manifestation of life forms has been changing all through these eons in form and function and also less obviously in the potential of each individual and species. While changing, all life forms have been exerting themselves to modify their habitat, both its living and non-living components, so that it becomes better suited for more species.

He maintained that we too have been doing it but a bit too successfully helped by our technology and the machines. Our interventions have been extremely selfish. These modifications are meant exclusively for ourselves and a handful of other species which we consider domesticated. And all the modifications have really not been for the better in our long-term survival but they have been effected for our short-term conveniences and comforts. This is the most tragic part of it. So automatically most of our inventions, discoveries and the intellectual assets have no survival value judged by the utterly impartial judge, selection for evolutionary continuity. No, not the continuity of the human species alone but the continuity of a biological species as an integral part of an ecosystem.

He argued that all human achievements also are to be judged on the criteria of enhanced security for the species. Food security and reproductive success are basic criteria for assessing the evolutionary success of any species. From this point of view human beings are confronting a disastrous failure at the end of a couple of lakhs of years of evolutionary venture. For the modern human being, food security is not a simple matter of finding enough energy through eating to ward off predators, to reproduce and to contribute to own species welfare. For the modern human being, at least since the dawn of agricultural revolution a couple of thousand years ago, food security has become an integral part of the complex social survival scaffolding. This scaffolding is supported by the other pillars namely social security, economic security and ecological security.

Currently only a small fraction of the human kind is directly involved in food production, essentially agriculture, animal husbandry and fisheries. Beyond the process of food production an extremely complex social institutional web is essential to reach food to whoever has the economic power to afford food. In a society rapidly descending to disorder, the food production as well as the distribution system and the even more complex economic system which makes money available to those who want to purchase food have all lost viability in the long-term. The concept of social security is nowadays re-designated as legal or policing correction or a downright violent disruptive social engineering.

Even if we can take care of food security along with social and economic security, maintaining ecological security to sustain the purely biological operation of plant and animal growth which are the basis of agriculture is highly uncertain. This is further magnified in the context of global climate change.

The hottest and the most widely discussed current topic, taken up in the widest range of fora across the world is global climate change. There has been a series of very high profile conclaves during the past couple of decades attended by the largest number of heads of nations representing practically the entire human population. There have been meetings in locations spread all around the world. Armies of scientists have formed panels, consultative groups and so on to work out the technical backup for discussions. The topic of discussion in all these assemblies have been global warming i.e., extreme climate oscillation. And of course all of this has been at an enormous cost. In any case most of us have realised or experienced firsthand by the end of 20th century that this is a serious problem confronting the humankind irrespective of race, nationality, political shade of government or the economic or military power of nations.

In spite of all the time, energy and expectations invested against the backdrop of the deepening crisis we have not dared to touch the core issue but have been going round and round the periphery. Specious arguments, dilatory measures, scientific evasions have been aplenty. On a political basis there has been a deluge of mutual recrimination between the traditional massive polluters whom we identify as the developed nations and the developing nations who are in reality those nations who hope to become even more massive polluters. But all the while we have been dancing around the periphery, within the central stage the real issue has been growing, mushrooming beyond definable dimensions and feasible answers.

Shorn of details, the crux of the problem is very clear. The earth's atmosphere is retaining more and more incoming solar radiation. The chemistry and dynamics of the earth's atmosphere is changing in an unforeseen manner. Regular cyclic processes have become unpredictable. For life in general the biosphere is becoming uncomfortable. Not only the atmosphere, but also the earth's surface is steadily warming up. The unaccustomed (at least for our species in recent times) amount of heat energy circulating within the biosphere is accelerating and altering patterns of flow of matter and energy. All atmospheric phenomena including wind, rain, snow fall and so on, are changing in intensity and pattern. Similarly the oceanic circulations are also changing rapidly. What is really happening within the lithosphere we are not very sure. Accelerated weathering for sure is happening but what else we can't say.

Within living systems everything is going haywire. While the normal population ranges of many species are collapsing resulting in uncountable species extinctions, in the case of few other species (including some undesirable species as far as we are concerned) numbers are increasing and ranges are expanding. Oldest and the most complex ecosystems are getting diluted and disintegrating. Many fragile smaller systems are literally imploding overnight. Naturally on earth all systems are interconnected and act as feedback circuits. Causes and consequences are so inextricably intertwined, reason is at a loss.

For us the writing on the wall is very clear. During the past couple of centuries our population has increased incredibly fast, occupying every bit of habitable earth. We have sucked in all that is of potential use to us labelling them resources and tied them up with a monetary priced consumer value system. This in a sense can be termed selling or sending them down the drain. Simultaneously we have built up an extremely complex but very vulnerable top heavy social structure. This human edifice requires unsustainably massive paraphernalia of artifacts and behaviour patterns. To keep this going we have to use subsidies, coercion and outright violence.

The current discussion on global climate change to some extent focuses on energy subsidy. That too on the fossil fuel dependent energy generation. Everyone is experiencing in some facet of their existence the consequences of this mode of energy development. The political as well as economic fallout of it is more immediate and tangible than the environmental where the spatial and temporal dimensions of impact are poorly understood. The consequences of the economic subsidies for the current human developmental design we are seeing as the neglect and collapse of basic critical social development sectors such as education, health care and so on. Most of the monetary investment gets diverted elsewhere. The environmental consequences of the social developmental debacle are less clearly articulated. The dilution, distortion and usurpation of the true human potential under pressure from collapsing economic and social order we see around us as greater violence in societies, deeper fault lines within families, communities and countries, denial of justice between cultures, nations and so on. But the consequences of the loss of true human potential which would have been channelized toward the corrective mechanisms to tackle global warming remains unexplored. The final outcome is the dearth (or is it really the death?) of hope. No one may try to change what is happening now even if the problem and the solution are clear.

In spite of all the econometric equations and political rhetoric, he maintained, the very simple fact is that the continuity and stability of human society depend on the interplay of food security, social security and economic security. Food security is possible if only the social structure remains stable. Social stability depends on cultural security. Economic security is essential if people are to buy food. We may have all the agricultural technology, energy and institutional mechanisms but we would not be able to guarantee food security. We may have high GDP, high industrial growth rate and a stable currency but these would be no guarantee for food security for all the citizens of the country. And now with States failing all over the world, not only Somalia, Haiti or Afghanistan, people may swarm across borders and security of any sense cannot be guaranteed by border guards or fences. Ultimately the basic hard foundation for the crop plant, for the civil society and even for the mirage of the financial institutions to survive, there must be environmental security. But the simple question is whether we will grasp this point in time. The current period is being called the Anthropocene because human activities have a most decisive impact on earth equivalent to a geological upheaval. And the sixth wave of extinction is actually extermination of species by direct and indirect human activity. Dwindling food supply, population pressure, uncongenial changes in the habitat and so on would have often pushed species to search for more secure living conditions. But in the case of Homo sapiens apparently these were not the prime motives for the simmering deep disquiet. Human kind moved out of Africa and within an extremely short time and behaving like an invasive species spread over all the continents except Antarctica. They also left a trail of deep dark devastating footprints, not a legacy to be very proud of.

He further argued that we evolved rituals which became the basis of religion and developed our sophisticated artistic aesthetic culture. But all the while the deeper disquiet gnawing at our innards deflected us from a peaceful and peaceable existence. We had to invent harsh and punitive patriarchal Gods and carry out senseless bloodletting to appease them. We had to negate the all giving Earth and fabricate a virtual heaven out in the cosmos. We evolved incredibly complex religious rituals and constructed powerful hierarchical social institutions to safeguard us from punishment after death. But these institutions only carried out witch hunts, crusades and inquisitions ably helped by horrendous torture equipment. With the same religious fervour we fabricated ideologies from which we expected solutions for all our worldly problems and erected hierarchical ruling institutions which then we had to suffer. But they also carried out bloody purges and ran death camps. None of these institutions contributed to our elementary survival needs. Our contorted fears and guilt taking control of our ability for innovation created rock paintings in the caves in Pyrenees 20,000 years ago. But our modern shamans ended up creating poison gas, nuclear bombs, biological warfare and star-war strategies. In short, most of what we proudly assembled during the last 12 or 20,000 years not only had very little biological survival value, but they also seriously undermined our very survival possibility.

He had emphatically pointed out that our insecurity has mushroomed to gigantic dimensions partly because of our sheer unsustainable numbers, deadly toxic technologies and our collective cynical negation of all ethical or altruistic values. The attitude that we used to refer to as humane has been erased effectively by our present day religions, our education and value systems. We began by being afraid of natural forces. Out of fear we decided to control them. So we began playing God. We deluded ourselves in our attempt to rearrange all the forces that frightened us. We claim we have control over nature. We may have left our footprints on the lunar dust but we have also been tearing apart the surface of the earth for our conveniences and have succeeded in damaging it seriously.

History, he says, is an essential critical perception to view anything, detached from frozen boundaries of space and time. A historical perspective alone can give us the ability to look closer and see the earlier stages of what we call the present. History alone will help us project the trajectory of the present into the future. Without this clearer and more tangible perception of the future, our steps would not merely be faltering but could very well be in the wrong direction. States competing for resources, markets and even manpower triggered war after war since the Industrial Revolution. 'The war to end all wars' was fought during 1914 to 1918 but after a gestation period of less than 20 years an even more destructive and wider ranging Second World War took place as the vanquished sought redress for the treatment they got from the victors. This war gifted to us Hiroshima and Nagasaki in 1945. The search for security with weapons produced a weapon and its parent technology which thereafter gave us the legacy of eternal insecurity, fear of radiation death. This insecurity is very real in war as well as during peace and it applies to everyone on earth. Impartially it will inflict friend as well as foe for a span of time measured in millions of years. Since 1945 periodically regularly, and from locations as distant as Three Miles Island, Chernobyl and Fukushima, the mourning bells ring to remind us of our very insecure fate.

He further noted that it was search for security during travelling and the need for cheaper ways to travel in comfort that created the first mass production lines and the Model T Ford way back in the 1920s. This was a significant change in industrial labour relationships. Within half a century, by the 1970s, this little machine of secure travel and its varied mutants had already shifted the survival balance fully against us. The fossil fuel this machine needed to burn and its excreted waste in the form of carbon dioxide have taken on dimensions of insecurity we face on earth to complexities beyond ordinary human comprehension. And it requires solutions which unfortunately are outside practical implementation because all nations do not consider it equally seriously as a threat. Many nations like India and China are still in the race for the riches emitting more and more carbon dioxide.

The American economic crisis or the so-called partial meltdown in 2006-8 periods, he argued, was heavily assisted by the increasing frequency of hurricanes and cyclonic storms ripping across the U.S. In 2005 Hurricane Katrina also contributed to a sliding economy by knocking out insurance companies and pricking the bubble of speculation trade on coastal lands. The Tsunami on Dec 26th, 2004 had not only impacted upon the coastal tourism but also impacted on the perception of threat in the minds of millions of coastal dwellers in the South and Southeast Asia. Because there is no predictability of when it will happen again. The fear has come to stay.

He concludes the well-articulated article by a cautionary note that now there is no other place for humankind to seek refuge. Nations, borders and armies are no longer relevant to fend off the threat of global disorder. Technology will not be able to recall all the toxins it is has spewed out. Actually we are not even very serious about finding a solution. Having collectively cried wolf so many times, apparently we are now too lethargic to care. What we really need is a simple collective species paradigm shift. Reworking human identity is the only solution and not possibilities of biodiesel or genetically manipulated seeds. To solve all our problems of energy or hunger, he suggests, we need a humbler human being in a Green Planet.

Dr. Nanda Kishor in his article on 'Examining India's National Security Semantics -A Theoretical Consideration' made an attempt to bring in the theoretical aspects of security. He argue that defining what constitutes national security is a herculean task in any part of the world, and in the case of India; it is much more complex due to its inherent values of multiculturalism, different schools of thought and differing perspectives on any issue of national importance. The policy makers have realized that the traditional security paradigm does not address the rapidly growing nontraditional threats to security like: the struggle for resources embedded in the pursuit of energy, security, environmental degradation, forced migration, international terrorism, insurgency ascendancy of non-state actors in drugs, arms, money laundering and financial crime organization. The former National Security Advisor of India asserted that "We now need to consider our energy security, food security, technology security, and social cohesion and institutions, to name just a few, when we think of national security". This understanding, he argued, has essentially come in India much later than some of the developed countries from the compulsion that national Security requires a stable economy with assured supplies of materials for the Industry. In this sense, frugality and conservation of materials are essential to national security. Security means more than safety from hostile attacks, it includes the preservation of a system of civilization. Something that we have all been witnessing has been the change in the mind set from the strict monoculture and sacrosanct traditional notion of security meaning military dimensions of national security being changed to include other non-military aspects of security in India. Think tanks and academicians working on strategic studies have started accepting this definitional change happening in a subtle way. One of the best examples that can be cited is the subject of climate change and environmental security which has almost become part of all the institutions working on strategic studies. This is a welcome alteration in an era where the possibility of physical war is meager. It is high time such several aspects which have influence on national security should be taken into consideration as the expected standards in the notions of national security has to be multidimensional, integrated, interest-based and not threat-based, grounded in hope, not fear, pursued inside out, adapted to the information age. In the verge of making the world a better place to live by hoping for peace and make wars and conflicts scanty, there is a necessity to move beyond the national security discourses surrounding national interest and the security of the individual country. No national security is comprehensive in the world without considering the global threats as we live in a world of complex interdependence and each other's actions can cause an equivalent amount of damage as well as bring positive results equally.

In his research article on 'Theorizing the Sino-Indian Ties in the Emerging Global Order' Dr. Harish Thakur had conceded that India and China have generated lots of debate in the international politics over their conflicting borders and interests and role as active players in Indian sub-continental, Asian and consequently world politics. In recent years both have reached newer heights in the domains of science, technology, space, economy, trade and military and hence invite larger global attention. This article endeavours at drawing certain lines of commonalities and differences over the decades between the bilateral ties of the two as also in respect of the world politics. There have been deliberate attempts on behalf of the two states in the past to follow short term and long term policies to fizzle out the pressure of the unresolved issues which in turn take the shape of short term and long term theories to be consistently followed by them. 'One China Theory', 'China's Growth Rate as a farce Theory', 'Contain China Theory', 'Balkanize India Theory', 'India's Tibet Theory', 'Destabilize India Theory', 'Trade Theory', 'String of Pearls Theory', and 'Iron Curtain Theory' are the ones which have been followed by the two states in general and US and its allies in particular. This article is an earnest attempt to assess these theories keeping in view the bilateral ties between India and China.

Professor B Vivekanandan in his well-articulated paper on 'The Defence Aspect of India's National Security' maintained that the most serious threat to India's security emanates from China's brazen claims on Indian territories, and the preparations Beijing is making to realise those untenable claims. In world politics today, China belongs to a special category. In the present day world, China is the only country which still shows an insatiable appetite for expansionism. Its leadership refuses to learn any lesson from history, that all imperial build-ups — from the Roman Empire down to the USSR — had become victims of their expansionist policy, and fallen apart under their own weight after some time. China will be no exception. Future will show. Yet China contrives and manipulates alibis for expansion with territories of neighbouring countries. In one go, the dragon had swallowed Tibet. After the revolution, China has made territorial claims on its neighbouring countries like India, Russia and Japan, and is systematically building up its army, navy and air force, and the nuclear missile systems, to realise those ambitions.

He further pointed out that New Delhi is not doing much, diplomatically or strategically, to counter these anti-Indian activities of China. The shrillness, which is often seen in Indian responses to Pakistani activities, is conspicuous by its absence when it comes against the Chinese misdemeanours and arrogance. India did not do much even when China did a very grave anti-Indian act of clandestinely assisting Pakistan's nuclear weapon programme, in order to prop up Pakistan against India in the nuclear field. Reportedly, even border road building, on the Indian side of the Indo-Tibetan border, has suffered a grievous neglect since 1962, on the basis of a foolish, unstated strategy that, if India has built its border roads right upto the front-line, it would help the Chinese invaders, to easily come down to the South, and occupy more Indian territories! Whether such an unstated approach is still in vogue, some one knowledgeable, from

The Changing Dimensions of Security: India's Security Policy Options

the Defence Ministry, should explain. It is reported that, because of this approach, some of our 'border roads' end at 60 to 80 Kms away from the border, making it impossible for India to take its troops to the borders instantly at short notice. That is not a satisfactory situation for India.

Dr. C Vinodan in the paper entitled 'Nuclear South Asia: Strategic and Security Dimensions' upheld that there is no place else in the world today where proliferation concerns are more acute than in South Asia. Major actors in the region possess nuclear weapons capabilities. The nuclear programmes in the region are rooted in the intense rivalries over power and territory and unresolved historical hatreds. There are no regional nuclear arms control regimes, and participation in global ones is sporadic. The danger with regard to these programmes is exacerbated by their lack of transparency and the growing influence of non-state actors in the regional security matrix. In South Asia, states have generally been poor at dealing with the insecurities of their people. The processes of nation and state-building in the region have proved long and arduous, and preoccupied state agendas for decades. Historically, the focus has been on efforts to protect the territorial integrity of the state, and the safety and stability of ruling regimes-usually at the cost of adequate socio-economic development and political freedoms for those living inside and across borders. This focus continues to dominate security policy-making in the region even today, and is also to an extent reflected in the bulk of the international relations and security studies literature on South Asia, which deals overwhelmingly with inter-state hostilities, wars and disputes over territories and international borders; intra-state conflicts including armed insurgencies and ethno-nationalistic movements, and the seemingly ever-present threat of nuclear conflict between India and Pakistan. Consequently, there exists relatively little scholarship from international relations and security studies perspective which attempts to grapple with those issue which are perceived as sources of deep insecurities by sub-state groups in South Asia, and the range of actors operating in these realms particularly in the absence of effective state led efforts.

In his article on 'Indo-US Nuclear Deal and India's Nuclear Policy' Mr Rajesh Kuniyil outlined India's nuclear policy from the beginning till the Indo - US nuclear accord. He had argued that the Indo - US nuclear accord provides a vital and probably enduring access to dual use technology, the best course is to operationalize it as fast as possible. After the arrangements with the IAEA and NSG it will be possible to do business with willing nuclear suppliers anyhow. The Civil Liability for Nuclear Damage Act, 2010 or Nuclear Liability Act is a highly debated and controversial Act which was passed by both houses of Indian parliament. The bill was the last hurdle for the government in opening up India's nuclear power industry to private investors in the USA, and proposed that financial liability for foreign suppliers – in the event of an accident – be capped at Rs.500 crore. This amount was far lower than demanded by other countries, and even lower than levels of damages sometimes claimed in weather storms. Much of the liability was also transferred to the operator – in this case the Indian government – meaning that compensation would be covered by the taxpayer. It indicated the government's disregard for the safety and wellbeing of Indian citizens in preference of foreign investment.

The article 'Sino-Indian Relations in the Era of Globalization' by Dr. Devender Sharma and Dr. Ved Prakash Sharma, upheld that India and China–the world's two oldest civilization-states, once great powers and now the most populous countries–are back as claimants to preeminence in Asia and the world. Both are heavily engaged in the global economy and possess nuclear powers with expanding military capabilities to match their growing ambitions. They also have a long history of bitter rivalry and an unresolved border dispute that erupted in war. Only during the last three years have India and China begun to shed their wariness toward each other by initiating measures to stabilize their relationship, including regular high-level visits. The rapprochement is based on a mutual need to focus on social and political stability, and strong economic growth and a sense of security, so each can avoid the perils of stagnation or decline. The incipient Sino-Indian entente has prompted some to argue that it has the potential to radically alter India's and China's security environment and restructure Asian geopolitics. Long-time observers of India-China relations, however, maintain that India- China ties remain fragile and as vulnerable as ever to sudden deterioration as a result of misperceptions, unrealistic expectations, accidents, and eruption of unresolved issues. Internal issues of stability and the external overlapping spheres of influence forestall the chances for a genuine Sino-Indian rapprochement. Indeed, the issues that bind the two countries are also the issues that divide them and fuel their rivalry. With their ever-expanding economies and widening geopolitical horizons, the bilateral relationship between the two rising Asian giants could be characterized more by competition than cooperation. As India and China proceed simultaneously on their relative power trajectories, geopolitical equations and power relations in Asia are bound to undergo significant realignment. This paper had made an attempt to analyze the Sino-Indian relations in Post-cold war Globalized era.

Dr. Sudhir Singh in his article on 'Pakistan's Afghan Policy in Post 2014 Scenario: Options for India' pointed out that Pakistan and Afghanistan relations have always been turbulent due to gamut of factors. Pakhtunistan is top among them. After 1979 Soviet intervention, Pakistan has adopted the policy to keep Afghanistan volatile to achieve strategic depth against India. In the backdrop of 9/11 terror attack the NATO led attack was commenced against Taliban in 2001. Since last 13 years despite part of coalition against terror, Pakistan has been supporting terror elements preciously to score points against India. Despite civilian regime in Islamabad, military has to sustain old Afghan policy which is bound to inflict collateral damage to India therefore, he exhorted that, we must reformulate our strategy to cope up with the impending dangers.

In his paper on 'Challenges and Options for a Maritime India in the 21st Century' Commodore R S Vasan had underscored that the transformation of the global maritime security landscape has been quite dramatic with the unfolding of events in different oceans of the world. On a global scale, it is done with the recalibration of the US pivot to Asia and the impact of the withdrawal of US and allied forces from Afghanistan. At the regional level, it is piracy that took centre stage in the West Indian Ocean and the Gulf of Guinea that brought the international community together to contain this scourge. The capture of a floating armoury off Tuticorin by the ICG recently brings out that not all the anti-piracy measures have been carefully thought out. In another region, it was the declaration of the ADIZ over disputed Islands in the East China Sea with potential to affect the maritime balance not only in the region but also elsewhere with the downstream effects. It is in the backdrop of such events that India needs to work on the options for its maritime forces to take on the challenges of this century. The growth of the maritime forces in India has been steady and is poised for greater role in the Indian Ocean and beyond. The recent commissioning of the Aircraft Carrier INS Vikramaditya in November 2013 and the ongoing sea trials of the INS Arihant, the restoration of the control of the strategically important A&N Islands to the Navy and the addition of new platforms, weapons and sensors are equipping the nation

Introduction

with a formidable strategic and diplomatic option for using the Navy as an instrument of foreign policy to serve national objectives. This paper had attempted to examine the full import of recent developments in the maritime arena in areas of concern to India's both long term and short term challenges.

The paper entitled 'Terror on High Seas' Dr Vibhuti Singh Shekhawat, expounded that we are infested with terrorists of many descriptions such as Indian Mujahidins, Maoists, Naxalites, secessionists in Jammu and Kashmir and the northeastern India including the seven sisters and terrorists coming from across the border from Pakistan. But we lack the will to tackle them and are only wasting the resources in the illusive mission to eliminate them. The more we try to eliminate them, the more we inadvertently strengthen and promote them by our ad hoc policies and simplistic solutions. We efface the symptoms but do not reach the bottom to identify the causes of malaise. Small wonder, there is a continuity of terror which manifests itself with intermittent intermissions. Blasts continue to occur in a sequence or periodically and these acts of unremitting terror show no signs of abating. While acts of serial bombings in several cities of India are still fresh in our memory, new forms of terrorist attacks occur that continue to baffle our security personnel. One can identify and explain one new addition to the existing forms of terror viz., the maritime terror which we did not visualize till the Mumbai 9/11 attack that was sea borne. For the first time, he upheld that, it awakened us to a danger from across the high seas.

'Emerging Maritime Threats and Challenges in India's Marine Domain: Post 26/11' Dr Mukund Narvekar maintained that with all challenges and threats perception, Indian maritime security policy has evolved in an age of globalisation. It's preparedness to deal with maritime threats has come to a mature. Its deployment of forces in piracy affected area since 2008 has earned world wild accreditation. By merely understanding the various maritime threats post 26/11 will not help, but it need a system and an institution in place to manage India's maritime security post 26/11. Need an integrated institution and infrastructure, which would monitor the development in and around India's maritime domain. Certainly, India has a wide maritime ground, which needs to be covered. It must match up with the need of the hour and to picture itself as dominant maritime power in the contemporary world. To achieve this objective, it is vital to maximise cooperation between the maritime authorities, institutions, stake holders and private industries in order to create enhanced maritime domain awareness. Therefore, India must develop a mechanism, wherein it takes all the agents and players into consideration which share the same understanding and its commitment to the maritime world, resources and environment. The security of India's maritime frontiers is challenged by non-states actor as well as rogue states. Primarily it is the task of armed forces to protect the integrity and sovereignty of India. Simultaneously it is equally the responsibility of the other stakes holders to share the information and security measures to build strong maritime policy.

'Post 26/11 Terrorist Threats in India – Is National Counter Terrorism Centre alone the Solution?' Mr. Unnikrishnan G, identified that the 26/11 terrorist attacks in Mumbai had more impact on public consciousness and state policy of India than any preceding incident or cluster of incidents in the past. A lot of initiatives were taken to curb terrorism and the notable among them was the proposed National Counter Terrorism Centre. It is a federal anti-terror agency modelled on the National Counter Terrorism Centre of the USA and it has intelligence, investigative and operational functions. But the crucial question is whether it is the only solution for countering terrorism in India. In India there is no scarcity of institutional arrangement for countering terrorism. But in these systems there are deficiencies in skills and capabilities. Moreover we focus more and more on meta- institutional reform and the creation of new institutions to monitor coordinate and oversee the largely dysfunctional apparatus.

Dr. Suresh R in the article entitled 'India's Security Challenges and Policy Options: A Human Security Perspective' had pointed out that human security or people's security focuses on the basic units of nation states, that is, the individual. People centred development would help to solve the problems of the individuals in a better way than the state centred development. In a state centered development paradigm the basic issues of individuals get less attention. Nation states were the creation of people who desired to protect and promote their security. It was one of the means to achieve people's security at a particular stage of human civilization when the threat to security of the people emanates mainly from external sources, that is, from other states. Security, therefore in the ultimate analysis means human security. In the post-cold war period the external threat perception has been diminished or even eliminated and new threat to security of nation states as well as people are evolved. These nontraditional threats to security of nations including terrorism, global economic slowdown and global climate change can be addressed only with multilateral effort. Again it is widely accepted that even if nations are secure people may not be secure. People are not secure in their daily life as long as poverty, illiteracy and hunger remains. Moreover unless the social economic and political rights of the people living in all nation states are not secured and protected there is no human security, national security and international security. Thus the blurred boundary between human security and national security on the one hand and national security and international security on the other hand again emphasis the significance of human security. The modern states are welfare states and the welfare state concept envisages a minimum standard of living to all individuals. Though India is celebrating the 68th anniversary of its independence nearly one third of its population lives in poverty and nearly forty per cent of the population are illiterate, the gap between rich and poor is alarmingly growing. The political equality was ensured with one man one vote, however social, economic and educational inequality is looming large in the Indian society. In a welfare state it is the responsibility of the government to ensure minimum standard of living to all. The failure on the part of the government to ensure people's security is gross violation of the constitution. Thus the threat to security emanates not only from external aggression but also from poor management of the scarce resources to ensure human security. It appears that the best option before India is to focus more on human security issues than pure military security. Since the threat to security of the nation emanates mostly from non-state actors with the support of some nation states the cooperation of other actors in the international system are required to address these issues. In the long run armament and arm race in the region is particularly detrimental to India both in terms of scarce resource use and also instability of the political system in the immediate neighbourhood having nuclear weapon power. In the present context it appears that India should focus more on addressing the human security concerns than on accelerating military built up in the region. This would enable India to solve most of the internal security issues by undertaking the various welfare measures to alleviate poverty and other human security issues. However the British colonial system entrenched strong bureaucratic and defence structure in India could easily resist any attempt to restructure the existing security policy by the political executive which is weakened through the compulsions of coalition politics and deeply drenched in corruption charges.

In the paper entitled 'The Changing Dimensions of Security and Emerging Nontraditional Threats in South Asia: A Human Security Perspective' Mrs. Rakhee Viswambharan maintained that the major functions of nation states is to ensure security to its people. Modern nation states maintain a large defence force to deter any threat from other nation states. However, in the post cold war period the threat to the security of nation states also emanates from nontraditional sources. The nontraditional security issues includes the challenges to the survival and well-being of peoples and states that arise primarily out of nonmilitary sources, such as climate change, cross border environmental degradation and resource depletion, infectious diseases, natural disasters, irregular migration, food shortages, human trafficking, drug trafficking, and other forms of transnational crime. The South Asian countries need to develop multilateral responses to mitigate the challenges of nontraditional security issues through the regional mechanism of the SAARC. Though a good beginning has been made in certain areas like disaster management, yet geopolitical competition and lack of trust are obstructing the adoption of a multilateral approach to deal with such nontraditional security challenges as transnational crime, drug trafficking, illegal migration, money-laundering and gun-running, and terrorism. The nontraditional security challenges also include climate change, cross border environmental degradation and resource depletion, and infectious diseases. The water security is another area where some instances of cooperation exist in the South Asian region. As in the global level, in the South Asian region also most of the nontraditional issues to security are transnational and therefore require a multilateral approach. In short, the existence of human security related nontraditional security issues pose a challenge as well as opportunity to the South Asian countries. The challenge is to tackle these common transnational problems through multilateral approach. And the opportunity is to evolve a common strategy to address these problems. In this paper the author made an attempt to examine the non-traditional security issues in South Asian region and the imperatives of regional cooperation to address these human security issues especially in the context of changing dimensions of security.

The above fifteen articles deals with the changing dimensions of security and a wide spectrum of security issues that India is confronted with and also certain policy options. In the theoretical section the strategic doctrine of India is well reviewed and policy options are also explored.

It covers areas such as biological perspective of security, human security perspective, energy security and maritime security. In addition it also deals with the theoretical aspects of security and also some of the bilateral security issues and concerns with neighbouring countries.

PART – I

THE CHANGING DIMENSIONS OF SECURITY - A THEORITICAL PERSPECTIVE

1 | India's Strategic Thinking And Policy Options

Mohanan Bhaskaran Pillai

Introduction

The Indian political state is just 67 years young although India as a civilizational entity cherishes the memories of many millennia. The young state's, threat perceptions, strategic thinking and policy options are not starting straight from the year of independence in 1947, but influenced and conditioned by the civilizational continuity and memories etched in the collective psyche of Indians. The partition of the subcontinent and carving out of Muslim majority areas as a separate state by the withdrawing imperial power curtailed its holistic geographic expression-the *Jambudipa* (the Island state) and that has had debilitating impact on the security of the remnant secular and plural state. In other words the very moment of the birth of the new state in 1947, along with her twin sister Pakistan, India's security issues surfaced with a bang.

Desire of sizeable sections of the Muslims in the Kashmir Valley to be independent from India, Pakistan's overt and covert support to the separatists in the valley is a major national security issue right from the birth of the Indian political state. Tribal insurgency in the North –East is another security issue that India has been facing ever since the withdrawal of the British. The North-Eastern Tribals think that they are different from the rest of Indians and therefore they are separate Nations qualified enough to be individual Nation States based on the merit of their distinct identities. Maoist extremism, in the tribal pockets, right from the eastern areas of West Bengal down to Warangal district of Telangana and from there to Western Ghats, is a major internal security problem. Cross border terrorism having its roots in Jihadi ideology in its different manifestations is again another major threat to India's national security. Sunni radicalism exported from Saudi Arabia to other countries in West Asia and other parts of the world including Pakistan is emerging as a major security concern for India with its sizeable Muslim minority population. Sunni radicalism in the Islamic crescent from Magreb to Indonesia is creating havoc in Pakistan and India's Kashmir. Pakistani Taliban operating from North Waziristan Mountains has been creating turmoil and dissensions in side Pakistan aiming at taking over of nuclear armed Pakistan (Karnad, 2014). Also Saudi- funded Madrassas within Pakistan are incubators of terrorism which has to be viewed with great concern. The Sunni-Salafi charitable trusts in Saudi Arabia and other gulf emirates are pumping money to different states in India, where there are sizeable Muslim population, particularly to the South Indian States of Kerala, Karnataka, Andhra Pradesh and Telangana. This fund flow from the Gulf has already communalized and destabilized South Indian societies known for its communal harmony. Contemporary India is really facing a severe security threat from this "Home Grown Islamic Terrorism"(Karanrd, 2014) as a result of the gradual replacement of moderate Sufi Islam, representing syncretic culture and rooted in local environs, by "Wahabi values and ideas redolent of desert Islam"(Karanrd, 2014).

The ever increasing presence of China in Gigit – Baltistan ,and in India's neighbourhood "adds to our anxiety"(Srinivasn, 2013).China's pro-active presence in the neighbouring countries in south Asia, border problems and the presence of Dalai Lama in India intensify India's anxiety with regard to China.

Various security agencies of Government of India has documented that the terrorist, insurgent and extremist groups operating in North – West, North –East and the tribal belts are aided and abetted by institutions and groups beyond the borders of India in certain neighbouring countries. Along with the above mentioned security problems we have to take into account the fact like India the other two major neighbours of the country, China and Pakistan, are nuclear weapon capable states. Issues like, poverty, energy security, environmental security, cyber espionage, communal violence, changes in the military technology are other major security concerns for India.

Thus it is very clear that the security environment of India is a complex and rough terrain; and a daunting task to our security machinery to deal with. Naturally the question is do we have a well-oiled strategy to manage, if not eliminate, these security issues? If the answer is yes, then comes the second question about the efficiency of the proclaimed and not openly stated strategies. Thirdly, the question is do we have a strategic Doctrine? If the answer is yes then comes the next question about the strategic culture of India up on which the strategic doctrine of India got constructed. Thus in the following sections the meaning and nature of strategic culture will be elucidated followed by brief examination of India's strategic doctrine. In the third section the strategic behaviour of India will be analyzed followed by concluding remarks.

Strategic Culture

What is the meaning of strategic culture and what is India's strategic culture? "Strategic culture is that set of shared beliefs, assumptions, and modes of behaviour derived from common experiences and accepted narratives (both oral and written),that shape collective identity and relationships to other groups ,and which determine appropriate ends and means for achieving security objectives"(Jones, 2006 p.4). Jones has identified the philosophical and mythological foundations as also instrumental implications of India strategic cultural profile and called it "Omniscient patrician strategic culture"(p.5). This strategic culture has taken its nourishments from the past civilizational values.

According to Johnstone "strategic culture is an integrated set of symbols (i.e. argumentation structures, languages, analogies, metaphors, etc.) that acts to establish pervasive and long-lasting grand strategic preferences by formulating concepts of the role and efficacy of force in interstate political affairs, and by clothing these conceptions with such an aura of factuality that the strategic preferences seem uniquely realistic and efficacious" (Johnston as quoted by Bajpai p.246). Taking cue from Jonstone's definition, Bajpai has constructed the three central paradigms of India's strategic culture as Nehruvianism, Neoliberalism and Hyperrealism (p.251).According to Bajpai Nehruvians are idealist, neoliberals' emphasize the primacy of economics and the hyperrealists are hardcore realists.

One of the pioneering works on India's strategic culture is by George K. Tanham (1992) titled *India's Strategic Thought: An interpretive essay*, in which he argues that virtually there is no evidence to prove that Indian elites have consistently thought about a national strategy. According to him this lack of a coherent strategic thought can be explained by analyzing four principal factors that have conditioned the thought process of the Indian strategic community viz., geography, history, culture and the British raj (pp.1-19).These factors have contributed largely to the absence of strategic thinking (pp.50-67).From among the Indian strategic community a few has partly and another section has fully agreed with the arguments of Tanham. Rejecting Tanham's argument Shiv Shankar Menon, former Foreign Secretary and National Security Advisor, has made a powerful intervention in the debate by stating that India possesses a strategic culture and the same has been consistently used in bilateral and multi-lateral diplomacy (Menon, 2013).

The above noted definitions and arguments of well-known scholars and strategic practitioners are based on their understanding of India's civilization, culture, colonial experience and geographic locations. It is very interesting to note that on the strength of a thorough study of India's past, Jones and Tanham arrived at two different views about India's strategic culture. Looking at the same historical, geographical cultural and colonial evidences, I would like to present the argument here that India's strategic culture branches out into two viz., Plural and Secular Democratic and Hindu Nationalist. Plural and Secular Democratic strategic culture represents two streams of thought sometimes merging, sometimes separating in certain locations and flowing independently of the other for some time and then converging again. These two mutually nourishing streams of strategic culture I would call as Nehruvian and Gandhian. Nehruvian strategic thought is syncretic in nature and inclusive of everything that is at the point of Indian independence. The Hindu cultural ethos, Jainist, Buddhist thought systems, form the inner core of Nehruvianism which has had the supplementary nourishments of Islamic, Christian values and modern western rationality and the ethos of representative democracy. Teachings of Gita, Jainism and Buddhism influenced Gandhi and his pacifist approach to national defence. The plural and secular democratic strategic culture keeps unstinting faith in democratic institutions and international organizations in conflict transformations and its basic approach to security issues is defensive. The core values of this stream of strategic culture are strategic autonomy, faith in regional and international organizations ability to mitigate conflicts as also calibrated use of weapons as the last resort to ensure national security. The mandala concept of concentric circles as codified by Kautilya in *Arthasastra* had influenced Nehru's views on nonalignment and its core value strategic autonomy.

The Hindu nationalist tradition on the other hand advocates, according to its proponents, a more realistic foreign policy and security strategy. The cultural nourishment for this tradition derives from Brahmanical Hinduism, M.S.Golvalker and other Hindu Nationalist leaders. It is exclusionary and based on a selective reading of Indian History. The Hindu nationalist strategic culture believes in hard core realism and advocates projection of India's military power beyond its borders. Instead of strategic autonomy this school advocates alignment with the lone super power to achieve national security goals. To Hindu nationalists preemptive strikes are not anathema and defensive strategy should be replaced with offensive advancements. The Hindu Nationalists do not accept the plurality of India and they think that India is the land of Hindus. Once the primacy of Hinduism is accepted by the minorities ,they will get respect for their traditions and way of life. Keeping in mind these two parallel streams of strategic culture let us have a look at the nature of India's strategic doctrine.

What is Strategic Doctrine?

According to a study of ORF foundation the word 'doctrine' stands for many meanings, mainly religious. In strategic literature it connotes a grand strategy of a nation. It "guides the higher purpose of a country's defence and security policies" (ORF).The strategic doctrine or grand strategy as per the Nehruvian-Gandhian tradition is that military power should be used only as the last resort. As noted above, Nehruvians and Gandhians favour strategic autonomy in the place of alliance and counter alliances. Shivshankar Menon stated that "our primary task now and for the foreseeable future is to transform and improve the life of the unacceptably large number of our compatriots who live in poverty, with disease, hunger and illiteracy as their companions of life. This is our overriding priority, and must be the goal of our internal and external security policies. Our quest is the transformation of India, nothing less and nothing more" (Menon, 2014). According to him in the defence sector options "range from defensive power through offensive capability to aggrandizement. With the aim settled, defence priorities are non –controversially arrived at. We need to work for a peaceful periphery. Our goal must be defence not offense, unless offense is necessary for deterrence or to protect India's ability to continue its own transformation. We must develop the means to defend ourselves" (quoted in Ali Ahmed, 2014) .

At the same time it has been noticed that India does not have officially pronounced strategic doctrine, despite the fact that the government of India has appointed the Naresh Chandra Task Force on national security in 2012 and the task force has reportedly submitted its recommendations. The ORF Foundation organized a workshop to highlight the need for a well pronounced strategic doctrine for the country. The authors of the background paper circulated by the Foundation identified certain policy options having a doctrinal import from the various decisions of the cabinet committee on security. According to Joshy and Mitra (2014), India's doctrine in relation to Pakistan is "strategic restraint and engagement" and the policy vis-a- vis China is "dissuasive defence"(p.3).The doctrine in respect of nuclear capabilities is "credible nuclear deterrent". However, according to Joshy and Mitra we should have a national security doctrine with official stamp on it mainly because of our new status as nuclear weapon capable state. (Joshy and Mitra, 2014,p.5).Of late the discussion is that a Modi Doctrine is in the making. This is based on an erroneous reading of his foreign policy overtures like inviting the Tibetan Prime Minister-in-exile for his swearing–in along with the SAARC leaders and his attempts to have strategic partnership with the US, Japan, Australia etc. However, from a close look at what Prime Minister Modi aims to achieve, we could see strikingly similar policies objectives pursued by his immediate predecessors Mahmohan Singh and A B Vajepaee. Neither of them constructed a doctrine of their own, but pursued a swing policy between Indira Doctrine and Gujral Doctrine, both aimed at strategic autonomy (Hall 2015).

It is worth mentioning here that at least a powerful section in our strategic community argues that pursuance of strategic autonomy has led India to strategic reduction. For instance, Bharat Karnard (2015) has compared India's strategic autonomy with *wei-qi* the template for Chinese state craft and he is of the view that "*Wei-qi* obviously scores over the less engaged mandala infused approach (nonalignment, strategic autonomy)".

We have come across two divergent views on India's strategic doctrine. One view is that India does not have a coherent strategic thinking due to various historical and cultural reasons. The other view is that India does have a strategic doctrine, but it has not been stated openly with official imprimatur. Some scholars expressed the view that a strategic doctrine officially declared would better serve the nation's security interest. Whether it is openly and officially declared or not we do have a grand strategy or doctrine to act swiftly when a threat to national security emanates internal and external sources.

India's strategic behaviour

Independent India is the inheritor of Imperial Britain's strategic policy in the region despite the fact that India is not a holistic geographic expression due to the partition of the country. Britain considered Tibet and Afghanistan as British India's buffer zone and Indian Ocean a private lake. This British strategy had influenced the Indian nationalist leadership while formulating its security policy and strategy. This is evident from the Indian strategic behaviour with regard to our border with China despite India conceded to Chinese claim on Tibet. Right from the days of independence India proclaimed that Indian Ocean should be declared a Zone of peace and believed that great power rivalry in the Indian Ocean region really would be a threat to India's national security. Similarly, India believes that its small neighbours fall within India's security penumbra and disliked if the small neighbourhood hobnobbed with outside powers. The small neighbours of India, except perhaps Bhutan, reluctantly accepted the security canopy unilaterally extended by India over the neighbourhood's horizon. But Pakistan challenged and continues to challenge India's security doctrine of including the small neighbourhood within India's security canopy.

In the overall security strategy of India non-alignment that got incubated in the nest of freedom movement, got a pivotal role to play. The experiment in strategic and foreign policy on the platform of nonalignment with its core value of strategic autonomy has been carried out to protect and promote the national interest of the new born state. It can be noted that right from the Nehruvian era 'strategic autonomy' has been the recurring theme in the foreign policy and strategic behaviour of India. The seemingly autonomous space that was carved out of nonalignment policy contributed to economic development and facilitated the growth of domestic capital, which was very fragile at the dawn of independence. Nehru's nonalignment placed immense faith in international organization, regional organizations and consensus building through discussions and negotiations. This is evident from India's initiative in hosting the first Asian Relations conference in New Delhi and the enunciation of the panchsheel principles for the conduct of relationship with neighbours. In this context it is worth remembering that it was India who took the Kashmir issue to the UN in 1948 thinking that the international body would look at the issue impartially and resolve the conflict amicably. In the matter of external aggression Nehruvians believed that resort to arms should be the last option after exhausting all peaceful mechanisms to resolve conflicts. In the matter of internal security Nehruvian approach has been to apply the principles of federalism by extending autonomy to different ethnic, language and cultural groups. Reorganization of the states on linguistic basis, the adoption of the three language formula and similar policies of federating the country was part of the conflict resolution/transformation framework for internal security.

Prime Minister Indira Gandhi's attitude towards India's small neighbours in South Asia was more assertive and sometime hegemonic because of the regional strategic dynamics. Her neighbourhood policy has been called "hegemonic interventionism"(Hall,2015). She entered into a treaty of peace and friendship with the Soviet Union during the peak of the East Pakistan crisis in 1971 when Bangladesh was on its birth pang. India's nonalignment was criticized as pro-Moscow. In a later period Prime Minister Gujral wanted to remove the tag attached to India as the big brother through his doctrine "restrained magnanimity (Hall 2015). He came out with the idea that India should be benevolent to the small neighbours and his neighbourhood policy came to be known as 'Gujral Doctrine'. In fact Indira Doctrine and Gujral Doctrine are two variants of the same grand strategy rooted in the plural and democratic secular culture.

A major shift in the international political economy occurred during 1978-80 period, much ahead of the disintegration of Soviet Union and the collapse of East European regimes. The shift from "Embedded Liberalism" to Neo-liberalism has stripped capitalism of its liberal –welfare façade, and, as a result, the welfare states in the west and the socialist pattern of governance as it was found in India and other third world countries paled into oblivion to pave the way for the thunderous entry of techno-capitalism which is dominated and guided by finance capital. In the context of such a massive shift in international political economy, India confronted a situation where it had no other go but to introduce the structural adjustment programmes at the behest of the Fund-Bank combine under the leadership of Prime Minister Narasimha Rao and Finance Minister Manmohan Singh. The UPA I and II under the premiership of Manmohan Singh further liberalised the economy and integrated it with the global economy. The non-congress governments that came to power in-between, including that of A B Vajpayee, continued the same policy with minor changes here and there in the operational side. However, due to the constraints imposed by coalition politics as also the pressure exerted by other social formations and leftist political parties, full integration did not take place at the desired level (Pillai, 2015).

The economic reforms initiated by Narasimha Rao government just in the aftermath of the crumbling down of the bipolar world order led to massive readjustment in India's foreign and strategic policy. For the first time India opened diplomatic relations with Israel and initiated the look-east policy with noticeable strategic overtones. It is appropriate here to take cognizance of the offer of Condoleezza Rice, the then US Secretary of State, to India that the US would facilitate the India to attain the great power status on condition of abandoning the nonalignment and getting on the bandwagon with the US. India which always favoured to keep away great powers from the Indian Ocean is now not averse to the presence of the US in the Indian Ocean region and quietly buried the concept of Indian Ocean a zone of Peace. Strategic partnership with the US has taken to new heights by signing the nuclear accord during Manmohan Singh's period. Vajpayee and Manmohan Singh followed some kind of a middle path between Indira Gandhi's 'hegemonic interventionism' and Gujral's 'restraint magnanimity' towards the immediate neighbourhood while operating from within the frame work of neoliberalism.

In 2014, for the first time in the history of independent India, a cultural nationalist party which considers secularism and pluralism of Indian National Congress party as minority appeasement has come to power with a massive mandate. The signals emitted by the foreign policy behaviour indicates that Prime Minister Narendra Modi would try to deepen further the policy of integration of the Indian economy with the capitalism of "financialized, generalized, and globalized monopolies"(Amin 2014) .

A quick look at the election manifesto of the BJP, and Prime Minister Modi's speeches, pronouncements and initiatives in foreign policy front for the last one year indicates the following:

(1) Maintenance of good relations with the SAARC neighbours are essential for transforming India into a major player in world

politics;

(2) A standalone strategy is required to manage relations with Pakistan, the sister country of India which thinks that Pakistanis personify 800 glorious years of Islam in the Indian subcontinent;

(3) Friendship with China cannot be sacrificed at the altar of the pivot strategy of the US;

(4) Japan and the other East Asian countries are vital links in the Act East strategy;

(5) Russia is an all-weather friend of India;

(6) Indian diplomacy in multi-lateral forms like BRICS indicates India's presumption that the world politics is moving towards a multi-polarity;

(7) Closer cooperation and friendship with the United States to balance China;

(8) The underlying thread of all the above initiatives is the 'Make in India' clarion call. It is also noteworthy that Prime Minister Modi has been trying to lure the influential Indian diaspora from the US and Europe to invest in India.

(9) Rediscovery of the Indian Ocean

It is very much astonishing to note that the foreign policy behaviour of Prime Minister Narendra Modi government with its Sangh Parivar background demonstrates a clear and striking similarity with the Nehruvian framework of nonalignment and strategic autonomy in its new and improved version pursued by Vajpayee and Manmohan Singh. The Nehruvian framework of nonalignment did not attempt to delink from the liberal capitalist world order. Instead, the flexibility that was embedded in liberal capitalism was leveraged by the Congress of Nehru and Indira Gandhi to fulfil the objective of import substitution industrialisation, the dominant paradigm of development during that period. Since the social structure of accumulation in contemporary capitalism of monopolies is totally different from that of embedded liberalism, such leverage was hardly available for the post reform governments in India. However, Narasimha Rao managed the switch over to the LPG with ease. Governments of Vajpayee and Manmohan Singh could not tune the Indian economy fully in accordance with the interests of monopoly capitalism only because of weak coalition governments and the stiff resistance offered by certain social formations in general and the left political parties in particular. Even then both of them promoted free-market economy to the extent possible.

The economic pronouncements of Prime Minister Modi indicate that he would continue, on a fast pace, with the reforms that was initiated in 1991 by Prime Minister Narasimha Rao and pursued by his immediate predecessors Manmohan Singh and Vajepayee. We can notice in Narendra Modi's approach of 'strategic interconnectedness' or 'multi- vectored engagement' a striking similarity with the Nehruvian non-alignment and strategic autonomy. At the dawn of independence, such an approach facilitated liberal capitalist economic development with socialist flavours on an upward trajectory. It shows that there existed symbiotic relationship between foreign policy strategy and domestic economic development. It seems that Modi's Make in India project would try to draw its nourishment from monopoly capitalism, and the politico-strategic doctrine will be constructed on the plank of multi alignment or strategic inter connectedness.

From the above, it could be gleaned that 'strategic autonomy', the quintessence of nonalignment is a fairly constant element in the foreign and strategic policy of India right from the days of Nehru, the architect of India's foreign and strategic policy. This is in fact a civilizational legacy, very well ingrained in the collective psyche of Indians. The most important aspect of strategic autonomy is that our games of autonomy are played in the lap of political economy of capitalism. Therefore, the natural course of action is that, India has to adjust and remodel its politico-strategic calculations in accordance with the shifts in the international political economy. Such an adjustment or remodelling started unfolding with the initiation of the LPG reforms in India. However weak central governments crippled by coalition's pressures could not facilitate the expansion of dependent peripheral capitalism in India as envisaged. In the last general election we witnessed the collapse of the Congress system and the definitive victory for the Hindu nationalist BJP under the strong leadership of Prime Minister Narendra Modi. It was perceived that BJP's Hindu nationalism in alliance with the comprador elements in trade and commerce would pressurise Modi to further accelerate economic neoliberalism.

It is very interesting to observe that Modi's continuous interactions in the last one year with the leaders from the neighbourhood, the Japanese

Prime minister, the Chinese President and, above all, with the US President Barak Obama did help him to rediscover the merit of strategic autonomy. It is worth mentioning here that immediately after inking the partnership agreement with the US President Obama, Prime Minister Modi asked his external affairs minister to go to China to prepare the ground for his visit to that country in May,2015. It has been noted that Prime Minister Modi's foreign policy objectives are very much akin to that of Manmohan Singh and AB Vajpayee. They in turn followed a policy of via media between Indira Gandhi's hegemonic interventionism and Gujral's restrained magnanimity (Hall, 2015).This is very much evident from the way he successfully solved the enclave issue with Bangladesh.

Concluding Observations

During the period of 'embedded liberalism'-precisely during the period of cold war — India's security concerns revolved around the threats emanating primarily from Pakistan. On a conventional analytical frame, China is also perceived as a threat to India's national security. However, the age of neoliberal globalization has added additional dimensions to the conventional threats. In the post-cold war period the major security concern of India emanates from cross border terrorism and Sunni radicalism.

All other traditional security concerns are overtaken by economic issues. The challenges posed by international terrorism, global economic meltdown and environmental degradation including climate change are also security concerns that India has to address seriously. The crisis in the energy sector is a major security challenge. On the domestic front India faces many challenges including poverty, illiteracy, social and economic inequality, communalism, regional imbalances and development based displacement, Maoist insurgency etc. The other most important security theatre, that requires a distinct treatment particularly in the aftermath of Mumbai terrorist attack, seems to be the Indian Ocean and the jihadi ideology.

Tuning the international and domestic situations favourable to India's security architecture is a daunting task. The post-cold war international power structure, is symptomatic of the overarching politico-military dominance of the US which turned out to be the protective shield of the international political economy managed by the Wall Street –WTO-World Bank complex. However, the US initiatives to curb international terrorism and actions against state sponsored terrorism suites to New Delhi's official positions on India's strategic objectives that were reformulated in the aftermath of the collapse of the Soviet Union. In official parlance, India's relations with the United States have acquired remarkable maturity and dynamism in the post-cold war period. Many developments created the conducive atmosphere for such a transformation, including the end of the Cold War. India's emergence as a dynamic economic force and an objective assessment of the strategic implications of a world dominated by knowledge-driven societies have also led to the same.

At present the India-US relations are moving beyond a bilateral partnership towards a global partnership, which is anchored not only on common values but also common interests of the dominant sections. The strategic dimension of India's relationship with the US underlines their common interest in combating terrorism, proliferation of weapons of mass destruction and enhancing global peace. There has been a convergence of views on strategic and security issues which extends to cooperation in defence, science and technology, health, trade, space, energy and environment. It is worth noting that the US counts India on its side in the execution of the newly crafted 'rebalancing strategy in the Indo-pacific region'.

On several counts US' rebalancing strategy in the Indo-Pacific region finds strategic convergence with India's "Look East" policy which was drawn up in the 90s to cement further its relations with the countries of South East and East Asia in the context of the disappearance of India's most trusted friend Soviet Union from the political map of the planet. More than an external economic policy or a political slogan, the look east policy is a strategic shift in India's vision of the world and its place in the evolving global political economy. It is also a manifestation of India's belief that developments in East Asia are of direct consequence to its security and development. Therefore, India is actively engaged in creating a bond of friendship and cooperation with East Asia; and that has a strong economic foundation and a cooperative paradigm of positive inter-connectedness of security interests. The LEP represents a reorientation of India's foreign economic policy in the aftermath of the demise of the Soviet Union and it signalled the end of the era of self-reliant growth strategy formulated by Nehru and ardently adhered to by his daughter Indira Gandhi.

It is to be noted here that India is part of multilateral interaction with its membership in the five nation grouping called BRICS (Brazil, Russia, India, China and South Africa) to strengthen collective relationships. This grouping's political interaction could help to alter the shape of the international financial system and the global economy. One of the objectives of the grouping is democratization of international financial institutions. The joint declaration at the first summit meeting held in Russia focused on global food security. The BRICS countries supported the adoption of a wide range of mid- to long-term measures in order to provide for a solution to the issue of food security. However India's capacity to take forward the momentum of multilateralism is doubtful because of deepening of integration with the capitalism of the globalized age.

From the above it is very clear that India's security environment is very much complex with its internal and external dimensions. To me two most important security issues are jihadi ideology with its various shades and utter poverty of teeming millions. The attempt has been to identify the most suitable policy options to tackle these two and other security concerns of India. Such an enquiry has naturally taken us to the strategic culture of India and the grand strategy/doctrine originated from the platform of the country's strategic culture. It has been found that extensive studies have been undertaken by foreign and Indian scholars to delineate the nature of India's strategic culture. Tanham is very emphatic in his argument that India lacks a coherent strategic thinking due to various factors. It has been assertively refuted by Shivshankar Menon, the country's foreign secretary and National security advisor during UPA regime. However many Indian scholars have pointed out that we do not have an explicitly stated security doctrine and it is a major drawback in framing policies for addressing complex security issues. From a quick overview of the foreign and strategic behaviour of India, it has been found that the recurring theme in India's policy behaviour is strategic autonomy despite the fact that there is a shift in our political economy from the import substitution industrialization of the embedded liberal period to the free market ideology of neoliberalism as also the Government in New Delhi is controlled by the Hindu nationalist party.

References

Ahmed, A. (2014). Towards a National Security Doctrine. *Internet sources retrieved 8/6/2015*

Amin, S. (1997). *Capitalism in the age of Globalisation.* Madhyam Books: New Delhi

Bajpai, K. *IndianStrategicCulture.*kms2.isn.ethz.ch/Serviceengine/files/ESDP/101069..dzfz./n/.pdf. retrived 16 January 2015

Hall, I. (2015). Is a Modi Doctrine Emerging in Indian Foreign Policy. *Australian Journal of International Affairs.*dx.doi..org10.1080/10357718.2014.1000263.

Harvey, D. (2005). *A brief History of Neoliberalism.* (Oxford)

Jaffrelot, C. (2014). A Modi Doctrine? *Indian Express* November 20.

Jones, R.W. (2006). *India's Strategic Culture.*SAIC:https:/fas.org retrieved 16 June 2015

Joshi, M., &Mitra, A.I. (2014). National Security:The need for a Doctrine. ORF

Karnad, B. (2014). America an unreliable partner. *The new Indian express,* 24 January.

_____ (2014). Home Grown Islamic Terrisom. *The New Indian Express,* 24 October.

_____ (2015). Bad Policy, Geostrategics will Go Against India. *The New Indian Express,* 13 May.

Menon, S. (2013). India has a Unique Strategic Culture and Diplomatic Style. New Delhi:MEA mea. Gov.in /articles-in-Indian media.htm retrived 16 June 2015.

Pillai, M.B (2015). Modification of India's Foreign Policy:A Political Ecconomy perspective. *ISDA Journal 25(1).*

Raju, R. (2013). India's security: Emerging frontiers of cooperation. In Mohanan B Pillai(Ed.) *India's National Security: Concerns and Strategies.* New Delhi: New Century Publications.

Srinivasan, K. (2013). India's security policy: Shifting paradigms and Emerging Frontiers. In Mohanan B Pillai (Ed.) *India's National Security: Concerns and Strategies.* New Delhi: New Century Publications.

Tanham, G.K. (1992) .*India's strategic Thought :An Interpretive Essay.* Santa Monica, C A:RAND

2 | Insecurity And The Search For Security: A Biological Perspective

S.Sathis Chandran

Preface

In these times we hear so much about security which possibly suggests that our overriding feeling must be fear. Everywhere we see security barriers, security guards, National Security Councils and so on. Winding a piece of black cloth around fashionably coiffured head, our obese super hero film star acts as an NSG commando, a sad burlesque. The word security has seeped into every conceivable sphere of human life. Health security, food security, social security, family security, it goes on and on. Very different from Hope or Care or Love, the other four letter word Fear has displaced all other primary concerns of humankind. Using word play we label all our short-term self-serving offensive actions as defence. In this offensive defence we have totally forgotten our earliest regular concern, food to keep us alive and the Earth which enables adequate photosynthetic fixation of light energy as biological energy.

Long ago when hunger was tangible we sought food security. We reordered the world around us, sought and gained social security. Societies were held together by the gravitational pull of cultural identity. We understood and maintained various dimensions of cultural security including language, religious beliefs and so on. When the axis of rotation of the anthropocentric world shifted to monetary prosperity and money, financial security became an overriding concern. The poorest citizens as well as mighty world powers were perpetually concerned about the strength of their currency. From the Kerala model Kudumbasree to the World Bank, everyone is now concerned about taking loans, capital building through giving loans and hopefully happily living thereafter on the interest.

In spite of all the econometric equations and political rhetoric, the very simple fact is that the continuity and stability of human society depend on the interplay of food security, social security and economic security. Food security is possible if only the social structure remains stable. Social stability depends on cultural security. Economic security is essential if people are to buy food. We may have all the agricultural technology, energy and institutional mechanisms but we would not be able to guarantee food security. We may have high GDP, high industrial growth rate and a stable currency but these would be no guarantee for food security for all the citizens of the country. And now with States failing all over the world, not only Somalia, Haiti or Afghanistan, people may swarm across borders and security of any sense cannot be guaranteed by border guards or fences. Ultimately the basic hard foundation for the crop plant, for the civil society and even for the mirage of the financial institutions to survive, there must be environmental security. But the simple question is whether we will grasp this point in time.

In the Beginning

For life to evolve into higher levels of structural and behavioural complexity, the compelling reason has always been the inevitable and constant change in the living surroundings. The response of all living things to the changing milieu is referred to as adaptation. The ever present changes in the habitat not only raise challenges for the smooth continuation of life but at the same time it also offers opportunities for the expansion of species numbers and compels modifications in the existing forms and functions. Between the interplay of insecurity and life striving to continue beyond those diverse limiting factors, what survives and adapts alone is true progression.

But periodically in the long passage of life across the eons there have been violent and abrupt encounters, geologic or cosmic, that push life back almost to the starting point. Yet again over long spans of time extending across millions of years, adaptation and expansion unfurls the magical carpet of Life. Whatever survives at a point of time is what is currently called biodiversity. Palaeontology and geology record specifically five episodes of mass extinction of life on Earth. More than 98 per cent of all forms of life existing on Earth at that time were wiped out in some of these mass extinctions. The earliest such cataclysmic event took place at the end of Ordovician Period 450 million years ago. Then during the late Devonian about 360 million years ago a second wave of mass extinction happened.

The third wave was at the end of Permian Period 250 million years ago and the fourth took place 200 million years ago at the end of Triassic Period. The fifth mass extinction took place at the end of Cretaceous about 65 million years ago. In all certainty we are currently sliding fast into a sixth wave of mass extinction. The current period is being called the Anthropocene because human activities have a most decisive impact on earth equivalent to a geological upheaval. And the sixth wave of extinction is actually extermination of species by direct and indirect human activity.

This long roller coaster ride of life stretches almost three billion years back into time. Against this enormous span of time, just a moment ago, approximately 2.5 lakh years ago, an ordinary primate species stepped out on to the stage of life in Africa. This species due to unknown reasons speeded up its own journey in search of security. It took control of its own evolutionary course and in rapid steps it lifted one after another all the environmental limiting factors that had so far restricted other species from a comparable explosive growth. This inconsequential species that we scientifically label Homo sapiens sought security in dimensions never before explored in the entire history of life.

Our Deep Disquiet – Roots of Our Insecurity

Dwindling food supply, population pressure, uncongenial changes in the habitat and so on would have often pushed species to search for more secure living conditions. But in the case of Homo sapiens apparently these were not the prime motives for the simmering deep disquiet. Human kind moved out of Africa and within an extremely short time and behaving like an invasive species spread over all the continents except Antarctica. They also left a trail of deep dark devastating footprints, not a legacy to be very proud of.

The anatomically exaggerated development of the human brain and the consequent hyper developed integrated neuronal circuits gave our species unusually complex capabilities of perceptions and responses. These stimuli triggered analytical thought streams which we call our 'rational' understanding. This in turn elicited quantum changes in perception and created what could be called consciousness and started off an innovation called language and all its associated creative symbolism. We evolved rituals which became the basis of religion and developed our sophisticated artistic aesthetic culture. But all the while the deeper disquiet gnawing at our innards deflected us from a peaceful and peaceable existence. We had to invent harsh and punitive patriarchal Gods and carry out senseless bloodletting to appease them. We had to negate the all giving Earth and fabricate a virtual heaven out in the cosmos. We evolved incredibly complex religious rituals and constructed powerful hierarchical social institutions to safeguard us from punishment after death. But these institutions only carried out witch hunts, crusades and inquisitions ably helped by horrendous torture equipment. With the same religious fervour we fabricated ideologies from which we expected solutions for all our worldly problems and erected hierarchical ruling institutions which then we had to suffer. But they also carried out bloody purges and ran death camps. None of these institutions contributed to our elementary survival needs. Our contorted fears and guilt taking control of our ability for innovation created rock paintings in the caves in Pyrenees 20,000 years ago. But our modern shamans ended up creating poison gas, nuclear bombs, biological warfare and star-war strategies. In short, most of what we proudly assembled during the last 12 or 20,000 years not only had very little biological survival value, but they also seriously undermined our very survival possibility.

These Dark Times

These are times of extreme stress and distress. It is a time of wars, pestilence and poverty in an unprecedented scale. Our insecurity has mushroomed to gigantic dimensions partly because of our sheer unsustainable numbers, deadly toxic technologies and our collective cynical negation of all ethical or altruistic values. The attitude that we used to refer to as humane has been erased effectively by our present day religions, our education and value systems. We began by being afraid of natural forces. Out of fear we decided to control them. So we began playing God. We deluded ourselves in our attempt to rearrange all the forces that frightened us. We claim we have control over nature. We may have left our footprints on the lunar dust but we have also been tearing apart the surface of the earth for our conveniences and have succeeded in damaging it seriously.

So now we have reached a juncture where not only the climate but also all the previously predictable cyclic biogeochemical processes upon which life continues in our planet are now going haywire. Ecosystems are collapsing all over the biosphere like card castles. According to scientists ecosystems almost as old as life itself, for example, the coral reefs in the oceans are now left with a maximum lifespan of twenty or thirty years.

Ecosystems on land as complex and rich as the rainforest which contain more than 70 percent of the biodiversity on land are getting wiped out for reasons as absurd as for the creation of football grounds. All the orderly social institutions we have so painstakingly established over time within human societies whether it is the fundamental family unit or systems of participatory governance starting with the Magna Carta written in 1215 CE are vanishing overnight to be replaced by Khap Panchayats in the Indus Valley and by the blind new Caliphates in the Middle-east deserts who have stockpiles of murder weapons.

In this juncture let us stand still for a moment and reflect.

Starting with History

History is not just the unreliable timeline, of uncommon people and unusual events from the past. History is a continuum, a constant stream of dynamism and subsequent happenings woven together, perhaps appearing linear and clear to us now on hind sight. History is an essential critical perception to view anything, detached from frozen boundaries of space and time. A historical perspective alone can give us the ability to look closer and see the earlier stages of what we call the present. History alone will help us project the trajectory of the present into the future. Without this clearer and more tangible perception of the future, our steps would not merely be faltering but could very well be in the wrong direction.

The Threat

Faced with any serious threat there are only two directions for us to move. Either we have to avoid the threat and run away from it or we have to confront it. The last three lakh years of human history has been simply a series of such moves, both avoidance and confrontation. Facing hunger, facing predators, threats by extremes of climate and so on, we took either of these steps. All that we consider as progressive steps of the humankind have been solutions coming out of such choices. Forging social groups, efficient hunting techniques and weapons, domestication of fire, domestication of wild species of plants and animals, invention of man-made ecosystems (agriculture), clothing, and fabrication of shelter and so on have been our answers to threats. Security in large numbers and assured food supplies followed by division of labour and settled existence provided the boon of markets, profits and prosperity. Are they not truly the serpent tempting us to eat the forbidden fruit which succeeded in expelling us from the relatively stress free subsistence existence? In any case, with our present day population, fast disappearing natural resource base and our weakened skills and capabilities to search for survival requirements, we have no possibility of going back to being hunter-gatherers.

In the bygone days our aura of culture held in check a host of elementary threats for a short while. But our numbers continued to increase and the deep disquiet compelled us to go on along the same destructive direction. Simultaneously new threats and fears also cropped up. They are of a larger magnitude and more difficult to tackle. In comparison, the earlier fears lasted but for a short duration and most of them had definite practical solutions.

Earlier when there were fewer of us and we had more empty spaces around us, we could run away from threats and need not confront other occupants of those lands where we sought refuge. We only exterminated plants and animals. The Dodo and the Cheetah were only the initial tally. Mass exodus of people had happened repeatedly in history at least during the last few thousand years. Hostile cultures had forced the most frequent mass migrations. Diseases such as the Black Death during 1347 to 1351 found survivors migrating en mass from southern and south-eastern Europe. They left behind countries which had lost 70 to 80 percent of their population due to this epidemic. Religious persecution shifted large populations from across Europe into North America, Australia and parts of Africa. The Irish Potato Famine during 1846 to 1849 apart from killing more than a million peasants, forced large-scale migration to North America. But the consequences of such relocations were not always simple. When Christopher Columbus crossed the Atlantic in 1492 there were more than five million people belonging to hundreds of distinct cultures in what is currently called North America. But within two centuries their numbers got reduced to less than one million. Within this short span of time more distinct and diverse cultures were almost intentionally wiped out than over the entire cultural evolutionary history of humankind. Anti-Semitism sweeping across Europe repeatedly since the Middle Ages shifted the Jewish population across Europe and it culminated in the pogrom during the 1930s to 1945 under the Nazis. Independence in India in 1947 triggered the largest forced human movement in human history across the new border dividing the now two different independent countries. And in the birth place of Abrahamitic religions in Jerusalem, they continue to kill children even today in the name of God.

The Current Crisis

Although we talk about global climate change and its impact on human society, it is not the first time the cooling or the warming of the Earth's surface has influenced the human evolutionary course. With more detailed scientific studies it is almost certain that our past has also been routinely and basically heavily influenced by climate change. Specifically our ancestors in the temperate lands had been affected deeply by global climate change. Global cooling and expansion of glaciers influenced the diet and clothing of our ancestors and forced them to change their hunting strategies. The requirement for body warmth moulded our concept of shelter and affected our house design significantly. On the other hand, drought and dry spells influenced agricultural communities and gave birth to irrigation technologies. This gave rise to the complex hydraulic civilisations in river valleys like the Euphrates - Tigris, Nile, the Indus and the Yangtze. Global dry spells very drastically influenced pastoral cultures and nomadic lifestyles in the vast grasslands of Central Asia, Europe and the Americas. The mobility requirements and self-protection measures in such exposed open terrain developed into martial cultures which in some specific instances had worldwide repercussions. Genghis Khan's forays across Asia and almost up to the Atlantic shores had the most far reaching consequences in human history. Mongol cavalry simply swept aside European foot soldiers. When vast empty spaces were no longer a threat due to the domestication of horses and the vicious competition for the limited foraging grounds in the Steppes gave birth to cavalry battle tactics, threats became pathways to conquest for some.

River valley civilisation, food surplus and urbanisation with its possibilities of consolidating diverse knowledge systems and the opportunity for conversion of commodities to monetary capital gave birth to the Modern Age. All further development of the so-called modern age of man came to depend on an enormous quantum of external energy. Energy requirements for survival were initially met from food. Later energy was required to regulate the micro milieu created in our immediate vicinity. Clothing was the first step and housing the second. As our social organisation expanded, our early complex urban landscapes needed huge quantum of bound energy as wood. Forests vanished from near urban centres. The urban civilisation also required extensive mobility. The quest for energy before fossil fuel and machines had prompted man to harness animal energy. Automatically the next step was to treat his own species brother also as draught animal. Slaves were a more widely traded commodity possibly even before spices or minerals. Hunting for slaves in various parts of the world, specifically in Africa and South America wrecked more nations and societies than any epidemic. Raids for capturing slaves and their marketing were carried out by enlightened people coming out of Europe with the blessings of religious heads. Vast tracts of Sub-Saharan Africa were depopulated by religious Arabs from various countries from the Mediterranean rim moving into capture slaves. Much before the fallout from the scramble for fossil fuel in the West Asian deserts, searching for energy had created the most destructive social, political and economic fault-lines in various parts of the world. Cutting down forests for melting metal ores created more destitute populations in countries as far apart as China, Central India and the British Islands. But more serious than the mere human tragedy, the dependence on excess fuel consumption disrupted the living world to such an extent that our search for energy security has created ecologically a most insecure world.

Search for Security through Polity

For the modern human society with very rare exceptions, evolution of the concept of State and the systems of governance offered a greater level of security than ever before. This is partly because of standing armies, the rule of the law and social support scaffoldings built into the governmental machinery. Units of governance in all parts of the world went through phases of consolidation and growth to reach maximum spatial expansion before disintegrating into smaller, often competing units. The Greeks, the Romans, the Mauryans, the Hindu empire of Vijayanagara, the Ottomans and in modern times the Soviet Union all experienced it. Balkanisation is not merely a literary term. It is one tangible result is untold human misery during the phase of splitting apart. Kosovo and Sarajevo are still living memories of events whose roots go back 600 or 700 years to the expansion of the Ottoman Empire. Alternating cycles of centripetal and centrifugal forces are often accompanied by waves of conquest, subjugation and not uncommonly widespread genocide. This has been a constant refrain in human history long before 9/11. Strong States offer physical security to most inhabitants, economic and cultural security to many but not all. So there will be some insecure who will have a grouse. There will always be a 'minority' feeling for some group or other and those feeling insecure retaliates by violence.

States competing for resources, markets and even manpower triggered war after war since the Industrial Revolution. 'The war to end all wars' was fought during 1914 to 1918 but after a gestation period of less than 20 years an even more destructive and wider ranging 2nd World War took place as the vanquished sought redress for the treatment they got from the victors. This war gifted to us Hiroshima and Nagasaki in 1945. The search for security with weapons produced a weapon and its parent technology which thereafter gave us the legacy of eternal insecurity, fear of radiation death. This insecurity is very real in war as well as during peace and it applies to everyone on earth. Impartially it will inflict friend as well as foe for a span of time measured in millions of years. Since 1945 periodically regularly, and from locations as distant as Three Miles Island, Chernobyl and Fukushima, the mourning bells ring to remind us of our very insecure fate.

It was search for security during travelling and the need for cheaper ways to travel in comfort that created the first mass production lines and the Model T Ford way back in the 1920s. This was a significant change in industrial labour relationships. Within half a century, by the 1970s, this little machine of secure travel and its varied mutants had already shifted the survival balance fully against us. The fossil fuel this machine needed to burn and its excreted waste in the form of carbon-dioxide have taken on dimensions of insecurity we face on earth to complexities beyond ordinary human comprehension. And it requires solutions which unfortunately are outside practical implementation because all nations do not consider it equally seriously as a threat. Many nations like India and China are still in the race for the riches emitting more and more carbon dioxide.

To Cut Short

The American economic crisis or the so-called partial meltdown in 2006-8 period was heavily assisted by the increasing frequency of hurricanes and cyclonic storms ripping across the U.S. In 2005 Hurricane Katrina also contributed to a sliding economy by knocking out insurance companies and pricking the bubble of speculation trade on coastal lands. The Tsunami on Dec 26th, 2004 had not only impacted upon the coastal tourism but also impacted on the perception of threat in the minds of millions of coastal dwellers in the South and Southeast Asia. Because there is no predictability of when it will happen again. The fear has come to stay.

There is a flip side to this coin. Divided we stood and faced all challenges so far. The able bodied male fought off the predator to safeguard his family or a group of men went hunting for the tribe. We built palisades around villages to keep off animals and hostile tribes. Nations had standing armies and armouries which grew larger and larger. This of course finally resulted in the collapse of both the nations considering themselves to be the leaders in the bipolar world. Long ago we could shift our villages when rivers rampaged. People of the Harappan culture shifted about seven times when mud and debris from the Aravallis and the Himalayan slopes buried their beautiful burnt brick structures. But Mohenjo-Daro is the hottest place in Asia with temperature reaching above $60°C$ and New Orleans still remain in shambles even though almost nine years have elapsed since Hurricane Katrina passed by.

Now there is no other place to seek refuge. Nations, borders and armies are no longer relevant to fend off the threat of global disorder. Technology will not be able to recall all the toxins it is has spewed out. Actually we are not even very serious about finding a solution. Having collectively cried wolf so many times, apparently we are now too lethargic to care. What we really need is a simple collective species paradigm shift. Reworking human identity is the only solution and not possibilities of biodiesel or genetically manipulated seeds. To solve problems of energy or hunger we need a humbler human being in a Green Planet.

3 | Examining India's National Security Semantics – A Theoretical Consideration

Nanda Kishor M S

Defining what constitutes national security is a herculean task in any part of the world, and in the case of India; it is much more complex due to its inherent values of multiculturalism, different schools of thought and differing perspectives on any issue of national importance. This essentially problematizes the very effort of trying to examine India's national security as it may lead to the perception of considering it a vague and even non-explainable phenomenon. The other major problem emanates from the reasoning of what theories should be used to analyse. There are certain prerequisites to make any analysis and in this case a readily available document on India's national security in terms of its objectives and strategy. There exists nothing of that sort and that makes this research more complicated. The way to analyse the topic is to observe and scrutinize India's behavioural pattern over a period of time through the prism of different academicians and their interpretations and arrive at some of the conclusions. The concern for the security of a nation is undoubtedly as old as the nation state itself.

Prior to plunging into the central theme of this research it is pertinent to decipher and understand some of the key concepts on which the arguments are built and furthered. Deconstructing the concept of national security would reach to the bottom layer of a term called national interest. National security is principally a subset of national interest. Examining national interest can lead us to understand security and subsequently national security in a much more comprehensive manner.

Reasoning National Interest

Many of the terms in International Relations are heavily contested and the list starts with nation, national interest, security, national security and many more. It is for sure that no agreement can be reached about its ultimate meaning unlike formulae in mathematics. In a way it is the magnificence hidden within the disciplines of social sciences. Analyzing it from the perspective of International Relations and Political Science and arriving at some demonstrable variables would be of some help, which otherwise might end up as a futile exercise. Objectively defined through some yardsticks and criteria would allow us to reach the probable use of it in political action. As an analytical tool, it is employed to describe, explain or evaluate the sources or the adequacy of a nation's foreign policy. As an instrument of political action, it serves as a means of justifying, denouncing or proposing policies. Both usages, in other words, refer to what is best for a national society. They also share a tendency to confine the intended meaning to what is best for a national society. Beyond these general considerations, however, the two uses of the concept have little in common' (Rosenau). The problem with even such a definition is that it does not allow us to draw a boundary as to when it is analytical and when it is an instrument of political action. Persons involved in national policy many a time play the role of analyzing it as well as implementing the aforesaid political action. Though there are realists thinkers who are blunt to moral claims of the term and assert that 'the interests of the national society for which government has to concern itself are basically those of military security, the integrity of its political life and well-being of its people. These needs have no moral quality....they are unavoidable necessities of a national existence and therefore not subject to classification as either good or bad' (Kennan). Somewhere these definitions also hint at the political class being entitled to take the decisions that are best for a nation and term them as national interest. There are also academicians like Raymond Aron who differ with these propositions and vehemently argue and conclude after thorough examination that 'the plurality of concrete objectives and of ultimate objectives forbids a rational definition of 'national interest'....' (Raymond Aron). Joseph Frankel proposes a new classification for the national interest dividing its usage into three: aspirational, operational and explanatory/ polemical categories (Joseph Frankel). According to him each set of use will overlap the other; he nevertheless attempts to provide contextual definitions. The aspirational national interest is rooted in history and the country wants to revive that past, operational rests itself predominantly on *specific, measurable, achievable, resourced, and time oriented* concepts and the polemic or explanatory usage essentially does the ground work to justify the actions of the nation as necessity and remain dominant in the intellectual space by using dominant discourse. In other words, "its main role is to prove oneself right and one's opponents wrong" (Frankel).

Needless to say, there might be several interests depending on the state and the society we live in a country like India. The plurality is much celebrated but there are binding factors which also makes it to look as one unit and then it is pronounced as India. It might be the Constitution to which the people of India vow their allegiance and abide by. Though even the Constitution undergoes change through amendments, still it certainly provides clarity in terms of the structure of governance and equally guides through sections such as Directive Principles of State Policy. There have been instances where India has taken a completely varied path in the direction of growth from the socialist path it idealized and diverse in the 90s, but at large it still continues to be a welfare state. In a vast country like India, however it may sound utilitarian, there is a need to make some distinction between interest as a nation and interest of the individual. The nation may also lack the resources to meet all the requirements and interests of its people. This does not mean that the interest of the nation and the individuals are not complementary. Some interests will certainly receive emphasis and some may have to wait for the suitable time to arrive. This job of making the choice on behalf of the national society is left with the policy makers. Though all citizens are capable of making decisions and equally enthusiastic, there is a necessity to keep it to a smaller number to arrive at consensus and the opposition parties are expected to keep the party running the government rational. As Antonio Gramsci opines, "All Men are Intellectuals, One could therefore say: But not all men have in society the function of intellectuals. Thus, because it can happen that everyone at some time fries a couple of eggs or sews up a tear in a jacket, we do not necessarily say that everyone is a cook or tailor" (Hoare and Smith). However, educated and enlightened society one may be, still it needs to rest some responsibility of the nation in the hands of the policy makers. Decision making is one of the prime duties of statesmanship to know when and how to make such choices of national importance translated to national interest. Moreover, the national interest cannot be equated with a list of state interests, then it can be reduced to the sum of demands by domestic groups. Most of the nations across the world would certainly make a distinction between domestic and foreign interests of a nation. This also in a way provides the leverage for the policymakers to make distinction and define national interests in terms of outcomes. Thus national interest of a nation is arrived by prioritizing what is best for the national society to progress and remain peaceful.

Understanding Security

There have been writings from the realist and neo-realist scholars which emphasise what is insecurity to understand security. Indeed, it is one of the ways of decoding the concept but essentially it believes in the negative image of the international order and push us towards imagining the Hobbesian state. This argument of insecurity essentially comes from quoting Hobbes where he emphasizes 'without security there is no place for industry... no arts, no letters, no society; and which is worst of all, continual fear, and danger of violent death; and the life of man, solitary, poor, nasty, brutish, and short' (Oakeshott). Needless to say, if it were to be true there should have been several wars and bloodbaths throughout, but it is not the case in the Twenty First Century. It is true that one of the meanings of the term security implies freedom from threat but it is a contested concept. The enquiry would move further and demand an explanation as to what is freedom from threat and whose freedom it refers to. Is it individual, national or international security? Further, security in what? From what? And to whom? These questions are rarely probed and nation states essentially evade from answering them. It is true that many of the terms revolve around the concept of state. This does not mean that security means the ultimate security of the state alone. Debates about security have traditionally focused on the role of the state in international relations. Different times with different notions of security have been witnessed and most of the time they are tuned in terms of military.

There are scholars who believe that rather than looking at security in all ages it is essential to see them through the time frame starting with security in pre, during and after the Cold War. This can be highly Western centered model which is often dubbed as the standard format of presenting. But there are no such evidences to show that it has been the same in all parts of the world. For example, nations which got liberated from the colonial rule would want least things to be remembered in terms of security under the colonial powers. They would want to count on their experience with security after independence and in this case the standard model might not be sufficient to explain the phenomena. Certainly, the end of the Cold War changed the notion of security from the heavily state oriented military security to the other dimensions of it and India was also a stakeholder in that. The specific section on national security would deal in detail about it.

National Security

The term security covers a range of goals so wide that highly divergent policies on minimum policing also can be interpreted as policies of security of a state. A normative view of national security is one predicated upon values, ideas and identities. National security is regarded as fundamentally normative because without it human life is reduced to a basic struggle for survival. National security also points to some degree of protection of values previously acquired by a nation state. This statement can be verified by some definitions of national security which echo the terms such as values and core values. Lippmann argues that 'a nation is secure to the extent to which it is not in danger of having to sacrifice core values if it wishes to avoid war, and is able, if challenged, to maintain them by victory in such a war' (Lippman). The definition to a large extent identifies that security rises and falls with the ability of a nation to deter an attack, or to defeat it. India too considers the concepts embedded in the Preamble of the Constitution as its core values. The problem in accepting the core values to understand India's concept of national security further complicates it. The day to day behavioural patterns cannot be assessed only through the core values she protects. Wolfers opines that 'security, in any objective sense, measures the absence of threats to acquired values and in a subjective sense, the absence of fear that such values will be attacked'(Wolfers). There are other academicians who have come with a more docile and social security theory that takes the view that 'stable security can only be achieved by people and groups if they do not deprive others of it; this can be achieved if security is conceived as a process of emancipation' (Wheeler and Booth). The instrumental approaches to security largely propounded by the realists and neo-realists believe in outcomes in the form of policy and actions and try to break away from the moral dilemmas embedded in the normative sense of security. But it is extremely difficult to comprehend as to what extent people are happy only due to some policy. Even if there is a policy it is a methodological challenge to measure it.

Wolfers termed the word National Security as an ambiguous symbol. He wrote this when people had lost hopes of researching on national security due to its vagueness inbuilt and arguments becoming endless. Wolfers did not dismiss the concept as meaningless or hopelessly ambiguous, but he was concerned about the ambiguity of national security. 'It would be an exaggeration to claim that the symbol of national security is nothing but a stimulus to semantic confusion, though closer analysis will show that if used without specifications it leaves room for more confusion than sound political counsel or scientific usage can afford'(Wolfers). This sounds sort of a political jargon but there is much more to what he observes. Morgenthau termed national security as "the integrity of the national territory and its institutions" (Morgenthau). The need to safeguard an accepted political system, society and its people has also become primordial to the overall national security architecture. But what complicates it further is the problem associated with the term national security itself as it does not offer itself to a precise definition. There is also nothing called *The National Security*. It also moves through the time swiftly apart from regular ideational perspectives on freedom from external and internal threats to sovereignty of a nation. Without doubt, over a period of time, there has been a discourse heavily centred on the realist interpretation of national security which is essentially associated with defence and survival of the state, which is also often dubbed as the military and state centric security. As mentioned in the previous section, there is semantic confusion all over in terms of understanding security as equivalent to defence and military. This view was accepted all over the world until the wave of globalization started creeping into several parts of the world. For common man, there is utter poverty in these connotations in day to day life. As there are no major wars happening in any part of the world and there are no such anticipations of any in the future too, it has led to suspicious of the state itself. The state is suspected to be working and using the state centric approach to keep itself at the center of discussion. As Brown opines 'it is used to justify the maintenance of arms, the development of, new weapon systems, and the manufacture of armaments. The overwhelmingly military approach to national security is based on the assumption that the principal threat of security comes from other nations' (Brown). Brown's contentions are clear, relevant and continue to find their space for the years to come. Ullman views 'national security as more than a goal with different trade-off values in different situations' (Ullman). But this military and state centric notion of national security comes at an extreme cost. This was anticipated by Adam Smith two centuries ago. He opined that national security is an expensive activity and demands the allocation of resources that are likely to remain unused. This is true for sure as most of the countries who top the list with their defence acquisitions are suffering from this problem and India too is in the spree. Many a time countries like India have justified acquiring weapons due to the 'security dilemma' they go through which is an essential source of conflict between states leading to the hyper notion of national security. In fact Wolfers has befittingly termed it as *hysterical apprehension*. This is due to the reaction of nations to the external situation of the country and its geopolitical position. Any threat perceived, some tend to exaggerate on the one hand and some underestimate it on the other. Objectively defining national security of a country may not be able to explain it all the time. These type of situations demand subjective reaction as there is a lot more to be imagined, analysed and involves great deal of perception. This leads to the problem which is double edged. If we assume the objective sense of national security, it may not lead to positive results anticipated in extraordinary situations. On the other hand, there is no guarantee inbuilt in subjective analyses in extraordinary situations which would bring success. If there is a minimal success in subjective understanding of national security, it would certainly lead to massive procurement of arms and ammunitions reminding us of Adam Smith who said that they may never be used. 'In any case, together with the extent of external threats, numerous domestic factors such as national character, tradition, preferences and prejudices will influence the level of security which a nation chooses to make its target' (Wolfers). This is the reality even in the twenty first century with all the nations across the world.

This ambiguity is not just with one nation or a few in the world. It is universal and has been dubbed by many scholars as one other concept which would keep the academicians busy all over the world. Though marked by considerable ambiguities and fuzziness (Buzan) the concept of national security did provide a dominating strand of security analysis, one that tended to equate "security with the absence of a military threat or with the protection of the nation from external overthrow or attack" (Halftendorn). Depending on the conditions in which the country is treading, it has been observed that states that still largely favour the state as *the* important and revolve around traditional notions of security tend to favour established realist and liberal approaches developed during the last century. But in contrast, some of the nations which have moved beyond the notions of the traditional approaches have shown large interest in unconventional and broader definitions of national security which include environmental security, economic competitiveness, human rights, or human welfare as an alternative analytical perspective to assess themselves. It has been argued that this is due to globalization and its ability to percolate into most of the nations. The differing view to such notion is, at that superficial level there is no doubt that one would be forced to believe that globalization has blurred the borders and the heavy reliability on the traditional notion of security. A close and in-depth scrutiny of the process of globalization would reveal the new security state which is emerging on the premises of neoliberal thought of demanding more freedom for economics to play in the forefront. Rather than speaking in terms of becoming an arms acquiring state for the sake of projecting power, now the state is acquiring new weapon technologies and buying arms in the name of protecting its economic freedom and those of the others that have invested in their country. Interesting examples emerge from several nations — to protect the maritime boundary and the movements of goods, countries are building their arsenal heavily. Surveillance in the name of protection has become the order of the day in the disguise of enabling security for the people.

India, in the post-colonial period struggled to work on everything from identifying her friends to enemies. There was no consensus on how the state would want to be. Nehru, the first Prime Minister had his own set of national goals starting with national unity, parliamentary democracy, industrialisation, socialism, development of the scientific temper, secularism and nonalignment (Parekh). This adequately does not speak of the national security and such importance was not given to the traditional notion of security of that time though the Indian military had won an important war with Pakistan in 1947 itself. Many have scathingly attacked India for not having a national security doctrine or a document due to its weak strategic culture and the leading one being George Tanham. Though his understanding has been criticized by a few scholars, the reality needs to be embraced by understanding and accepting the history. The strategic culture or thought was interrupted several times due to the invasion by some of the external powers for centuries together. Essentially, strategic thought is also a civilizational value which travels with the coming generations and there have been situations where it did not find conducive regimes to flourish. The fractured strategic thought had its complete change over during the British rule. Occupying the mind space was the ultimate victory for the British as it would serve the purpose of keeping people slaves not just physically but would become the symbol of victory for the British Empire even after their departure from India. It is extremely difficult to understand India's behaviour to term what has been its understanding of national security due to its compatibility with the age old realism of Kautilya through Arthashastra and the latest being the concept of non-reciprocity of Gujral. Generally used theories for analyzing India's national security such as structural realism, liberalism or constructivism may be not be sufficient to explain all the traits of India and its perception of national security. India has not relentlessly pursued a hegemonic policy when structural conditions were conducive to her and allowed domination. The most cited example is that of victory over Pakistan and the liberation of Bangladesh in 1971 (Cohen). The concept of strategic restraint has held her in much more control (Cohen and Dasgupta). It also equally reminds us of some more incidents which are hard to comprehend and analyse India's behaviour such as its withdrawal from Sri Lanka in 1990 and exit from Maldives in 1989 without consolidating power to boost its national security. In the first case with regard to Sri Lanka it succumbed to the pressure of the Tamils at large but this would also take us to the fundamental question: why India could not imagine such a situation forthcoming at the very outset prior to making a decision to move in? Could not she understand her own domestic situation? Was she in such dearth of strategic understanding? Was it not too obvious? In the second case, India could have played a very constructive role and could have added a lot of strength to her own consolidation of power which could have got translated into its better position in the SAARC meetings. These two examples apart, India also has some examples to show that she does not fall only under the category of a defensive realist state. The takeover of Goa from the Portuguese in a successful combat codenamed 'Operation Vijay' was condemned by the United States and six others including the British made no impact on India. The Indian representative at the UNSC declared 'Charter or no Charter, security Council or no Security Council' that Goa, Daman, and Diu are inalienable part of India unlawfully occupied by Portugal'. This event being one of the most successful by India in projecting its strength to protect its national security is a startling example of her strategic culture. India continues to host Dalai Lama, being aware of the tensions with China. It does not also fit into the liberal strategy too as it does not follow the ideals of countries like the United States, which are always in the run for spreading democracy in as many countries as possible irrespective of the returns. India has not tried ever to spread its democratic credentials to even its neighbours who are less powerful. This is quite strongly advocated by scholars like Mehta who opine that 'policies that are too norm driven will make problematic countries even harder to engage. Thus, despite India's own democratic example and sense of desirable regime forms, it is unlikely to sign on to democracy promotion as a *big idea*' (Mehta). Apart from these, India is fiercely combating the naxal movement yet is offering them space for joining the mainstream to achieve peace makes it tough to understand her national security objectives. As Wolfers points out to national character, tradition, preferences and prejudices being great influence on national security character of a nation is befitting to understand India. India's behavioural pattern can be best understood under three schools of thought named as *Nehruvian Idealism* (moving beyond nation and adopting a world view), *liberalists* and *hyper nationalists* by adopting it to reconstruct the national security thought.

The first school of thought, Nehruvian Idealism is characterized by traits such as Nehruvian world view predominantly, which is cooperative in nature. It emphasizes that India should be able to defend itself from its enemies but should not dispose of so much force that it frightens others. It underscores a multifaceted process of communication and contact to solve national security issues. Indian exceptionalism on issues involving national security issues might have suited Nehru's world view and his statesmen traits but they essentially did not go great with India's national security. Seeking the moral high ground on most of the issues hurt India in her initial years, which have continued to haunt India even today. The strategic decisions have had a great impact on India's geopolitical position and its maneuverability on national security issues. May it be Kashmir or Sino-Indian issue or even that of Tibet. Nehru could not make any distinction between idealism and utopianism in many of his decisions. Nehru grappled with challenges of domestic nature; he hoped India's new-found independence and freedom would galvanize her to rise to greater acceptance on the international scene. His desire to become a champion of the Third World blinded him to the essential national security objectives of India, rather, his focus was on national goals which do not speak anything on national security per se. The decisions taken by Nehru during his long tenure were not essentially that came from consensus rather by his own imagined self-merit. Some of the strategic thinkers like K. Subramanyam have summed up his personality as 'on the whole, Nehru's attitude must be summed up as of one who wanted to avoid war, who abhorred it, yet who would not hesitate to fight to defend his country's interests, in this he was like many western liberal statesmen and thinkers'(Subramanyam). There are other observations made by some scholars who opine differently on Nehru especially on Sino-Indian war being one of the major blows in the history of India - 'Nehru was right when he spoke in the early 1950s about India and China being blessed with an absence of possible grounds of conflict, claiming to envision a future of Sino-Indian amity. It was his own irrational, self-defeating policies-his folly-that doomed that aspirations, and their lasting effect leaves the two huge powers still estranged, with festering enmity against China harbored by the Indian political class, first duped, now self-deceived' (Maxwell). Subramanyam drubbing Maxwell wrote that the concept of forward policy was not anyway a mistake by Nehru. Needless to say, whether pro or against Nehru, the argument is very well taken that he as an individual and as a personality shaped tenets of India's national security around his own beliefs. This is being accepted even by Subramanyam knowingly or unknowingly in one of his works regarding the Sino-Indian War of 1962, which says that 'history will record that Jawaharlal Nehru's perception of India's problems of security was accurate. The polices he pursued were also perhaps the best under the circumstances. But he failed partly in their implementation and partly for reasons which could never have been anticipated, such as the local command failure in the 1963 war. If we take into account the magnitude of the crisis that India faced, it would seem that Nehru pulled her through it at a relatively low cost' (Subramanyam). Some scholars from the liberalist tradition dispel the aura around Nehru in some of their writings. They opine that 'though no one doubted Nehru's sincerity, many questioned the correctness of his policy. Yet no one had the courage to defy him either out of respect for his position or for the fear of becoming unpopular and losing positions of power' (Narayanaswamy). The nonexistence of *realpolitik* in the policymaking as well as the limits of Nehruvian idealism was apparent in many instances. The thought of Nehruvian Idealism laid the foundation for several decisions taken in the future too regarding India's national security. In fact, one can even say, the strategic restraint found its birth in the post independent India through Nehru.

The second school of thought constitutes the liberalists who believe in individual liberty, free trade (not all as few liberalists have adopted the Indian version of liberalism), and moderate political and social reforms. The liberalists heavily rely and stress on human rights and democracy. They have a different notion of security and are often dubbed as less nationalistic and less patriotic by the hyper nationalists. For liberalists, the human nature is basically good and that innate goodness makes societal progress possible. States are, and always have been, embedded in a domestic and transnational society, which creates incentives for economic, social and cultural interactions. Evil or unacceptable human behaviour, such as war, is, according to liberals, the product of inadequate or corrupt social institutions and of misunderstanding among leaders (Mingst). The regulation regime and high value given to the rules, acts and security is not very well accepted though they respect all of these when they are minimal and mild. Though initially even Nehru was a liberalist soon he moved towards championing socialism. One best example to differentiate between Nehru's ideology and liberalism is Chakravarthi Rajagopalachari's anecdotes and his life. Though Nehru and Rajagopalachari were together during the freedom struggle, soon after independence Nehru's obsession with Socialism troubled Rajaji and his colleagues and they went on to start a new political outfit called Swatantra Party opposing Nehru's policies. In fact 'Rajaji was the first person to hoist the flag of open revolt against Nehru's polices (Narayanaswamy)'. Still scholars like Ramachandra Guha hold Nehru as a liberalist as against the group of scholars led by Partha J Shah. To be precise, the Congress party led government in India and its leadership at different intervals starting with Nehru until recently to Manmohan Singh have been a confused lot. Unlike Nehru, Narasimha Rao and Manmohan Singh thought that it is best to be liberals by including the trade component to it. This might be one of the main reasons Manmohan Singh struggled with the issues of national security. At the most he did was to condemn such instances. The liberalist thought in India thinks that the inherent value of rationality will work and there is no need for intervention of the state every time on every issue. The fact that needs to be emphasized here is that the Liberalists need certain conditions remaining constant to flourish. This has led to a tension between the liberalists and nationalists. If the country is strong in its foundation and is a stable state, the liberalist tradition would flourish. The problem with a country like India since its independence till date is that of its security. Volatile boundary issues with Pakistan, China and Bangladesh have always demanded a strong state and concurrent laws to deal with it. The politics of welfare state and planning also to a large extent remains as an irritant to the liberals. Needless to say, the liberals had their time, but were always threatened by the hyper nationalist thought.

The third school of thought consisting of hyper nationalists is the right wing of India. Though on the surface they appear to be the most unpopular among the intellectuals, their stand is always clear and straight forward. The hyper nationalists do not want any compromise on the security of the state. For them the motherland becomes the most important. They also demand strong action against the nations opposing India like Pakistan. It is to be noted that the hyper nationalists derive their ideology from organisations such as the RSS, the VHP and the Bajarang Dal, which base themselves on the protection of Hindu religion essentially invoking motherland as part of it. They always have an opinion that India was glorious but was looted and brought to a bad situation because of invaders. The revival of the past glory seems to be a primordial idea, be it Sanskrit as a language or heroes of mythology. The striking change in their path is the interest they have been showing with regard to the neo-liberal culture towards commerce but equally conservative in terms of culture as such. Possessing strong military and strong reactions to perpetration by the enemy remains the basis of their imagination of national security. Hindu nationalists have also generally been more hawkish, calling for a commitment to military strength and often favouring the use of force and have been advocating the acquisition of nuclear weapons since the 1960s' (Swamy). Though they have had a chance to be in power only twice including the present regime, they have been vocal in their approach to India's national security. Many academicians term hyper nationalists as realists. There are scholars who make a distinction and opine that 'where Hindu nationalists depart with Western realists like Thucydides, Morgenthau, and Waltz is with their insistence that for a country to be strong it must cultivate a strong sense of national identity' (Panda). The hyper nationalist group always uses the instance of India going fully nuclear in 1998 under Vajpayee's regime as their symbol of nationalism. The present government led by Narendra Modi is also seen as a continuing stream of Vajpayee's legacy but with some changes such as high importance to trade, make in India, unleashing the soft power strength of India and quick decision making process. Though there have been few instances to prove the rhetoric to reality, they have been significant from India's national security point of view. The retaliation to the actions of Pakistan would serve as a good example. The economic times reported saying 'in another example of how decision-making process has changed under the BJP-led government, Prime Minister Narendra Modi did not convene a meeting of the Cabinet Committee on Security (CCS) before deciding to aggressively retaliate to Pakistan's shelling last week. The decision was taken by Modi himself in consultation with the National Security Advisor (NSA) Ajit Doval'. This is exactly the result the hyper nationalists have looked forward under Modi's leadership. His criticism of the previous Prime Minister's national security policy during the electoral campaign as "weak where we needed to be strong, insensitive where we needed to be sensitive" can be aptly recalled. Modi and his team branded as hyper nationalists due to his background have no hesitation to accept that India has been timid in relations with China and weak on counterterrorism and cyber warfare (Nanda). In the coming five years, India will witness the hyper nationalists at the helm of affairs on decisions pertaining to India's national security.

There is a flaw in each of the school of thought as they suffer from one or the other type of extremity. One needs to also make a distinction between the notion of national security that was prevailing in India before 2000 and later. The policy makers have realized that the traditional security paradigm does not address the rapidly growing nontraditional threats to security like: the struggle for resources embedded in the pursuit of energy, security, environmental degradation, forced migration, international terrorism, insurgency ascendancy of non-state actors in drugs, arms, money laundering and financial crime organization. The previous National Security Advisor of India (NSA) asserted that "We now need to consider our energy security, food security, technology security, and social cohesion and institutions, to name just a few, when we think of national security" (Menon). This understanding has essentially come in India much later than some of the developed countries from the compulsion that national Security requires a stable economy with assured supplies of materials for the Industry. In this sense, frugality and conservation of materials are essential to national security. Security means more than safety from hostile attacks, it includes the preservation of a system of civilization (Huddle). Something that we have all been witnessing has been the change in the mind set from the strict monoculture and sacrosanct traditional notion of security meaning military dimensions of national security being changed to include other non-military aspects of security in India. Think tanks and academicians working on strategic studies have started accepting this definitional change happening in a subtle way. One of the best examples that can be cited is the subject of climate change and environmental security which has almost become part of all the institutions working on strategic studies. This is a welcome alteration in an era where the possibility of physical war is meager. It is high time such several aspects which have influence on national security should be taken into consideration as the expected standards in the notions of national security has to be multidimensional, integrated, interest-based and not threat-based, grounded in hope, not fear, pursued inside out, adapted to the information age. In the verge of making the world a better place to live by hoping for peace and make wars and conflicts scanty, there is a necessity to move beyond the national security discourses surrounding national interest and the security of the individual country. No national security is comprehensive in the world without considering the global threats as we live in a world of complex interdependence and each other's actions can cause an equivalent amount of damage as well as bring positive results equally.

References

Acharya, Amitav (1995) "The periphery as the core: The third world and security studies." YCISS Occasional Paper.

Aron, Raymond (1966) Peace and War: A Theory of International Relations . Garden City, NY: Doubleday & Company

Ayoob, Mohammed (1995) .Regional Security and the third world: State Making, Regional Conflict and tthe International system. New York: Lynne Rienner

Bajpai, Kanti.(2002) "Indian Strategic Culture." Chambers, Michael R. South Asia in 2020: Future Strategic Balances and Alliances. Carlisle, PA: Strategic Studies Institute

Beard, Charles A. (1966) The idea of the National Interest. Chicago: Quadrangle.

Brown, Lester R (1977) "Redefining National Security." Worldwatch Papers. Washington, D.C: Worldwide Institute

Buzan, Barry (1991) People, States and Fear: An Agenda for International Security Studies in the Post-Cold War Era. New York: Harvester Wheatsheaf

—. (1991) People, States and Fear: An Agenda for International Security Studies in the Post-Cold War Era. New York: Wheatsheaf

—. (1991) People, States and Fear: An Agenda for International Security Studies in the Post-Cold War Era . New York: Harvester Wheatsheaf

Cohen, Stephen P. " India, Pakistan and Kashmir." Journal of Strategic Studies (2002): 32 - 60

Dasgupta, Stephen P. Cohen and Sunil (2010) Arming without Aiming: India's Military Modernisation. New Delhi: Penguin Viking

Frankel, Joseph. (1970) National Interest. London: Pall Mall Press Ltd.

Halftendorn, Helga. "The Security Puzzle: Theory-Building and Discipline-Building in International Security." International Studies Quarterly (1991): 3 - 18.

Hobbes, Thomas. (1946) " Leviathan." Oakeshott, Michael. Oxford: Basil Blackwel,.

Marshall, Charles Burton. "National Interest and National Responsibility." Annals of the American Academy of Political and Social Science (1952): 85.

Maxwell, Neville. " Forty Years of Folly." Critical Asian Studies (2003): 99 - 112.

Mehta, Pratap Bhanu. Journal of Democracy (2011)

Menon, Shivshankar. " India's External and Internal Security." Raja Ramanna Memorial Lecture . 21 January 2013.

Mingst, Karen (2003) "Essentials of International Relations." New York: W W Norton & Company

Morgenthau, Hans J. (1948) .Politics among Nations: The Struggle for Power and Peace. New York: Alfred A. Knopf

Narayanaswamy, G. (2001) "Rajaji: Man with a Mission in profiles in Courage: Dissent on Indian Socialism." Shah, Partha J, Profiles in Courage: Dissent on Indian Socialism. New Delhi: Centre for Civil Society

Parekh, Bhikhu. " Nehru and the National Philosophy of India." Economic and Political Weekly (1991): 1 - 2.

Renner, Michael. (1989) " National Security: The Economic and Environmental Dimensions." Worldwatch Paper. Washington D.C: The Worldwatch Institute

Rosenau, James N (1968). " National Interest." Sills, David L. International Encyclopedia of the Social Sciences. New York: Macmillan Free Press

Rothschild, E. " 'What is security?'." Dædalus (1995): 53–98.

Smith, Quintin Hoare and Geoffrey Nowell (1971) Selections from the prison notebooks of Antonio Gramsci. London: Lawrence & Wishart

Subramanyam, K. (1976) " Nehru and the Sino-Indian conflict of 1962." Indian Foreign Policy: The Nehru Years. Nanda, B. R. Honolulu: University Press of Hawai

Ullman, Richard. "Redefining Security." International Security (1983): 129 - 153.

Wolfers, Arnold. ""National Security" as an Ambiguous Symbol." Political Science Quarterly 67 (1952): 483

4 | Theorizing The Sino – Indian Ties In The Emerging Global Order

Harish Thakur

Abstract

India and China have generated lots of debate in the international politics over their conflicting borders and interests and role as active players in Indian sub-continental, Asian and consequently world politics. In recent years both have reached newer heights in the domains of science, technology, space, economy, trade and military and hence invite larger global attention. The current paper endeavours at drawing certain lines of commonalities and differences over the decades between the bilateral ties of the two as also in respect of the world politics. There have been deliberate attempts on behalf of the two states in the past to follow short term and long term policies to fizzle out the pressure of the unresolved issues which in turn take the shape of short term and long term theories to be consistently followed by them. 'One China Theory', 'China's Growth Rate as a farce Theory', 'Contain China Theory', 'Balkanize India Theory', 'India's Tibet Theory', 'Destabilize India Theory', 'Trade Theory', 'String of Pearls Theory', and 'Iron Curtain Theory' are the ones which have been followed by the two states in general and US and its allies in particular. The current paper intends to assess these theories keeping in view the bilateral ties between India and China.

I

India and China are the two largest states of Asia and world both in terms of population and territory. However, owing to different reasons the relationships between the two states have never been normal since their coming into existence as independent states. The ideologically different planes over which the politics of the two states has evolved over the decades may have moved a bit closer, the bilateral trade ties may have strengthened enormously but the role and the influence of the two in the continent of Asia and Indian sub-continent seems to be undefined largely and the two are engaged in a silent war of spreading their areas of influence and control.

It has been customary in the field of international relations to theorize the bilateral and multilateral ties among states based on the policies and practices they follow in the exercise of their relations. It's not that attempts at such theorization are futile and insignificant since the relations among states are fluid and dynamic rather they represent the set of events spread over a specific time with common elements of origins and causations. They also provide yet another way of looking at the relations of states through placing them under the *'short theoretical norms'* cropping up from the specificities of time and space that help better understanding of the relationships duly situationalized and contextualized.

The relations between India and China also deserve to be studied on the bases of such piece-meal perspectives since the nature of the problem between the two is quite complex on account of the overlapping of history, culture, geography and people. The failure of the two states to resolve the border issue and the continuing stalemate has forced many to present small piece-meal propositions as gradual moves in the direction of the resolution of the larger issue.

Besides such propositions there have been deliberate attempts on behalf of the two states to follow short term and long term policies to fizzle out the pressure of the unresolved issue which in turn take the shape of short term and long term theories to be consistently followed by them. 'One China Theory', 'China's Growth Rate as a farce Theory', 'Contain China Theory', 'Balkanize India Theory', 'India's Tibet Theory', 'Destabilize India Theory', 'Trade Theory' and 'String of Pearls Theory', and 'Iron Curtain Theory' are the ones which have been followed by the two states in general and US and its allies in particular. The current paper intends to assess these theories keeping in view the bilateral ties between India and China.

II

India and China are considered to be the oldest civilizations and it is customary that they are taken as two big Asian giants. However, the idea of the Sino-Indian parity seems to have ebbed down over the years as China statistically outpaces India economically. However, the figures don't bear static appearance for all the times and this is what makes the things interesting to the world. There has been a lot of debate these days about the resurgence of India vis-à-vis china so far as economic development and technological advancement is concerned. Statistics apart the increased malignant polemic on behalf of China to undermine the Indian assertion seems to have been guided by certain concealed motives, of course the prime one to establish itself as the undisputed power of the continent. China's foreign policy towards India appears to be directed by these very motives.

After independence, China largely remained obsessed with the idea of ideological expansion and socio-economic reconstruction with opposition to the developments reeking of western capitalist cult. Its foreign policy remained broadly confounded with the domestic that intermittently smacked against the acronyms of disagreements. It spanked all such developments, which were detrimental to the communist legacy of China so much so that even the fellow riders in the shape of USSR also kept it alarmed, partially because of undefined borders and primarily due to the larger geopolitical stratagem. Although, the ideological culture seems to have subdued a lot these days as China attracts immense FDI from the West yet the emergence of a strong China as a global power (economically and militarily) has lead many a thinkers propound 'China Threat Theory'.[1]

This theory bears a dual character as economically strong China would inflate militarily and tend to expand geographically to overcome the lingering disputes. This might take into its fold Taiwan, Hong Kong, and certain territories of India and Mongolia thus threatening the strategic interests of the West on the one hand and Japan and Korea on the other. "A state dissatisfied with the status quo will seek changes through territorial, political and economic expansion until the marginal costs of further changes are equal to or greater than the marginal benefits".[2]

There is another dimension of the theory that makes the situation imminent. In case of China's collapse, as predicated by many, it would reemploy the older tool of aggressive nationalist policies to recuperate from the scenario and this might cause a significant flashpoint in the international politics. The possibility of such probable irks West which has aligned against China's expansion thus leading to '*Contain China Theory*'.

China that had border disputes with about 14 states has so far settled almost all of them except few with India or Taiwan. The reasons are not far to be noticed. The question of Tibet ails the bilateral understanding between the two. Its policy of exercising control over Tibet is centuries long and any skepticism about China's withdrawal from the same would be a grave error. It has exercised control over Tibet intermittently in the past. Historically, it has laid claim to Tibet as it walked out of the Simla Conference held on July 14, 1914, thus denying the British doctrine of McMahon line. The same did the later regimes and the onus to settle the issue lies more with India than China. Against this India has placed the things as they received from the colonial masters, which the former would disagree to approve.

"Historically China's regions of Tibet and Xinjiang had been considered as its soft underbelly where China had been repeatedly hit by expanding empires be it Russians or the British in India or the Mongols or Muslims from the North-West Asia or the nomadic warlords from Central Asia. In more recent period, Western powers had come to be communist china's sworn enemies. Indeed, from the very inception of communism in the former Soviet Union their opposition had been the guiding force in their decision to support the KMT government against China's Communists and this was to become the most critical determinant of New China's world view after its liberation in 1949".[3]

The march of China over Tibet in 1950 and the consequent ratification of Chinese move by India, though a bit hesitant, portrayed an expansionist and much ambitious China. It showed to the world that China is not going to compromise over the issues relating not only with national interests, which every state tend to do, but also with geographical history it carries. This is the chief principle together with the ruse work done with Nehru (Panchsheel) that formed the bases of China's Foreign policy in the early fifties and even today.

The foreign policy of China towards India has undergone slight shift as China disowns certain commitments made earlier and adds more recalcitrance to its negotiations. Immediately after the signing of 'Five Principles' it not only kept on infringing the borders but also provoked the ill-equipped India to follow its line. However, since 1960 one can observe some evenness in its approach so far as the ideas of Zhou En Lai were expressed again by Deng Xiaoping in 1981 and Jiang Jamin in 1997.

During the summit talks of 1960, Zhou En Lai not only established officially that a serious border problem exists between the two but also offered "reciprocal acceptance of present actualities in both sectors and constitution of a boundary commission". But this had happened when China had forcefully occupied hundreds of miles of territory over the border through recurrent incursions thus humiliating India. Almost in the same vein spoke Deng Xiaoping in 1981:

"China has never asked for the return of all the territory illegally incorporated into India by the old colonialists. China suggested that both countries should make concessions. China in the East Sector and India in the West Sector on the basis of the actually controlled borderline so as to solve the Sino-Indian border question in a package plan."[4] The same opinions are expressed by his successor Jiang Zemin who also expressed the willingness of the China to resolve the dispute based on mutual trust and concessions. One thing is evident from the repeated pleadings on behalf of China is that they dissociate the independent Indian governments from the actions of their colonial masters. The undefined borders, which the two have inherited, need to be settled vigorously and for this China would employ all the means its domestic strength allows. It is in no mood to bargain what it thinks belongs to China, however much time it takes. And this is the crux of the foreign policy of a state that it follows in the pursuit of national interests. In the case of India the deliberate pending of the resolution serves China's additional purpose too i.e. keep India preoccupied with regional and domestic problems to check it grow as an economic giant, a challenge for China. In the struggle for hegemony in Asia India seems to be the challenge number one to China.

The foreign policy thus conceived by China in the early fifties has received a different touch from the new masters who belong to a new generation more sensible to the post-cold war neo-globalized world. "The New (Jiang Zemin and now Hu Jintao) leadership is likely to be very pragmatic. Engineers (most of the members of Polit Bureau of CPC are engineers) see political issues as problems to be solved based on hard data and hard interests, not as conflicts driven by ideological principles. In many ways, if the larger economic and political context permits, the new leadership is likely to push fundamental reform of the economy dramatically farther than was politically feasible in the Deng period. At a minimum, in the hands of this leadership the era of egalitarian social revolution in China is over. However, the foreign policy of China won't turn hyperbolic and repugnant to the past as Jian Zemin would continue to quote the adages of Confucius and other national heroes in his speeches. At an ASEAN summit held at Kuala Lumpur In December 1997 Jiang suggested that East Asian peoples generally share cultural traditions that value the virtues of "self-respect and self-strengthening, arduous effort, industriousness, frugality, modesty and eagerness to learn" as well as "harmony in human relations and peaceful coexistence in international relations."[5]

India has repeatedly endorsed the theory of 'One China' thus making its stand clear over Tibet and Taiwan accepting them as part of China. However, China would differ over the same when it comes to 'One India Principle' keeping its options open over Sino-Indian border and Jammu and Kashmir. It has played Tibet card quite successfully to gain concessions from India whereas India has miserably failed to do so. Its grant of asylum to Dalai Lama only irks China thus placing India at the same footing as Pakistan vis-à-vis India.

Now quite recent in origin is the theory of 'Balkanize India', a Chinese assertion of breaking India into 20 to 30 separate states, a dream that might be untrue even for Indians if they opt for this. The theory is guided by the long standing fear of China about India as the major stumbling block in the Chinese intent of becoming the undisputed Asian power number one. It has been a long policy of China to keep India circumscribed by assisting the neighbouring states like Pakistan, Bangladesh, Nepal and Myanmar. The separatist elements in the North-East too have clandestine links with China and Myanmar.

China Institute of International Strategic Studies (CIISS), a semi-governmental body published in its website a news entitled 'A Warning to the Indian Government: Don't be Evil'.[6] The article alarms India of the same consequences that it met in 1962, if it keeps on drawing 'arrogant' posture against China. The same piece was re-circulated before the 13th round of border talks in New Delhi in August 2009, an old act of China consistently followed to stall the dialogue.

After the resurgence of a strong China economically which has a growth rate of 8 per cent, it dreams of becoming a leading global actor, a dream that has alarmed the West too. Indian economy, which has also kept a sustained growth rate of 6 per cent in the last many years, is sure to vie with China in the future that the latter would not digest. China's settling the same McMahon Line with Burma speaks of its well thought out foreign policy i.e. not allowing India grow strong economically by impeding its advancement through the leverage of its contending neighbours and keeping the issue of unsettled borders alive. China's 'Tibetization'[8] of Burma is also seen quite detrimental to India's security interests. China's special interest in Burma is primarily guided by containing India become the sole naval power in the Indian Ocean.

Yet another theory in the air is about the genuineness of the growth rate shown by China. In the early 1990s China registered double digit growth rate which has gradually weakened over the years that smacks of near collapse in the future. "The fact that India is increasingly building from the ground up while China is still pursuing a top-down approach reflect their contrasting political systems. In utilizing of resources and facilitating home entrepreneurs India is doing a superior job. India's ground–up approach may indeed be wiser."[9] Theories apart, there has been a visible transformation in the policy stand of China against India in the post-Pokharan era. It has become more vociferous about its stance on Eastern and western sectors of Indian borders. In the Western Sector (border areas of Jammu and Kashmir and Himachal) very recently (January 2010) Chinese soldiers not only intruded into Indian territories of Ladakh but also marked their sovereignty over the land by painting rocks and stones. They also forced the J and K border road authorities on November 29, 2009 to stop work over the construction of a road under National Rural Employment Guarantee Scheme at Demchok in South East Leh.[10] Even in Sikkim that China has virtually accepted as part of India it is raking up the border issue by committing about 90 incursions only in the year 2008. It is also trying to press Thimpu for the exchange of two posts which near the state of Sikkim. On June 16, 2008 Chinese troops almost entered more than one kilometer inside the Indian territory in the northern most point of Sikkim called Finger Point.[11]

In August 2007 China also demanded removal of two Indian bunkers at Batang La near India-Bhutan-China Tri-Junction. Interestingly, as per 1890 Anglo-Chinese Convention that defined the border between Tibet and Sikkim, Beijing had no objections till now. But now its insistence to move the line southward along Torsa Nala seems to be guided by its desire to gain advantage over the Chumbi Valley under Indian control. On

October 10, 2007 when India refused to remove the bunkers China called it the violation of 'Agreement on Maintenance of Peace and Tranquility' signed in 1993. It accused India of building 'facilities' on the Indian side of the border.[12]

Its claim to whole of the state of Arunachal Pradesh from where it pulled back its forces in 1962 is a startling development of major concern. For India China has forcefully occupied about 43,180 sq. kms. of territories in the Aksai Chin area of Jammu and Kashmir including 5,180 sq. kms. illegally ceded to China by Pakistan under the Sino-Pakistan Boundary Agreement in 1963. Against this China lays claim over 90,000 sq. kms. of territory, mostly in Arunachal Pradesh and about 2000 kms. of area in the Middle Sector. As per the broader understanding reached in 2005 by the two that due care shall be taken of the populated areas while the settlement of the unfinished task of borders China seems to have forgotten the same when it lays claim for Tawang town in the light of selection of successor of Dalai Lama (However, Dalai Lama has also expressed his willingness to end the choice of successor, as the tradition is not imminent) Since Tawang is a significant place from religious point of view of Lhasa, its being the birthplace of 6th Dalai Lama Tsangyang Gyatso, China claims its ownership that first officially took place in 1984. In 1987 there was a border skirmish at Sumdorong Chu in Arunachal. "China's assertion of claims over Tawang is getting increased over the years. On the eve of Chinese President Hu Jintao's visit to New Delhi in Nov. 2006, Beijing's ambassador to India, Sun Yuxi told an Indian Television Channel that the whole of the state of Arunachal Pradesh is Chinese territory and Twang is only one of the places in it".

There seems to be the other dimension of the claim over Tawang as it is said to have good mineral sources and fertile land that can boost Tibetan economy. Militarily its passing into the hands of China would provide it a critical leverage over the north eastern states and Brahmaputra valley.[13]

China's harping over the issue of Tibet speaks of its neo-invented strategy of impeding the process of dialogue. Its claim to Tawang becomes weak in the light of its first capturing it together with the other territories of NEFA and then withdrawing broadly around the Mc Mahon Line, thus accepting it as a *de facto* arrangement. "If Beijing needed to hold on to Tawang for religious or security reasons or felt that their legal claim was rock solid, they would not have withdrawn. Its demand of the town now seems to be 'sheer political effrontery'. Its claim shows absence of any real desire for a border settlement and the tactic is to contrive an issue so as to transfer the responsibility for an impasse on to the Indian side".[14] One reason for China's now insisting over Tawang is to cut into the area of Dalai Lama's influence. If it succeeds in getting Tawang it now believes that a major support to the Dalai Lama's following would be pruned.

China's attitude seems to be governed by the elements of indomitable instinct of dominance and recalcitrance as it presses upon India to accept the unacceptable at the point of its military might thus forcing India to reinforce its armed strength. Moreover, it will not feel comfortable if India goes on for the wholesale modernizing of the arms and spends dollars over the programme.

The recent multiplying of trade output (though enormously in China's favour) has led the two to soften their attitude on the border issue. This is what the last two visits (December 2010 visit of Chinese Premier Hu Jintao to New Delhi and April 2011 visit of Prime Minister Man Mohan Singh to Beijing) give the impression. It is believed that more the trade grows more the two would be forced to soften over the border deadlock and the *Trade Theory* or *Trade Diplomacy*.

Around the 'String of Pearls' Politics

Of late with the unleashing of global forces, especially after the disintegration of Soviet Union several new aspiring actors have thrown their hats into the ring. The chief stake is regarding the natural resource rich Central Asia, the disintegrated units of former USSR. While the struggle to acquire influence over these states has increased there has been a persistent effort on the behalf of the actors engaged to keep the others at the fringe to ensure better prospects and a secure zone of rich harvest in the future.

In their search to develop better commercial avenues and network the states are engaged in extending their area of operation by building new trade links and commercial bases around the world especially in the Indian Ocean and Arabian Sea. While the US and NATO have solid foothold in the far eastern states of Asia and South China Sea the counter result of the buildup seems to have forced China to spread its network, though officially declared of commercial nature (but inherently military in intent too) from South China sea to the North African zone thus covering several strategically significant areas and waters.

In the Indian Ocean region (IOR) India and China are engaged in a silent war for over decades. While Indian interest in the ocean is visible for all its commercial activities rely on its sea ports the China's increased interest speaks of its rivalry with India on both economic and military grounds. A strategic analyst Mr. Mahan had predicted the significance of Indian Ocean long back in 19th century since the world politics would hinge upon it.

For India the ocean is important because of its dismal history for providing sea routes to the naval powers like Britain, France and Portugal. India now can't afford the presence of anti-India powers in the region and has to build up and modernize its navy accordingly. India also views the security of the IOR as prime responsibility of it geographically and politically. The Indian Naval Maritime Doctrine expressed in 2004 is crystal clear about the major Indian role in the region which irks China who would pronounce 'Indian Ocean as not India's Ocean'. In this regards Indian efforts to develop economic and strategic relations with Indian Ocean Rim states are significant. India has solidified its relations with Maldives, Mauritius, Seychelles, Madagascar, South Africa, Tanzania and Mozambique in the last few decades by improvising bilateral economic ties. It also extended double taxation exemption to Maldives and several such sops to the rim states. India's role in suppressing the coups against President Abdul Qayyum in Maldives in 1998 and Albert Rene in Seychelles is well known. Recently the India adventures into South China Sea in 2014 on the invitation of Vietnamese Prime Minister adds more spice to the 'forward naval policy'. Though China strongly objected to it and warned India to stay away from its bilateral disputes with neighbours India has given a strong message that it won't succumb to the China's policy of expansion and circumventing India through the so called 'string of pearl policy'. China also alleges India of developing an 'iron curtain' in the Indian Ocean to stall Chinese activities in the region.[15]

One such design devised by China is to surround India and increase its influence in Asia and Africa is what has been popularly called "The String of Pearls", a coastal chain of commercial centers and ports. It's a network of Chinese military and commercial facilities (though China would call it purely commercial) and relationships along its sea lines of communication starting from the South China Sea (Hainan Island) to the Port of Sudan in the North-Eastern part of African Continent. The above mentioned string or line of communication extends through several significant sea ports, maritime centres and strategic locations like the Strait of Mandeb, the Strait of Malacca, the Strait of Hormuz, the strait of Lombok as well as other strategic maritime centers in Pakistan (Gwadar), Srilanka (Hambantota), Bangladesh (Chittagong), Myanmar (Sittwe), Maldives (Marao), and Somalia. The term as a geopolitical concept was first used in an internal US department of Defence entitled "Energy Futures in Asia".

The String of Pearls is part of China's modernizing of its army programme and reflects its plans of increasing the area of influence to its trading partners who can be instrumental in meeting its energy needs in the future. The programme is multi-phased aiming at turning Chinese Navy from Green Waters to Blue waters. Although China has time and again allayed the skeptics of the regional actors over the peaceful intent of its naval policy yet the commercial act seems to have something more to a state like India who feels garlanded from the India ocean by China.

September 2014 was a remarkable month in Indo-Sino relations when the two Asian adversaries China's President and Vietnam's Prime Minister visited India. The visit was also important in the backdrop of Indian Prime Minister's Japan visit of August-September 2014 when the two countries entered into several agreements of commercial and strategic significance. The Indian security concerns are strengthened by the fact that when India cooperated with Vietnam over oil exploration activity in South China Sea the latter threatened India of entering into its security zone and stop the collaboration. During the Modi regime in the last six months India has taken more bold initiatives with cementing of its ties with Vietnam further. India has signed several agreements with Vietnam. In September 2014 Indian President signed six agreements with Vietnam followed by seven more when the Vietnamese Prime Minister Nguyen Tan Dung visited India On October 28, 2014. This is Indian response to China's string of pearl politics which, according to China is a commercial act in response to Indian dominance in the Indian Ocean region. China also placed its naval submarine *Changdjheng* and two warships at Hambantota port in Srilanka in September 2014. It also continued its old strategy of keeping the pressure on in the borders while paying official visits to India when it intruded in Chumar sector of Ladakh while China's President Xi Jinping was on official visit to India. Indian response to China regarding its collaboration with Vietnam is seen from the same perspective and a lot depends now how the two leaderships move ahead in the future.

III

The contemporary geopolitical and strategic dynamics of the world demand for the rational mutual adjustments and measures of building mutual trust and confidence. The significance of these theories lies in their utility in grasping the real crux of the issues. The relations between India and China have witnessed an era of confrontation and thaw. Their history is such that what they have inherited in the form of undefined borders is one of the most complex questions of the time. Since China withdrew from the Shimla Conference held in 1914, resulting in the McMahon Line, India needs to understand the traditional complications implied in the resolution of the borders. The geo-strategic plans and requirements of the British were different. India needs to settle them differently.

The major questions that India and China face today must be addressed by entering into strong Confidence Building Measures (CBMs). The key areas regarding this are the military modernization plans of India and China. While India's massive military modernization plan irks China, China's military strength outweighs India's thus forcing India to gain parity. While Pakistan feels imbalanced because of Indian programme, India feels outweighed by Chinese one, which in turn feels eclipsed by the US presence in the pacific.

Therefore, the core area that requires strong CBMs is the removal of mutual mistrust and fear. The better trade relations can make the environment more conducive to other areas of dispute. The issue of border can be placed at the backburner to be resolved by rational adjustments where the two have to be flexible in approach also. While India should evaluate the Chinese claims to the territories southward of McMahon line sincerely, China should also understand the post-independence implications of the settlement for India giving due honour to its claims northward, especially to areas of religious significance. Given the circumstances it's the need of the hour to evade the theories of mistrust and confrontation and go for the ones which strengthen the relations and add to the mutual trust and faith.

It's not the time when one can impose settlements forcefully since this theory works against the ethics of international peace. The string of pearls, the iron curtain, and India's forward policies require to be understood in the frame of the history and the actual position of the two. The September episode and the attitude of Modi government towards China have to be studied accordingly and the sensitive issue of border can be discussed as and when the circumstances are conducive. If China brushes away Indian role in Indian Ocean it shouldn't have objections in purely commercial forays of Indian company ONGC working for Vietnam in South China Sea. Its consistent intrusions on the borders need to be dealt diplomatically until some significant changes at border occur. The utility of such piecemeal approaches or theories to understand the bilateral ties between the two and also the multilateral dynamics could not be denied since they help us draw better insights into the core of the problems.

Notes and References

1. Russel Org, **China's Security Interest in the Post-Cold War Era**, (Surrey: Curzon Press, 2002), pp.161-167, See also James R. Lilley and David Shambaugh, (Eds.), **China's Military Faces the Future**, (Washington D.C., AEI, 1999); Chandran Jehurun, (Ed.), **China, India and Japan and the Security of South East Asia**, (Singapore: Institute of South-East Asian Studies, 1995) and K.R. Singh, **The Indian Ocean**, (New Delhi: Manohar Publications, 1977).

2. Robert Gilpin, **War and Change in World Politics**, (Cambridge: Cambridge University Press, 1981), p.106

3. Swaran Singh, **China-South Asia: Issues, Equations, Policies**, (New Delhi: Lancer's Books, 2003), p 331

4. Neville Maxwell, "Sino-Indian Border Dispute Reconsidered", **Economic and Political Weekly**, April 10, 1999

5. H. Lyman Miller and Liu Xiaohong, "The Foreign Policy Outlook of China's 'Third Generation' Elite," in David M. Lampton, (Ed.), **The Making of Chinese Foreign Policy in the Era of Reforms**, (Stanford: Stanford University Press, 2001), pp.136-137.

6. Ibid., p. 149

7. "A Warning to the Indian Government: Don't be Evil", at http://www.strategypage.com/militaryforums/69-30747.aspx , See also Barun Das Gupta, "Renewed Threat from China", **Mainstream**, September 11-17, 2009, p. 31

8. J. Mohan Malik, "China India Relations in the Post-Soviet Era: The Continuing Rivalry", **The China Quarterly**, No 142 , June 1995, p 338, See also Dan Twining, "Could India and China go to War over Tibet"?, See also at http://

shadow.foreignpolicy.com/posts/2009/03/10/could_china_and_india_go_to_war_over_tibet and Raviprasad Narayanan, "India's Foreign Policy Towards China: The NDA Experience-Dominant issues in Sino-Indian Relations", at http://www.asianqurterly.com/content/view/141/40/

9   Yasheng Huang and Tarun Khanna, "Can India Overtake China?", at http://www.foreignpolicy.com/story/story.php?storyID=13774

10 http://www.indianexpress.com/news/work-stopped-on-ladakh-road-after-chinese-troops-object/547903/

11 Sudha Ramchandran, "China Toy's with India's Border", **South Asia**, June 27, 2008, see also at http://www.atimes.com/atimes/South_Asia/JF27Df01.html

12 Pushpita Das, 'India Has to be Wary of Chinese Intrusions', at http://www.idsa.in/idsastrategiccomments/IndiahastobewaryofChineseIntrusions_PDas_191007

13 Sudha Ramchandran, **op.cit**.

14 Kanwal Sibal, Indian Defence Review, at http://www.rediff.com/new/2008/feb/03tawang.htm

15 See also http://www.indiandefencereview.com/news/chinas-string-of-pearls-vs-indias-iron-curtain/

PART – II

INDIA'S SECURITY CONCERNS IN THE EMERGING GLOBAL ORDER

5 | The Defence Aspect of India's National Security

B. Vivekanandan

When we look at India's security policy options, it is important to keep in view the determinants of India's security policy. A key determinant of India's security policy is the nature of relationship between India and its seven neighbours, with whom India shares its 15,000 Km long land border. Another key determinant is the state of affairs in the Indian Ocean, which washes India's 7,516 Km long coastlines.

Of the seven neighbouring countries, India shares a common culture and heritage with six of them. The one country with which India has no commonality of any kind, but with which India shares 4,000 Kms of its borders, is China. It is the only country in modern times which still demonstrates its insatiable instinct of expansionism, and systematically stirs up border disputes with most of its neighbours, including with India.

Before I come to India's security policy options, I would like to familiarise you with the security architecture which India's first Prime Minister Jawaharlal Nehru had bequeathed to his successors. In this context, I would like to draw your attention to four critical decisions Jawaharlal Nehru had taken personally during the first decade of India's independence, which sowed the seeds of all important security problems India is faced with today.

The first one was Jawaharlal Nehru's refusal, in May 1948, to permit Major General Kalwant Singh to continue, for five more days, his mopping up operations in Kashmir against the tribal intruders and to allow the Indian Army to reach Pakistan's international border. This was Jawaharlal Nehru's personal decision. If Gen. Kalwant Singh was permitted to continue his operation for five more days, as he requested for to Nehru, there would have been no Kashmir problem today to bedevil India's relations with Pakistan.

The second personal decision of Nehru was in the context of China's annexation of Tibet and the negotiations that followed between India and China on the subject. When the Chinese invaded Tibet in 1950, Nehru underestimated its implications for India's security. And, he did not do anything to preserve Tibet's independence, and quickly conceded China's sovereignty on Tibet, without even asking China to clarify its position regarding the status of the Mc Mahon Line as the border between India and Tibet. During the 3-year long negotiations between India and China on Tibet, between 1951 and 1954, Nehru repeatedly refused permission to Indian officials like Girija Shankar Bajpai, K.P.S. Menon and T.N. Kaul, to put the status of the Mc Mahon Line as an item on the agenda of discussion between India and China. And thus Nehru had kept alive the seed of a costly territorial dispute between India and China.

The third personal decision of Jawaharlal Nehru was regarding India's first atomic test. In 1957, Nehru refused permission to Homi J. Bhabha, India's nuclear scientist, to conduct India's first nuclear test, and to make the Hiroshima type atom bombs, at the cost of Rs 5 lakhs per piece at that time. If Nehru permitted Bhabha to go ahead with his plan, India would have been the 4th nuclear weapon power in the world, after the United States, Britain and the Soviet Union. It was only a few years later that France conducted its first nuclear test. And, China conducted its first nuclear test only in 1964.

Therefore, when the nuclear non-proliferation treaty (NPT) was finalised in 1968, the treaty gave the legal nuclear weapon state status only to those countries which had conducted nuclear tests before April 1968. As a result, while China got recognition as a nuclear weapon state, with the right to make, refine and stockpile nuclear weapons, India remained with the status of a non-nuclear weapon state. The reason for India's lower status vis-a-vis China under the NPT, is again due to Nehru's decision not to permit Bhabha to conduct India's first nuclear test in 1957.

"Buddha Smiled" in Pokhran only in 1974. But, so far India has not been recognised as a nuclear weapon state. That recognition requires an amendment to the NPT, by shifting the cut-off date of nuclear testing from April 1968 to a date after May 1974. But China and US are opposing any amendment to to that effect to accommodate India, and want India to sign the NPT as a non-nuclear weapon state, and roll back its nuclear programme.

After launching the Comprehensive Test Ban Treaty (CTBT) in 1996, the United States made a serious attempt in late 1990s, during the Clinton Presidency, to cajole India to sign the CTBT. As part of it, the US Intelligence surreptitiously used even the services of American academics, like Stephen Cohen, to build up a lobby of Indian academics to argue in support of India's signing the CTBT. Sadly, as a result, Stephen Cohen and the CIA had succeeded to net some Indian academics like Kanti Bajpai of JNU, for example, in that Indian lobby for doing that unpatriotic job to please the Americans. Yet they did not succeed mainly because many of us stood up firmly against such US moves, and defeated the US attempt to cajole India to sign the CTBT.

The fourth personal decision of Jawaharlal Nehru, which jeopardized India's security interests, was in 1955. In 1955, when People's Republic of China was not even a member of the United Nations, The United States came up with an offer that, instead of Taiwan, India should take the permanent Asian Seat in the UN Security Council. But, to the surprise of everybody, including of the United States, Jawaharlal Nehru rejected that offer, saying that let that permanent seat be there for the People's Republic of China to take when it would become a member of the United Nations.

China became a member of the United Nations 16 years later, in 1971, and instantly became a permanent member of the UN Security Council, with all the privileges attached to it. It had suddenly lifted up China's diplomatic leverage in world politics, and in South Asian politics.

It is pathetic to see India today knocking at the door of China, seeking its permission to join the UN Security Council as a permanent member. If you ask me, who had gifted this prowess to China in a platter, for using it today against India, my answer is: none other than Jawaharlal Nehru.

Therefore, keeping in view all these four personal decisions of Jawaharlal Nehru, between 1948 and 1957, and the disastrous consequences they entailed since then, it is fair to say that Jawaharlal Nehru was the architect of India's insecurity. So there is a built-in architectural defect in India's security design Nehru had bequeathed to his successors. We have not yet succeeded to undo those serious damages.

The defining factors of India's security environment today are its territorial disputes with two of its neighbours -- Pakistan and China. For solving amicably the Kashmir problem with Pakistan, India had two opportunities in 1970s. The first one was after the 1971 Indo-Pak war on Bangladesh, when the Pakistan Prime Minister, Zulfikar Ali Bhutto, came to Simla to negotiate with Prime Minister Indira Gandhi, the release of 96,000 Pakistani Prisoners of War in the Indian custody. During their meeting, Bhutto and Indira Gandhi discussed the question of an amicable settlement to the Kashmir issue, which revolved around the conversion of the LOC in Kashmir into the international border between India and Pakistan. But, their talks reached a stalemate as Bhutto needed personal consultation with his colleagues in Islamabad on this issue. It meant another round of talks between the two leaders on a later date. So the formal meeting ended in failure, and an announcement was made to that effect. But, before the two Prime Ministers left Simla, there was an one-to-one meeting between them. It was at this one-to-one meeting that Indira Gandhi gave in to Bhutto's bluff, and suddenly agreed to release all 96,000 Pakistani Prisoners of War unconditionally, and wasted a golden opportunity we got to amicably solve the Kashmir problem.

The second opportunity was during the Janata Party Government, led by Prime Minister Morarji Desai. Morarji Desai once narrated to me an inside story. He said that once he got an intelligence report that the Pakistani President, Gen. Zia-ul-Haq, was planning to increase the size of the Pakistan Army. But, Morarji did not leave that matter for the diplomatic channels to deal with. He picked up the telephone and dialled Zia-ul-Haq and asked him straight: "General, why do you want a large army for Pakistan? If Pakistan is in trouble, you tell me. My army will be at your disposal." Zia was thrilled and stunned. He could not believe that he was listening to the voice of the Indian Prime Minister, who was promising him the Indian Army's support to defend Pakistan. That day, the Pakistani President became a great admirer of Morarji Desai. He trusted Morarji Desai's words, and gave up his plan to expand the Pakistan Army. It also gives an indication why President Zia-ul-Haq conferred "Nishan-e-Pakistan" the Pakistani equivalent of "Bharat Ratna", on Morarji Desai.

It is my conviction that if the Morarji Desai Government continued in office for a full term of five years, the Kashmir problem would have been solved amicably forever. But, that process was not allowed to mature since

Indira Gandhi pulled down the Morarji Desai Government, when that Government's tenure was only half way through.

Despite these missed opportunities to amicably solve the Kashmir problem, I am optimistic about a close friendship between India and Pakistan in future. If we make a hard assessment of the future course of Indo-Pakistani relationship, inspite of its present nuclear capability and its Chinese proximity, it would be a grave mistake to treat or consider Pakistan as India's enemy or potential enemy. On the other hand, a hard assessment would show that Pakistan is India's potential friend. We should remember the supportive attitude Pakistan had adopted towards India during the Chinese aggression of India in 1962. It is my conviction that, before long, India and Pakistan will pool their destinies together and march forward hand-in-hand by giving more content to their symbiotic existence,

Therefore, the most serious threat to India's security emanates from China's brazen claims on Indian territories, and the preparations Beijing is making to realise those untenable claims. In world politics today, China belongs to a special category. In the present day world, China is the only country which still shows an insatiable appetite for expansionism. Its leadership refuses to learn any lesson from history, that all imperial build-ups – from the Roman Empire down to the USSR – had become victims of their expansionist policy, and fallen apart under their own weight after some time. China will be no exception. Future will show. Yet China contrives and manipulates alibis for expansion with territories of neighbouring countries. In one go, the dragon had swallowed Tibet. After the revolution, China has made territorial claims on its neighbouring countries like India, Russia and Japan, and is systematically building up its army, navy and air force, and the nuclear missile systems, to realise those ambitions.

With India, China raised dispute over India's 4000 Kms former border with Tibet, and fought a war with India in 1962, and annexed 80,000 Sq.Kms of Indian territory. In addition, it has made claims over another 1000 Sq.Kms of oil-rich areas of Arunachal Pradesh. And, it is engaged in a systematic military build up to encircle India, by land and sea, to intimidate New Delhi to accept China's claims on Indian territory. It has prepared Tibet, with all kinds of infra-structure for military operations – like roads, railroads and airfields – for making it a launching pad of attack on India, and to enable the Chinese to deploy troops and military hardware right up to India's border regions, at short notice. Adjacent to

Tibet, in Delingha in the Quinghai Province of China, China has built up more than 60 nuclear missile launching pads, for launching medium-range nuclear ballistic missiles against India. In Delingha, China has positioned its DF-21 medium-range nuclear ballistic missiles, which have a range of 2,150 Kms. All North Indian cities come within the firing range of these medium-range nuclear ballistic missiles positioned in Delingha.

These land-based Chinese military preparations against India in the North – in Tibet and Delingha – is complemented by China's gaining port facilities for the Chinese Navy in several littoral states of the Indian Ocean in the South for encircling India. Politically China has cultivated several Indian Ocean littoral states in India's neighbourhood, like Myanmar, Bangladesh, Sri Lanka, Maldives and Pakistan, and has obtained port facilities for its navy in all these countries. China has obtained port facilities in Oman also. India cannot, and should not, remain complacent over these systematic unfriendly moves of China.

But, it seems that India is pussy-footing against this growing grave situation. New Delhi is not doing much, diplomatically or strategically, to counter these anti-Indian activities of China. The shrillness, which is often seen in Indian responses to Pakistani activities, is conspicuous by its absence when it comes against the Chinese misdemeanours and arrogance. India did not do much even when China did a very grave anti-Indian act of clandestinely assisting Pakistan's nuclear weapon programme, in order to prop up Pakistan against India in the nuclear field. Reportedly, even border road building, on the Indian side of the Indo-Tibetan border, has suffered a grievous neglect since 1962, on the basis of a foolish, unstated strategy that, if India has built its border roads right upto the front-line, it would help the Chinese invaders, to easily come down to the South, and occupy more Indian territories! Whether such an unstated approach is still in vogue, some one knowledgeable, from the Defence Ministry, should explain. It is reported that, because of this approach, some of our 'border roads' end at 60 to 80 Kms away from the border, making it impossible for India to take its troops to the borders instantly at short notice. That is not a satisfactory situation for India.

While China pursues its encirclement policy against India vigorously, since 1981 it has also engaged India in phoney talks on the border question. Obviously, it is a deceptive exercise to hoodwink India. 34 years have passed since this phoney exercise has been going on between the officials of the two countries. But the outcome remains virtually a big zero.

So the real standing security threat to India today is from China, and not from any other country. We have to exercise our security options, keeping this reality in view.

In the end, I would say that, as all major security problems of India today have originated from the unwise decisions of Jawaharlal Nehru, it is imperative to suitably remedy the damages caused by those decisions, whichever way possible. A key remedial measure will be to help restoration of an independent Tibet as the buffer state between India and China. Keeping that in view India will have to extend steady support for the ongoing freedom struggle in Tibet. Similarly, India should stop supporting Beijing's 'One China Policy' with immediate effect.

With Pakistan, India should explore the possibility of a con-federal set-up with it, as a first step for pooling their destinies together and live in peace.

And, finally, a word about defence production. Import of defence equipment is a big drain on India's resources and foreign exchange. A lot of corruption is also going on behind these imports from abroad. Therefore, I would urge the Government of India to indigenise equipment production for India's Army, Navy, and Air Force.

6 | Nuclear South Asia: Strategic And Security Dimensions

C. Vinodan

There is probably no place else in the world today where proliferation concerns are more acute than in South Asia. Major actors in the region possess nuclear weapons capabilities. The nuclear programmes in the region are rooted in the intense rivalries over power and territory and unresolved historical hatreds. There are no regional nuclear arms control regimes, and participation in global ones is sporadic. The danger with regard to these programmes is exacerbated by their lack of transparency and the growing influence of non-state actors in the regional security matrix. In South Asia, states have generally been poor at dealing with the insecurities of their people. The processes of nation and state-building in the region have proved long and arduous, and preoccupied state agendas for decades. Historically, the focus has been on efforts to protect the territorial integrity of the state, and the safety and stability of ruling regimes-usually at the cost of adequate socio-economic development and political freedoms for those living inside and across borders. This focus continues to dominate security policy-making in the region even today, and is also to an extent reflected in the bulk of the international relations (IR) and security studies literature on South Asia, which deals overwhelmingly with inter-state hostilities, wars and disputes over territories and international borders; intra-state conflicts including armed insurgencies and ethno-nationalistic movements, and the seemingly ever-present threat of nuclear conflict between India and Pakistan.[1] Consequently, there exists relatively little scholarship from IR and security studies perspective which attempts to grapple with those *issue* which are perceived as sources of deep insecurities by *sub-state* groups in South Asia,[2] and the range of *actors* operating in these realms particularly in the absence of effective state-led efforts.

Nuclear Security Debate and South Asia

Most existing literature on nuclear proliferation focuses on the acquisition of nuclear weapons, viewing the ability to assemble a single functional nuclear weapon as the critical threshold in a state's ability to deter conflict.[3] But it is argued that mere acquisition of nuclear devices, however, neither constitutes an operational nuclear arsenal nor produces a uniform deterrent effect.[4] It is the incorporation of some number and type of nuclear warheads and delivery vehicles into a state's overall military structure and the rules and procedures governing how those weapons are deployed, when and under what conditions they might be used, against what targets, and who has the authority to make those decisions that broadly constitute a state's nuclear posture and that generate a specific deterrent effect. One of the most significant missing elements of the nuclear debate is the stable nuclear posture by the nuclear weapon states.[5] The 1998 nuclear tests in South Asia rise serious challenges to global and regional security environment. The post 9/11 developments and the growing menace terrorism worsened the regional security environment in South Asia. The nuclear security debate in South Asia raises serious questions. Scholars and practitioners began to pose the strategic effects of nuclear weapons developments in the specific regional security context? Will the spread of nuclear weapons to South Asia bring stability to the region or lead to nuclear war?. Scholars and security policy analysts sharply divided over the issue. A major section argues that the spread of nuclear weapons to South Asia will significantly reduce, or even eliminate the risk of future wars between India and Pakistan.[6] Following the logic of rational deterrence theory, these "proliferation optimists" argue that statesmen and soldiers in Islamabad and New Delhi know that a nuclear exchange in South Asia will create devastating damage and therefore will be deterred from starting any military conflict in which there is a serious possibility of escalation to the use of nuclear weapons. Other scholars and defence analysts - some in India and Pakistan , and many more in the United States - argue the opposite: nuclear weapons proliferation in India and Pakistan will increase the likelihood of crises, accidents, and nuclear war.[7] For 'proliferation pessimists, South Asia represents the worst of two worlds: small nuclear powers operating under conditions of security scarcity, where fierce animosities and rivalries do not bode well for rational or stable deterrence.[8] These "proliferation pessimists" do not base their arguments on claims that Indian or Pakistani statesmen are irrational or that the Indian and Pakistani governments are weak.

Instead, these scholars start their analysis by noting that nuclear weapons are controlled by military organizations and civilian bureaucracies, not by states or by statesmen. Organization theory, not just rational deterrence theory, should therefore be used to understand the problem and predict the future of security in the region. This organizational perspective leads the proliferation pessimists to focus on the pathways by which deterrence could fail, due to common organizational bias and errors, despite the unacceptable costs of any nuclear war. These two theoretical perspectives thus lead to very different predictions about the consequences of nuclear proliferation in South Asia. Fortunately, a new history of nuclear India and nuclear Pakistan is emerging, a history by which scholars and policy makers alike can judge whether the predictions of the deterrence optimists or the organizational pessimists have been borne out. Unfortunately, the emerging evidence strongly supports the pessimistic predictions of organizational theorists.

As the menace of terrorism increases day by day the security of the state and its people has come under severe challenge in South Asia and around the world. The very nature of terrorism in South Asia has a strong transnational and cross-border context and content, which is at the core of any discourse on South Asian security. The complexities and uniqueness of its approach in the present day sets it apart from traditional forms of terrorism. South Asia has had a long and diverse experience of dealing with terrorism. This experience dates back to the late 1940s and 1950s. Terrorism then was understood differently from today. The forms and patterns of terrorism experienced in South Asia since those early years have been varied ranging from religious extremism to those resulting from ethnic, regional, systemic and politico-ideological rebellions and conflicts. In many of these conflicts terror has been employed as one of the important instruments of revolt, and terror has also been employed in strategies to curb and counter these revolts by the state. Terror emerging out of these revolts in a given South Asian context has also been endorsed, employed and even encouraged by state actors to advance its specific strategic and foreign policy objectives. This has given rise to the phenomenon of 'cross border' terrorism. This type of terrorism existed in the early 1970s, it was mainly a coercive tactic adopted as part of territorial nationalism fighting to achieve a political objective and contained within regional borders. Established under a well-defined chain of command, it had defined political and economic objectives. Terrorist groups engaged in highly selective acts of violence that included many people watching rather than dead. The principal goal, therefore, was to raise public awareness over grievances, and not necessarily to cause a high number of casualties.

South Asia is increasingly referred to as the most volatile area of the word, as the epicentre, the 'new locus' of terrorism, as the venue of a resource – sapping and futile arms race and of a possible and devastating nuclear confrontation (Vijaykumar 2009: 74). Analysing the players at the core and peripheral levels, the Indian strategic role is highly significant. That is why most of the scholars argue that South Asian can also be characterized as an Indo-centric region due to India's overwhelming superior power in relation to its neighbours (Harshe 2005). Two important characteristics of the South Asia as viewed by Prasad Singh are South Asia is an Indo – Centric region and South Asia has an unbalanced and asymmetric power structure (Prasad Singh 2009: 217). The inclusion of China into the South Asian system may perhaps uphold the Chinese role. Encompassing china in top the regional power structure Sushil Kumar finds that the levels of relative power remain approximately unaltered, with China at the top, India in the middle, and Pakistan at the bottom (Kumar 2003: 117). This strategic triad has become very significant as these powers have nuclear capability. But the geographic significance along with many common shared historic and cultural features, place India at the core. India shares a boundary with most of the nations in the subsystem. The security system of this region is very much interweaved with its socio-politico character. The socio-economic backwardness has also caused the rise of militant groups in the South Asian region. The countries of South Asian region face the constant threats of irredentism and internal fragmentation arising from unresolved disputes over nationalist, ethnic, religious, cultural and secessionist issues within and between their territories. The most enduring examples of these are: the civil war in Sri Lanka, sectarian violence in Pakistan and the Kashmir conflict. Analyzing the stability of the South Asian security system, Sushil Kumar finds that the system is less stable. He says *"If systemic stability is absence of major war, or absence of threats to territorial security, combined with peace, or peace based upon the acceptance of a legitimate political order, then what has been witnessed within the South Asian region is less than systemic stability. Implied instead within the region—reinforced by the evidence regarding the dynamics of change on state power cycles—is political conflict, territorial insecurity and a contested political order"*(Sushil Kumar 2003).

The Non State Actors and the Regional Security in South Asia

The South Asian security can't be thought only on the inter action of the state actors of this region. The activities of a number of militant groups have been a notable threat to the South Asian Security system. In fact, South Asia has been remarked as the abode of many militant groups. Pakistan which has been called by the U.S. President Barak Obama as 'the cradle of terrorism' is a central nation of the South Asian system. *"The rugged mountainous terrain dividing Afghanistan from Pakistan provides a hiding place for Taliban terrorists, who, because they cross the border at will, are an equal headache for Pakistan"* "(Ali 2006). There is no exception that, almost all the countries of this region have been facing the dreadful deeds of the militants. "Much of Asia's terrorist violence is concentrated in its southern belt, which in the past decade emerged as the international hub of terrorism. This southern part of Asia, encompassing Afghanistan, Pakistan, Uzbekistan, Tajikistan, Chinese- ruled Xinjiang and Tibet, India, Nepal, Sri Lanka, Bangladesh, and Burma, is wracked by terrorist, insurgent, and separatist violence in a manner unmatched elsewhere in the world. The number of annual fatalities in terrorist- related violence in southern Asia far exceeds the death toll in the Middle East, the traditional cradle of terrorism (Chellaney 2001: 96). LTTE in Sri-Lanka, ULFA, Maoist and Naxalites in India, Maoists in Nepal and a number of terrorist groups operating in Pakistan, show that this region is highly vulnerable to militant threat. South Asia has dealt with conflict-generating terrorism for more than 20 years. The experience has been marked by state sponsorship of terrorism and, in other cases, controlled by elements outside the disputant countries. Pakistan finds terrorism as a more capable weapon than the nuclear weapon that could be used against India to persuade India on its Kashmir policies (Bajpai 2003: 118). But to India terrorism is most savage deed to threaten its security. Even though terrorist groups are operationally separate, they share many similar dynamics and goals (Raghavan 2004). Issues related to ethnicity and cultural assertions are among the other factors contributing to the rise of Non state actors and militants in the South Asian sub-region.

A number of terrorist attacks have been taken place in this region. South Asia is a fertile land for terrorism and terrorist activities. It is in fact is the culprit as well as the victim of many terrorising events. The state sponsored terrorism helps Pakistan challenge the Indian strength without involving greater efforts. The US government estimates that India has 400,000 troops in Indian-held Kashmir. This is a force more than two-thirds as large as Pakistan's entire active army. The Pakistani government thus supports the irregulars as a relatively cheap way (terrorism) to keep Indian forces tied down (Jessica 2000:116). Pakistan's *jihad* culture has created a plethora of radical Islamic groups, many of them involved in the export of narcotics and terrorism. Fundamentalism and militarism feed on each other, with the Islamists and the military serving as partners in drug and gun running, protection of domestic bandits, and export of terror (Chellaney 2001: 103). The terrorist activities have caused several security challenges both within and outside the nation states of this region. In the last decade the South Asian Region faced several bomb blasts carried out by the militant groups. Indeed this militancy has challenged not only the security domestic circles of each state but the security of the entire region, especially by creating international disputes. There are many such incidents that have deteriorated the India –Pak relation. "*On the evening of July 11, seven bomb blasts on five separate commuter trains killed more than 200 people and injured more than 700 in Bombay, India. The government accused the banned organization Lashkar-e-Toiba, reportedly based in Pakistan and the disputed Kashmir territory, of having placed the bombs*" (Ali 2006). In 2000, U.S. Department of State, analysing the Patterns of Global Terrorism has pointed out that facing mounting terrorist violence, Asia already accounts for 75 percent of all terrorism casualties worldwide (Chellaney 2001:96). The most dreadful problem is that the Pakistani militant groups are exporting their version of Jihad to all over the world. Most of the states in the south Asian region are victims of this cross boarder danger (Jessica 2000:123). This has induced arms race and violence to the other parts causing severe security crises. The arms race in the region, whether small or large has been a great threat to the security and peace. The role of small arms, especially used by the militants, has made the South Asian security really panic. "South Asia had only minimum of 45 regular military to military wars in the region. But it doesn't mean as many as peace. There have been over 42 wars of irregular type by 1995, besides a much larger number of armed conflict going on due to terrorist acts" (Kant 2003).

Nuclear South Asia: Changing Contours and implications.

It has been well agreed by many scholars that the nuclear tests conducted by India and Pakistan in 1998, has brought about a noticeable shift in security environment in South Asia. "The Indo – Pakistan nuclear test of May 1998, however, bought an 'equilibrium change' rather than a radical transformation of the existing regional strategic environment" (Tellis 2003:19). "On May 11 and 13, 1998, India conducted a series of five nuclear tests. On May 30th and 31st" Pakistan followed it by six tests of its own (Ganguly 1999: 45). The nuclearistion of the South Asian region by these central powers of the region received both bouquet and brick bats at the national and international realms. Many scholars had argued that the South Asian security is found to be at its worse with its nuclearisation. On the contrary, many availed it as a security shift which would be beneficial to the South Asian security environment. In fact the region was brought into the international concern with an active involvement of the big power into the sub systems. The nuclearistaion programme by India and Pakistan can't be treated as something odd. As Kissinger points out the nuclear challenge is inescapable. *"The challenge of the nuclear age is not only enormous but also inescapable. Within a generation the peaceful uses of atomic energy will have spread across the globe. Most nations will then press the wherewithal to manufacture nuclear weapons. Foreign policy henceforth will have to be framed against the background of a world which the "conventional" technology in nuclear technology"* (Kissenger 1957). Though India and Pakistan have different geographical environment, both these nations perceived the nuclear weapons something indispensable for their security. Indian interest in nuclear bomb was grounded in security consideration relating to China and Pakistan and its vision of itself as a major power (Alagappa 2009). Indian military modernization is aimed at restoring conventional superiority over Pakistan, building a strategic deterrent capability against China and building a regional force projection capability in support of its major power stations (Gill; 2005) The nuclear weapon programme by these nations may be observed as a reaction. The Indian nuclear programme was a response to the Chinese and the Pakistani nuclear programme was to that of the Indian. Vernon Hewitt find that, "While the Pakistani bomb was evolved in the regional context of growing Indian conventional superiority and Pakistan's cynicism in the 1970s over US nuclear guarantees; India's nuclear ambiguities are part of its wider rivalry with china" (Shastry 2001: 229). As Kanti Bajpai remarks "within the frame work of deterrence thinking, this is logical – if a rival or adversary has nuclear weapons, then one must invest in a retaliatory capability (Bajpai 2007 in Sing 2007). For India the nuclear weapon would provide retaliatory capability against nuclear Chin and for Pakistan against

India. Pakistan conducted the nuclear explosions in a sudden retaliation. It took only two weeks after the Indian nuclear explosion for Pakistan to retaliate with one more than the Indian explosion. (Pakistan conducted 6 explosion and India 5). It was retaliation not only in the same manner but also in a more powerful way.

The Indian nuclear science had its origin before its birth as an independent nation. Developing nuclear bomb was delayed due to the Indian disarmament policy, particularly during the regime of Nehru. However, many factors had driven the Indian nuclear weapon ambition. "Among the factors that influenced India was its quest for great power status, the operative security environment the bloody engagement in Kashmir, the existing world order, and the Bharatiya Janata Party's commitment to acquiring nuclear weapons. Similarly, the factors that motivated Pakistan to go nuclear included security considerations for its survival, in effective sanctions imposed on India, mounting devastating pressures and threatening statements issued by some B.J.P. leaders (Jetly 2009: 48). The Chinese factor as a driving force behind the Indian nuclear ambition can't be discarded. India viewed Chinese conventional and nuclear supremacy a great threat to the Indian security. The humiliation in the 1962 war with China, the border disputes, the Chinese pro-Pakistan policies and the Chinese threat to the Indian hegemony in the sub continent were certain factors that forced India to go nuclear. The Indian nuclear weapons program began shortly after India's failure to obtain a nuclear guarantee from the great powers following two events that had a profound impact on national security concerns. The first was India's disastrous defeat at the hands of the People's Liberation Army in 1962. The second was the Chinese nuclear test of 1964 (Kapur 2005). India had really feared the Chinese supremacy and the Indian subordination if it lacked the nuclear power. Over the years, Indian and foreign analysts have revealed that Pakistan and China co-operated on nuclear matters. Pakistan has allegedly received a substantial amount of both intellectual and material help from China in building its nuclear programme. It is a fact that China sees in Pakistan a strategic counter weight or balance to India, and that a nuclear Pakistan is therefore, is Beijings interest. The Indian pro-nuclear argument was to a greater extent was based on this China – Pakistan nexus.

The Indian factor marginalises all other factors in case of the Pakistan nuclear ambitions. "The 1974 Indian nuclear explosion thus had a decisive impact on Pakistan's perception of the need for nuclear weapons. The Indian nuclear explosion reinforced Pakistan's sense of urgency and its determination to build a nuclear deterrent potential to counter Indian nuclear threat and intimidation (Chakma 2009: 22). The prolonged enmity with India always resembled in the security policies of Pakistan. Feroz Haisan Khan and Peter R. Laroy contented that since the early 1970s, Pakistan leaders have consistently seen nuclear weapons as crucial to deter the existential threat from India, which they believe is real. (Alagappa 2009: 218). Pakistan perceived the Indian superiority in all respect, a challenge to its very survival. Hence it considers nuclear weapons as a means to compensate for Indian conventional superiority and to win on the battlefield (IISS 2007). Though it was a genuine mistake the pear of Israeli attack which accelerated the nuclear explosion by Pakistan, "the fact that the Israelis had used an air strike to destroy Iraq's Osirak nuclear plant, just outside Baghdad in 1981, added to Islamabad's fears". Of course the Israeli scare was either a mistake or deliberately planted by the pro-nuclear lobby (Jones 2002). After the second (1965) and the third (1972) Indo – Pakistan wars with their continuing tensions throughout the seventies, the Sino-Indian border conflict of 1962, and the secret preparation at the end of the sixties for entente between the US and China, the political rationale for a Pakistan bomb was obviously India, and India alone" (Vanaik 2001). To some extent, fundamentalist idea also influenced the nuclear ambitions of Pakistan. It was expressed by the late Prime Minister Zulfikar Ali Bhutto "we know that Israel and South Africa have full nuclear capability. The Christian, Jewish and Hindu civilizations have this capability. The communist powers also possess it. Only Islamic civilization was without it, but, that position was about to change" (Bhutto 1979). So Pakistan viewed itself to be a dominant power in the Islamic world.

Analysing the incentives for nuclear weapon programme, high degree of similarity, with the global trend could be found in the South Asian case. Like with nuclear weapon states (US, Russia, France, Britain, China), the South Asian states demand for the nuclear weapon was based on security threat, emanating from mutual rivalry and upholding prestige. Yoshiaki Nakagawa identifies the nuclear necessity with the strategic capabilities such as 'to counter a massive conventional attack, to offset any political or geo-strategic superiority and to deter a nuclear attack. "The most powerful factors behind a nuclear weapons programme may be national security concerns, reflecting a country's perception of external threats, but political and prestigious consideration is also be important" [Nakagawa, 1994 in Taylor 1994]. It is a fact that the military power and security consideration overrun many other considerations while developing the nuclear weapon. The poor socio-economic fabric of the South Asian region was criticized by many scholars as to be given priority than the nuclear weapon programme. The socio-economic conditions of India and Pakistan, when compared with the nuclear weapons states (US, Russia, China, Britain and France), are poor and need to be focused much. However, military strength and secure environment could foster greater socio-economic developments. Having the desire to become nuclear powers is not enough. It requires the capability to afford the economic cost and technical know-how of manufacturing the weapon. The peaceful nuclear programme is the shield that covers the nuclear weapon programme. In fact, the two South Asian nations began their nuclear programme for meeting the energy needs, which was constructive and peaceful. The clandestine development of the nuclear weapon was carried out by these nations. Both the nation had received foreign assistance in their peaceful nuclear programme. India had received the foreign assistance for development of peaceful nuclear programme from Russia, Canada and France. This was part of the developmental programme to meet the growing energy requirement of this big South Asian nation. The failure of the global Non- proliferations regime has been attributed as one cause of the nuclear development in South Asia. U.S. application of its own nonproliferation policy is inconsistent. Besides the case of Israel, the United States has taken no action to stop Japan, France, Germany, and other countries from extracting plutonium for commercial purposes. This technology has a proliferation problem (Makhijani 1999: 149).After India has proved to be a responsible nuclear power, the co-operation of the nuclear supply group has increased a lot. The Indo – U.S. nuclear deal 2006 is a better instance to this. The 2006 US – India agreement on civilian nuclear co-operation is restricted to the peaceful use of atomic energy (Arnold 2010). *"The Manmohan Singh – George Bush joint statement of 18th July 2005 on Indo – US nuclear co-operation resulted in signing of the agreement in march 2006, and followed by legislation later that year under which the United States would supply nuclear fuel to India"* (Jetly 2009: 53). Pakistan is in fact worried about the emerging Indo US relations, especially in the nuclear spheres. Pakistan strongly opposes the Indo-US nuclear agreement and their belief that the agreement will help India to build a bigger nuclear arsenal (Ramana 2011). Unlike Pakistan, what could be noticed is, India is more credible both in the acquisition and use of the nuclear power. India has crossed important threshold and acquired extraordinary range of capabilities in nuclear technology. It has successfully developed indigenous sophisticated technology to sustain the critical nuclear chain; fuels of various kinds, sufficient heavy water, reactors of ranging degree of sophistication for both civilian and military use and reprocessing facilities capable of making weapons – grade plutonium from spent fuel". (Malhotra 1997)

Pakistan also began its nuclear programme as part of nuclear energy development programme. From 1954 – 71 the official policy of Pakistan was to have purely civilian nuclear programme (Srivastava 2002). It was the Canadian plant at Karachi (KANUP), that Pakistan started its nuclear energy programme in 1965. For the Western powers France, US, Canada smelled the possibility of Pakistan using these technology for nuclear weapon programme and cancelled their collaboration with Pakistan nuclear energy programme. Therefore Pakistan had to develop the nuclear weapon by hook or crook. A key scientist in this process was a young graduate from the University of Leuven in Belgium, Dr A.Q. Khan, who began importing centrifuge technology he had stolen from his job in the Netherlands (Bruce 2008). Even Pakistan authors have said that, during 1975, A.Q. Khan plundered the Almdo facility to provide Pakistan with "blue prints of the enrichment plant, design and literature relating to centrifuge technology and lists of supplies, equipment and materials (Jones 2002: 199). China supplied a nuclear power reactor for the micro reactor at Chasma in 1988 which was put into operation in 1989 (Srivastava 2002). A sizable portion of Pakistani scientists were trained in the U.S., Canada and West Germany. Pakistan's early suppliers of nuclear materials were the U.S. and Canada. Whereas the Canadian provided a small, heavy water type power reactor, uranium and technical assistance, the U.S. initially provided a research reactor and heavy water. Later, however, the number of nuclear supplier countries substantially increased. Among them, there are West Germany, France, Italy, the Netherlands, Niger, Norway, Spain, Switzerland, Turkey and the U.K. Private firms of these countries has sold Pakistan the nuclear materials (Caldecott 2002: 420). China has provided assistance to Pakistan in its nuclear and missile programme. "In fact, China has not only supplied weapons grade uranium to Pakistan but also deployed, according to the claims of the Indian military officials, intermediate range missiles in the Tibetan plateau (Tellis 2003: 51). The clandestine nuclear weapon programme of Pakistan was either directly or indirectly supported by the foreign assistance. A very visible fact about the clandestine nuclear weapon programme is that civilian nuclear programme was the shield that covered the weapon programme in these two nations. The strategy of nuclear ambiguity followed by these nations until the nuclear tests in 1998, helped them to carry out the weapon programme behind the curtain. Unlike India, Pakistan had to heavily depend on the foreign support in their nuclear programme. Also Pakistan had to take up the greater challenge as the nuclear non-proliferation by the major powers was very active by the time it had started the development of nuclear weapon programme. Despite the international pressure and domestic socio economic backwardness these nations could achieve their nuclear power ambition. This nuclear weapon programme further added to the asymmetrical geopolitical environment of South Asia, with India ahead of Pakistan in nuclear weapon venture too. Indeed, this is an important movement in the geopolitical stability of South Asia.

Nuclear weapon and Deterrence in the South Asian Security Environment

It was expected by many that the nuclear South Asia is going to face a new security environment with the advent of nuclear weapons into the region. There was a large volume of articles and scholarly opinion that expressed the danger of nuclear weapon in South Asia. They viewed that any kind of confrontation between India and Pakistan will lead to nuclear war. The continued enmity between these two nations further escalated the possibility of the nuclear war. South Asia that had witnessed three wars between India and Pakistan, is the most likely area of the world to explode and wage a nuclear war in the near future (Malhotra 1997: 91). Although a major conflict in South Asia is unlikely in the present circumstances, this is one area of the world with the potential for a nuclear exchange between states (India and Pakistan) and such a development would have devastating consequences in the region and beyond (Raphel 1995: 222). Several scholars gave an analogical observation on the South Asian deterrence with the cold war period. Majority of them contented that the South Asian scene is different from that of the cold war posture and there is a high chance for the failing of nuclear deterrence. *"When compared with the close proximity of India, with religious differences, and with historical animosity unparalleled even during the cold war, it is not difficult to imagine an undesired nuclear war starting"*(Tkacik 2010, (Cheema 2004). Brown and Arnold imagines that the nuclear posture in South Asia is quite different from the cold war posture. "The nuclear risk in this region is really high". The nuclear world now has more pronounced regional tensions in areas such as the Indian sub continental and Middle East, where deep-seated and bitter enmities between densely populated, neighbouring states dominated the political landscape. (Brown and Arnold 2010: 300). Hence the presence of nuclear weapons in South Asia threatens to make regional conflict catastrophically costly. Further the subcontinent remains volatile, with recent violence ranging from a Pakistan-supported guerrilla war in Indian Kashmir invites military combat between Indian and Pakistani armed forces (Kapur 2005)

There are a number of factors that distinguishes the South Asian nuclear deterrence from that of the cold war deterrence. Geographical proximity between nuclear rivals, role of militants, terrorists, religion and extra-regional powers, and the political stability are some of the most influential factors of nuclear stability in South Asia. In a pessimistic perception, Scott Sagan argues that there exists a condition conducive to the nuclear failure in South Asia. He finds the overwhelming role of the military in the region, particularly the organisational behaviour of the military, lack of civilian control over the military and rising military budgets may lead to nuclear fallout in the region. Also he suspects the command and control of nuclear weapon in Pakistan (Ganguly 2008: 47). India- Pakistan nuclear confrontation cannot be regarded as nuclear rivalry that existed between the US and Russia, the US and China or Russia and China. Rather than a nuclear rivalry the India Pakistan confrontation is manifestation of the born enmity between them. The acquisition of the nuclear weapons in the 'childhood' by these two nations (India and Pakistan became independent in 1947)[9] still escalates the risk. Political and economic turmoil is great challenge to the operation of the nuclear deterrence. Political stability is viewed to be an important criterion for nuclear stability. Perhaps the Indian stand in this respect may be justified. But it cannot bring nuclear stability as the other power, Pakistan, is a victim of frequent political turmoil. Political stability is inevitable in ensuring a strong and rational command and control of the nuclear weapon. Timothy Hoyt argues that the command and control of the nuclear weapons under the military in Pakistan is safe and efficient. He analyses this from an organisational theoretic frame work. However, the frequent change of civil-military regimes in Pakistan really questions the command and control system the nuclear weapons. Further there is a tug of war between the political and military leaders in the exercise of power in Pakistan. Moreover the likely chance of the use of nuclear force, whether by misperception or right perception, is really high in praetorian states than under democratic regimes. Nuclear stability between India and Pakistan has so far unfolded two distinct patterns: a pattern of relative and conditional deterrent stability in the absence of crises and conflicts, and a pattern of recurrent crisis instability in conflict-situations (Cheema 2006).

The use of the deterrent strategy and the idea of Kenneth Waltz that, the spread of nuclear weapon did not have to be a terrifying project, denounced the danger of nuclear weapons in the sub-continent. Analysing the last 12 years of nuclear South Asia, nuclear weapons were involved to deter or end the conventional war in the conflicted situation between India and Pakistan. "In 1999 they fought the sharp Kargil War in Kashmir, amid great international concern that it could escalate into a nuclear conflict. The war ended suddenly, and senior military officers from both sides now believe the nuclear threat was salutary – a success is so far as nuclear weapons prevented further escalation" (Brown and Arnold 2010: 307). The supporters of the nuclear deterrence in South Asia also argue that the nuclear weapons did succeed in preventing a vigorous conflict between India and Pakistan. There have been no major wars between these two nations because of the involvement of the nuclear weapons. What make many to suggest a positive effect of the nuclear deterrent in South Asia is the historic lessons from the US – USSR cold war relation. But it's a fact that there are many differences in the geopolitical elements of both these conditions. To this reason many scholars have criticized this analogy. The geographical proximity is an important impediment in working out the nuclear deterrence. Neither India nor Pakistan has either the geographical distance that the US and USSR had from each other, nor the prolonged period of time they had to learn from their experience of innumerable false warning (Vanaik 1999).Another differentiating factor that drove to the nuclear option in South Asia is the religious consideration. Some elements of Islamic and Hindu fundamentalism gave incentive to the nuclear progress in Pakistan and India. Pakistan military government too have used religion against domestic foes, especially pro democracy groups. Pakistan used jihad to wage irregular war against India in Kashmir. Finally in the late 1990, India itself began to increasingly use religion as a method of mobilizing the masses. Thus Hindu fundamentalism as manifested in the nationalistic BJP in India, met Islamic fundamentalism (Tkacik 2010: 178). Though the nuclear weapon programme was more over a political decision, the continued rivalry of Hindu – Muslim elements also influenced the decision making process. Pakistan nuclear weapon is very often remarked as 'Islamic Bomb'. Analysing the Islamic Bomb Controversy Caldicott finds the revival of Islamic Fundamentalism, deterioration in the U.S. Pakistan relation, Pakistan nuclear shopping in many countries, close military and economic link between Libya and Pakistan and the international conference on the defence of the Muslim World as the reason for the suspicion of the 'Islamic Bomb' (Caldioct 2002). Therefore, there is considerable reason in religious influence in the nuclear weapon programme.

The nuclear threat, in fact, is centred on India and Pakistan. However, it would be more precautious to consider the other nations of this region. There are no clear evidences that the nations other than India and Pakistan have made their quest for nuclear weapons. Also these poor and puny nations cannot afford to the nuclear weapons by themselves technically and economically. But foreign assistance may help them to acquire the nuclear capability. The illegal connections between Pakistan and Afghanistan may be considered in this respect. The illegal nuclear trade of Pakistan is reported very often. Bumitra Chakma denotes Pakistan as a 'horizontal proliferator' of nuclear weapons (Chakma 2009: 103). "*It seems logical that Pakistan would trade nuclear technology with France and North Korea in exchange for help with missile development*"(Tkacik 2010: 192). Nuclear proliferation by Pakistan, authorized, or unauthroised, has been expressed by many scholars as a growing to the nuclear non-proliferation system – Washington has absolved Pakistan of involvement in proliferating nuclear technology to many of the most loathsome regimes on Earth, hiding behind the fiction that Pakistani nuclear black marketer A.Q. Khan was a one-man industry. (The evidence suggests the opposite: that Khan's activities, especially his dealings with North Korea, flowed from state-directed policy with high-level support.), (Bruce 2008). "*More stunningly, Libya informed the US, the UK, and the IAEA in Cate 2003* **that A.Q. Khan and his associates** *had provided centrifuge machinery, components technology, servicing facilities, training to the Libyans in how to operate centrifuges, and even bomb designs*" to assist Libya in its drive to build nuclear weapons" (Chakma 2009: 105). These incidents, in fact, question the credibility of Pakistan in non-proliferation of nuclear weapons in South Asia. The non – nuclear states of South Asia have already expressed their wish to have peaceful nuclear programme to meet their growing energy requirements. However, the possibility of converting these nuclear technology and materials for nuclear weapon programme cannot be discarded. Indeed, there are ample evidences in the world, like in the case of North Korea, about the conversion of the peaceful programme to nuclear weapon programme. Basically, a country might wish to engage in a peaceful nuclear programme to show it can achieve a significant level of technological advancement. However, it is not a big step to move from a peaceful nuclear programme to a programme of weapons development (Nakagawa 1997: 26).

Terrorism and Nuclear Insecurity in South Asia

Analysing the security threat in Nuclear South Asia, the concern now goes beyond a nuclear war between the two states. The nuclear danger emanating from ethnic-sectarian violence and terrorism have been repeatedly expressed by many scholars. Brahma Chellaney views South Asia as a "centre of transnational terrorism". She argues that the fight against terrorism in southern Asia will prove to be a long and difficult one, spurring further instability and violence, before a sustained campaign can bring a satisfactory degree of order (Chellaney 2001: 94). If there is what is called nuclear terrorism, a high degree of possibility is found in nuclear South Asia. Non-state actors can employ a range of tactics to achieve their goals, including conventional weapons, hijackings, suicide bombings, and the acquisition of weapons of mass destruction. Fortunately, only a minority of these groups seeks nuclear weapons (Jenkins 2006). An impoverished political administration would definitely lead to unauthorized or accidental use of the nuclear weapon. The proclaimed policies, doctrines and the nuclear strategies would no more be in a condition to use. The Indian context does not point to such a political turmoil and the nuclear threat from its effect. However, the Pakistan political instability and insecurity always point to this nuclear risk. This in fact, questions the reliability of nuclear deterrence in South Asia. Terrorism that has its root in Pakistan has turned against itself. The terrorist organizations have targeted the state institutions and rulers. Most of the leaders in Pakistan had to undergo terrorist threats and attacks. After Lashkar-e-Jhangvi, a Sunni sectarian gang, attempted to assassinate then Prime Minister Muhammad Nawaz Sharif in early 1999, Sharif proposed to expand the special military courts that try terrorist crimes from Karachi to the rest of the country (Jessica 2000:124). Former Prime Minister Benazir Bhutto was assassinated by the terrorists. General Parvez Musharaff was attacked repeatedly and unsuccessfully by the militants.

The reality of the nuclear terrorism is reasonable. As long as nuclear weapons are viewed as instruments of power and prestige and as valuable bargaining chips, non-state actors will want to acquire them (Jenkins 2006). As John Deutch observes about the US security complex "over the last decade, the nature of the nuclear threat has fundamentally changed, from large-scale attack to the use of one or a few devices by a rogue nation or sub-national group against the United States or one of its allies. Countering the proliferation of nuclear weapons-by slowing the spread of nuclear capabilities among states, assuring that nuclear devices do not get into the hands of terrorist groups, and protecting existing stockpiles-has thus become as high a priority as deterring major nuclear attacks (Deutch 2005). The International Atomic Energy Agency (IAEA) has documented close to two dozen cases of nuclear smuggling, raising the terrifying question of what might have gone unnoticed. (Wolfsthal 2005). Mathew Bunn in his mathematic modeling of possibility of nuclear terrorism estimates 30 to 50 percent probability of nuclear terrorism over the next decade (Bunn 2006). The Challenge that the terrorists are raising inextricably linked to the threat of proliferation of nuclear weapons. There are many reports about A.Q Qhan's network with the terrorist. The nexus between terrorism and proliferation was addressed by Washington immediately after the 11 September terrorist attack (IISS 2007). Allison makes clear the important link between state arsenals and terrorist ambitions with his "three no's" to prevent nuclear catastrophe: no loose nukes, no new nascent nuclear states, no new nuclear weapons states. The even countries that currently have no nuclear ambitions may feel compelled to rethink their nuclear options so as to avoid being the last to join a rapidly enlarging nuclear club." This prospect is eerily reminiscent of the mobilization race that led to World War I, and it must be avoided. (Wolfsthal 2005)

Role of the terrorist in escalating the nuclear danger could be perceived from two angles. One is the use of the nuclear arsenal by the terrorist or an attack on the nuclear reactors and the other is the combating terrorist by the state actors. The terrorist may occupy nuclear weapon by theft, illegal trade or by ceasing political power in a Nuclear weapon state. Over the years, however, there have been a number of incidents—from terrorists attacking a U.S. nuclear weapons base in Germany in 1977 to terrorist teams carrying out reconnaissance at Russian nuclear warhead storage facilities in 2001(Bunn 2006). The efficiency and responsibility of states in safeguarding their nuclear materials from the terrorist is very essential in avoiding nuclear terrorism. Concerns also exist about the level of security of the nuclear weapons in Pakistan (Jenkins 2006). Political instability and the overwhelming role of non-state actors in Pakistan have been pointed by many as an easy access terrorist to nuclear materials. President George W.Bush is among those who see this acquisition path as the dominant danger. "Rogue states," he has said, "are clearly the most likely sources of chemical and biological and nuclear weapons for terrorists".

Since terrorism has international networks it is likely to invite cross-border military actions by the state victims. In fact there are clear evidences of the state military actions against the terrorist, culminating into war. The US action on Iraq and Afghanistan are better examples of this. Analyzing the involvement of terrorist in Indo-Pak conflicts South Asian security is at stake. India views Pakistan as the centre of terrorist activities threatening the Indian security. In the future, India may use air strikes to take out terrorist bases in Pakistani territory (Raghavan 2004). If the activities of the terrorists are intensified and become inescapable threat, there is high chance for the Indian military action in Pakistan. This may lead to another war between India and Pakistan perhaps culminating in nuclear war. The scholarly opinion about nuclear potential in south Asia differs even to paradoxical lines. Some recognize that factors such as the nuclear stability-instability paradox may cause low-level conflict among nuclear-armed states but still argue that ultimately nuclear deterrence would keep the peace (Dinshaw 2009: 50). To some even the low level wars and conflicts would be averted due to the fear of an all out war. These nuclear optimist perception remains to be relevant so far as the nuclear detonation does not take place. On the contrary the other scholarly debate has evolved to focus on a few key points that depict a dreadful picture about the nuclear potential in South Asia. Amarjit Singh observes that in the Indo-Pakistan context the nuclear weapon has increased the level of conflicts and not brought in good amount of peace in the subcontinent (Singh 2010: 234). Pessimists maintain that the possibility of preventive war, command and control problems, accidents, the organizational biases and offensive inclinations of militaries that control nuclear weapons, and the fact that one or both sides do not have invulnerable second-strike forces could cause deterrence failure among nuclear-armed rivals; optimists contest these claims (Dinshaw 2009: 51). Blacket views, in a similar fashion that the incompetence of the state mechanism would lead to in inextricable security system due to accidental or irresponsible nuclear use. "*Clearly, the more nuclear weapons there are in the world, the more nations which posses them, the more will all the defence system become inextricably found up with nuclear weapons, so that the nuclear of figures on nuclear triggers will grow and risk it the danger of accidental or irresponsible nuclear war*" (Blacket 1962:143). The disparity in the conventional military power further escalates the nuclear risk in the sub region. Paul Kapar argues that readers may weigh their strategic options and reasonably conclude that risky behaviour best serves their interests. Nuclear weapons do enable Pakistan, as a conventionally weak, dissatisfied power to challenge the territorial status quo with less fear of an all out Indian military response (Kapar 2008). This could also be visible in the earlier confrontations between India and Pakistan. Pakistan began to employ, albeit in an ambiguous fashion, a nuclear deterrence strategy against the perceived Indian conventional threat from the early 1980s (Chakma 2009: 41).

India- Pakistan confrontations and Security Dynamics in South Asia

South Asia has undergone some conflicted and confrontations in the last 14 years, which were expected by many, would invite a nuclear war. Though the two nations had not completely acquired the nuclear weapon capability, Nuclear weapon was involved in the Brasstacks Crisis of 1987. Though the crisis was ended without the use of nuclear weapon, a number of scholars and analysts have claimed that Pakistan delivered a veiled nuclear threat towards the end of the Brasstacks Crisis (Devin 1998). Nuclear weapons capabilities were invoked at their militarily incipient stage in the winter of 1986-87 and the spring of 1990 – both in the first era of non-weaponized deterrence. (Cheema 2009:).The Kashmir crisis of 1990 alarmed the international community about the nuclear war that might occur in South Asia. There were reports about the nuclear capability of Pakistan. Most experts viewed that Pakistan in all probability developed its capacity sometimes in the early to mid – eighties. In 1987, Abdul Qader Khan gave his famous interview to Indian Journalist Kuldip Nayar, when he publicly declared that Pakistan had the bomb, or to the more precise, could assemble it immediately if required (Vanaik 1999: 110). The crisis originated with the Pakistan support for an indigenous insurgency in the controlled portion of the disputed state of Jammu and Kashmir. Most of the Indian and Pakistani armoured capabilities were not mobilized and remained in their peace time deployments. But the growing inability within Kashmir and the increasing bellicose rhetoric from both India and Pakistan caused growing anxiety all around the world especially that both sides had made significant strides in their efforts to acquire nuclear weapons. Till 1998, a kind of 'non-weaponized deterrence'[10] prevailed in the region.

The Kargil crisis of 1999 in fact, reveals the influence of nuclear weapon, though not used, in originating and ending the crisis. The crisis took place immediately after the Indo – Pakistan nuclear test of May 1998. Therefore, there is considerable reason in stating the involvement of the nuclear weapon as a causal factor in the crisis. Professor Timothy Hoyt wrote: "*Indian and Pakistani officials and leaders exchanged direct or indirect nuclear threats no fewer than 13 times between May 26 and June 30 during the Kargil conflict in 1999*"(Timothy 2010). Like the earlier plans, the Kargil operation was facilitated by Pakistan's nuclear capacity. Gilani explained that the nuclear tests increased Pakistani leaders' willingness to challenge India in Kashmir and that the nuclear weapon played a dual role in Pakistani strategy at Kargil. Analysts such as Ganguly, Hagerty, Kapur and Mazari observed that Pakistan would not have undertaken the Kargil operation if it didn't have the nuclear weapons (Ganguly 2008, Hgerty 2008, Kapur 2008 and Mazari 1999). On the other side it has been also noted by many analysts that the Kargil crisis did not escalate into a full scale war because of the presence of the nuclear weapons. Pakistan could not easily concede ground in the crisis because Prime Minister Sharif risked confrontation with his military if he ordered a withdrawal without obtaining at least some of Pakistan's objectives. The Army and the public found any kind of yielding to India would demon the Pakistani state. Also elections were due by the end of the summer (the government had lost a vote of confidence in April), and the government risked political losses if it appeared weak, especially after the Indian media had extensively publicized the intrusions, and opposition parties declared evidence of the government's weakness on national security. Indian political elites viewed Kargil as a "stab in the back" and were wary of making any concessions to Pakistan in exchange for its withdrawal. Because in February, just a few months before the Kargil crisis, Vajpayee had signed the Lahore peace accords with Prime Minister Sharif (Dinshaw 2009: 154)

Once again the confrontation between India and Pakistan rose up in the 2001 – 02 crisis which took place in two phases. The first phase began with the militants attacked the Indian Parliament on December 13, 2001 and the second one started on 14th May 2002, when tourists killed thirty two people at an Indian Army Camp at Kaluchak in Jammu. Outraged Indian leaders formulated a military response considerably more ambitious than the plans adopted in January. Now, rather than simply attacking across the Lo C., the Indians planned to drive three strike corps from Rajasthan into Pakistan, engaging and destroying Pakistani forces and seizing territory in the Thar Desert (Kapur 2008: 81). However, with the active involvement of the international community, especially the US, India avoided the plan to strike Pakistan. "Pakistan's nuclear capability did play a role in stabilizing the second phase of the crisis in May 2002. The existence of Pakistan's nuclear weapons prevented the Indian government from planning an all-out attack against Pakistan (Ibid: 22). Nevertheless the international pressure, Pakistan pledge and the US promise against terrorism helped to culminate the crisis, the role of nuclear weapon in this respect cannot be discarded.

Nuclear weapons played an important role in either commencing or culminating these frequently occurred crises in the region. On the one side it gave impetus to begin the crisis and on the other side it managed the crisis from becoming a full scaled one. Nuclear deterrence "has the ability to not only prevent a major war but also limit the area of conflict while using the threat to avoid it in other areas" (Raman 2006: 11). Analysing the role of nuclear weapon in these crises it could be noticed that nuclear deterrence worked out to some extent. *"The outcomes of the 1999 and 2001 – 02 crisis show, nuclear deterrence is robust in South Asia. Both crises were contained at levels considerably short of full –scale war"*. (Ganguly 2008: 65). The game in the nuclear deterrent area is different, especially between unbalanced nuclear powers. If it is balanced nuclear powers the same may be zero sum game. It is observed by many that the strategy of Pakistan had marginal gains. As Gilani points out nuclear weapons "deterred India from all out conventional retaliation against Pakistan. And they sent a message to outside world regarding the seriousness of the Kashmir dispute" (Kapur 2008:76). The Pakistan strategy with its inferior conventional power was successful. Analyzing over the last 6 decades of Pakistan's history, it could be found that Pakistan was less concerned of its international reputation. Of course, the conflict with India had reduced the international status of Pakistan. With a nuclear asymmetry and non – use strategy, it may be argued that, the small nation would have the gains. The Indian gain was limited to raising its international prestige. The pledge and promise what was offered in the crisis resolution was broken. The Mumbai attack on September 11, 2006 reveals the failure of the resolution. The infiltration and the Kashmir issue are still continuing. The same has moreover showed the Indian strategic failure. As Pakistan is not committed to a no – first use of the nuclear weapon and India is committed the no – first use, India should be precautious of a nuclear strike from Pakistan if it is defeated in a conventional war. However, superior the convention power, the nuclear power has a greater role in the confrontation. For instance, despite India's conventional military superiority, Pakistan's nuclear weapons complicate India's security calculus (Rajagopalan in Alagappa 2009). In the crises before the nuclear explosions in May 1998, the Brasstacks Crisis 1987 and Kashmir insurgency 1990, Pakistan used the strategy of ambiguity to win the game. It was not certain for the Indian whether Pakistan had the nuclear weapon capability. However, the overt nuclear capability proved to be successful for Pakistan in the crisis after the nuclear tests. Analysing the stability/instability Paradox in the nuclear South Asia, Kapur argues that nuclear weapons, far from providing stability in the region, have given Pakistan a compelling incentive to provoke India, with the former seizure in the knowledge that its possession of nuclear weapon will limit any Indian retaliatory action (Kapur 2007). The stability, what may be found today, may not last long unless the ongoing tensions to some extent may prevent the escalation of these tensions into full-fledged war. However, its role in finding a peaceful resolution to the tensions is very limited. The ugly stability, as denoted by Sumit Ganguly, which always has the threat of a war or a nuclear war cannot be relied on much. Nuclear war can easily occur without either side actually intending it, simply because the one misreads the signs or misinterprets the intentions of the other (Windsor 2006: 57). It may also be noted that the pressure of nuclear weapon may bring in minor crises and limited war in the region because it gives an impetus to smaller nuclear and revisionist power like Pakistan to begin a crisis. But as Kapur contends these Pakistani incursions may eventually lead India to respond with substantial force, thereby contributing to a wider war fraught with the possibility of escalation to the nuclear war (Kapur 2005). *"A qualitative transformation of Indo-Pakistan relations from hostility to cooperation is theoretically possible, but few Pakistanis believe it is within their power to bring it about, and few expect it in their lifetimes. Thus, the second alternative, relying on nuclear deterrence, stands out. That a nuclear posture is dangerous in its own right is appreciated, but it seems the least unpalatable of the alternatives* "(Jones Rodney 2000: 68)

Framing the security strategy devoid of the nuclear weapon in sub region perhaps may be expressed by many scholars. Analyzing the stability crisis in South Asia Presslar Larry says that "*In the end, the issue really is in the hands of the government of Pakistan. It has the ability to make a dramatic contribution to peace and stability in South Asia by voluntarily dismantling its nuclear weapons program*" (Presslar 1994). However there is a very seldom chance for such a situation. Examining the nuclear aspirations, its development and last 13 years of overt nuclear status of these nations, South Asian Security Environment is highly linked to the nuclear force. Many South Asian experts generally agree that a state of mutual deterrence has been established between India Pakistan and China but what the history reveals is decades of hostility and distrust characterize the relations between India, Pakistan, and China. But it would be disingenuous and imprudent to suggest that stable deterrence will inevitably evolve in South Asia as the region lurches from crisis to crisis. Human error, misperception, mis-judgment, and miscalculation could undermine the ragged stability that exists in the region (Gnaguly 2001). Analysing whether continuing violence in a nuclear South Asia has in fact resulted from the stability/instability paradox, Kapur finds that it has important implications for the regional security environment. If the nuclear stability/instability paradox is responsible for ongoing conflict, attempts to stabilize Indo-Pakistani relations at both the nuclear and the sub-nuclear levels could be futile, or even dangerous. It is because strategic stability allows more low-level conflict that has occurred so far in the region. On the other hand this stability/instability paradox does not create an ongoing violence then ongoing conflict suggests that danger inheres in current attempts to minimize the likelihood of nuclear war (Kapur 2005). Put it another way that the unstable peace has danger embedded within it.

The south Asian nuclear risk has been contented by many scholars as emanating from the nuclear triad (India-China-Pakistan) rather than nuclear dyad. China as a geographically close as well as nuclear weapon capable nation has been actively involved in the regional affairs. The recent developments in the Chinese policies towards South Asia are really relevant. In the India-Pakistan-China Trilateral Dialogue held in 2011, the Chinese responded positively that the NPT could be amended in favour of India. Also they made it clear that their relation with Pakistan would be brought under international legal covenants (Ramana 2001). The attitude of China now accepts the Indian stand to the International nonproliferation Regime and the failures in their earlier relation with Pakistan, especially in the nuclear field. The South Asian Nuclear politics stands in favour of India. The nuclear risk in South Asia emanates from different circumstances. The prolonged hostility between India and Pakistan, Political turmoil, strategic failures, terrorism, Human errors and natural calamities are the contexts under which the nuclear threat becomes logical. Under the above conditions the application of the nuclear strategies becomes a challenge. Therefore, the advent of the nuclear weapon has further challenged the security of South Asia. The last 14 years stability, which is remarked as many as 'ugly stability' may continue. But this cannot bring a resolution to the conflicted situation and a peaceful atmosphere in the region. It may also be noted that any kind of confrontation with in this region would invite an active involvement of the big powers so that it will not lead to an all-out war. The International community would demand the present condition to be continued especially in the Indo-Pak frontier because any alteration may escalate to nuclear war. Pakistan therefore has to stop sponsoring terrorism in the region as well as claim over Kashmir. On the contrary if Pakistan neglects the international pressure and even take up the risk of a nuclear war, the South Asian Security will be in deep trouble.

Notes

1. For example, see S. Gangualy, *ConflictUnending: India Pakistan Tensions Since 1947*, New York: Columbia University Press, 2001; R.G.C. Thomas (ed.), *Perspectives on Kashmir: the roots of Conflict in South Asia*, Boulder, CO: Westview Press, 1992; C.K. Tiwari, *Security in South Asia: Internal and External Dimensions*, London: University Press of America, 1989.

2. In the last decade or so, a small but growing number of scholars have started to focus on non-military threats to states and communities in South Asia. For example, see P.R. Chari, M. Joseph and S. Chandran (eds.) *Missing Boundaries: Refugees, Migrants, Stateless and Internally Displaced People in South Asia*, New Delhi: Manohar, 2003; Chari (ed.), *Security and Governance in South Asia*, Colombo: Manohar, 2001.

3. See Ganguly and Kapur, *Nuclear Proliferation in South Asia;* Kapur, "Ten Years of Instability in a Nuclear South Asia"; Kapur, "India and Pakistan's Unstable

Peace"; Kapur, *Dangerous Deterrent*; Ganguly, "Nuclear Stability in South Asia"; and Sagan, "The Perils of Proliferation in South Asia." For a discussion of the quantitative literature's approach, see Alexander H. Montgomery and Scott D. Sagan, "The Perils of Predicting Proliferation," *Journal of Conflict Resolution*, Vol. 53, No. 2 (April 2009), pp. 302–328, especially pp. 307–310.

4. See, for example, Keir Lieber and Daryl Press, "How Much Is Enough? Nuclear Deterrence Then and Now," paper presented at the annual conference of the American Political Science Association, Toronto, Canada, September 3, 2009.

5. The term "nuclear posture" refer to the capabilities, deployment patterns, and command and control procedures a state uses to manage and operationalize its nuclear weapons capability. Nuclear posture is best thought of as a state's operational, rather than declaratory, nuclear doctrine; it is a state's operational doctrine, or nuclear posture, that generates deterrent power against an opponent—states care more about what an adversary does with nuclear weapons than what it says about them. For more details see: Vipin Narang, Posturing for Peace?: Pakistan's Nuclear Postures and South Asian Stability, *International Security*, Vol. 34, No. 3 (Winter 2009/10), pp. 38–78.

6. For more discussion on the issue see :Devin T. Hagerty, *The Consequences of Nuclear Proliferation*, (Cambridge, MA: MIT Press, 1998); David J. Karl, "Proliferation Pessimism and Emerging Nuclear Powers," *International Security*, vol. 21, no. 3, (Winter 1996/97), pp. 87-119; John J. Mearsheimer, "Here We Go Again," *The New York Times*, May 17, 1998; and Kenneth N. Waltz, "More May Be Better," in Scott D. Sagan and Kenneth N. Waltz, *TheSpread of Nuclear Weapons: A Debate* (New York: W.W. Norton, 1995) pp. 1-45; Brahma Chellaney, "Naiveté and Hypocrisy: Why Antiproliferation Zealotry Does Not Make Sense," *Security Studies*, vol. 4, no. 4 (Summer 1995), pp. 779-786.

7. For examples see, Kanti Bajpai, " The Fallacy of an Indian Deterrent," in Amitabh Mattoo, ed., *India's Nuclear Deterrent: Pokhran II and Beyond*, (New Delhi: Har-Anand Publications, 1999), pp. 150-188; Praful Bidwai and Achin Vanaik, *South Asia on a Short Fuse* (New Delhi: Oxford University Press, 1999); and P. R. Chari, "Nuclear Restraint and Risk Reduction," *The Hindu*, October 19, 2000. Also see Samina Ahmed, "Security Dilemmas of nuclear-armed Pakistan", *Third World Quarterly*, Vol. 21, No. 5 (September 2000), pp. 781-793.

8. Victor D. Cha (2001): The second nuclear age: Proliferation pessimism versus sober optimism in South Asia and East Asia, Journal of Strategic Studies, 24:4,

79-120.

9. Unlike the other nuclear powers USA, France, Britain, China and Russia, India and Pakistan are newly Independent states. India and Pakistan are in the childhood of Social economic and political development. This has lead many scholars to question the nuclear development as responsible state powers.

10. 'Non-weaponized deterrence' is condition where deterrence derives from the power of each to construct nuclear weapons quickly. India and Pakistan negotiated a detailed, largely verifiable settlement based on "non-weaponized deterrence" That is fundamentally distinct from the minimal deterrent in which nuclear weapons and ballistic missiles would be deployed in small numbers under the rubric of a "Nuclear Weapons Safe Zone (See. Perkovich; 1993:86).

Reference

Ahmer, Moonis (ed.) (2001) : *The Challenges of Confidence Building in South Asia*, The Foreign policy Peace and Security Series, Har Anand Publishers: New Delhi, India: 28-39,115-188,204-253 and 401-433

Alagappa, Muthaya (ed.) (2009): *Nuclear Weapons and Security in 21st Century The Long Shadow*, Oxford: New Delhi

Alam, Mohammed, B. (2007): *Constructing Nuclear Strategic Dscourse South Asian Scene*, India Research Press: New Delhi

Ali, M. M. (2006): "Uncertainty and Crisis in India, Afghanistan and Pakistan" ,*The Washington Report on Middle East Affairs*, 25 (7).

Arnold, Lorna and Brown, Andrew (2010): "The Quirks of Nuclear Deterrence", *International Relations*, SAGE, 24 (43)

Bajpai, Shankar, K. (2003): "Untangling India and Paksian", *Foreign Affairs*, 82(3), May - June: 112-126

Banerjee, B. and Sarma N. (2008): *Nuclear Power In India: A Critical History*, Rupa & Co: New Delhi

Blinkenberg, Lars (1998): *India and Pakistan The History of Unresolved Conflicts* Vol.II, Odense University Press: Odense, 11-108

Booth, Ken (ed.) (1998): *Statecraft and Security the Cold war and Beyond* , Cambridge University Press: Stamford Australia

Brenner, J. Michael (1981): *Nuclear Power and Non – Proliferation The Making of U.S. Policy*, Cambridge University Press: US

Bunn Mathew (2006): "A Mathematical Model of the Risk of Nuclear Terrorism", *The annals of the American Academy of Political and Social Science.* http://www.sagepublications.com

Caldicott, Helen (2002): *Nuclear Danger George Bush's Military Industrial complex* , The New Press: New York

Chari, P. R , Gupta, Sonika and Rajain Arpit (ed.), (2003) : *Nuclear Stability in South Asia*, IPCS, Manohar Publishers: New Delhi, 19-60,99-18

Cheema, Zafar, Iqbal (2006): *Conflict, Crisis and Nuclear Stability in South Asia* ,Oxford: Pakistan

Chellaney, Brahma (2001): "Fighting Terrorism in Southern Asia The Lessons of History" *International Security,* 26 (3), Massachusetts, 94–116

Clarance, William (2007): *Ethnic Warfare in Sri Lanka and the U N crisis*, VIjitha Yapa Publication: Colombo

Cortright, David and Lopez A. George (ed.) (2007): *Uniting Against Terror, Coperative Non Military Response to Global Terrorist Threat*, MIT Press: Cambridge

Datta, S. K. and Rajeev Sharma (2002): *Pakistan From Jinnah to Jihad*, The Pakistan Trap, UBSPD Publishers: New Delhi

Davies, Simon J. (2004): "Community Versus Deterrence: Managing Security and Nuclear Proliferation in Latin America and South Asia",*International Relations*

Dholkia, Amit (2005): *The Role of Mediation in India –Pak Conflict: Parameters and Possibilities,* Manohar Publishers: New Delhi, 87-126

Douglas, Peers, M. (2006): "The State at War in South Asia", *The Journal of Military History*, 70 (2), 566-568 (Review) , Published by Society for Military History ,http://muse.jhu.edu/journal

Farooq, Agha, M. U Brigadier (2005): Nuclear stability in South Asia A Strategic Failure or Beginning of Regional Stability

Freedman, Lawrence (1981): The Evolution of Nuclear Strategy , The Mac Millan Press: London

G. Katyal and Bhushan K. (2002): *Nuclear Biological and Chemical Warfare*, A.P.H. Publishers: New Delhi

Ganguly, Sumit (2008): "War, Nuclear Weapons, and Crisis Stability in South Asia", *Security Studies*, http://www.informaworld

Ganguly, Sumit (2001): "Beyond the nuclear dimension: Forging stability in South Asia", *ArmsControl Today*, Washington, 31(10), 3- 5

George, Timothy, Litwak Robert and Chubin Shahram (1984): *Security in South Asia*, Inter national Institute for strategic Studies, Gower Publishers: Hampshire, England

Gray, Collin S. (1999): *The Second Nuclear Age*, Lynne Rienner: London: 115-123

Hussain, Rifaat (2005): Nuclear Doctrines in South Asia, South Asian Strategic stability Unit, *December 2005* SASSU Research Report No. 4

IDSA (2008): National Conference on "Non-State Armed Groups and Indian Security in the 21st Century" April 8-10, 2008

IISS Strategic Dossier (2007): *Nuclear Black Markets: Pakistan, A. Q. Khan and the Rise of Proliferation Networks A Net Assessment*, IISS: UK

Jalal, Ayesha (1995): *Democracy and Authoritarianism in South Asia A Comparative and Historical Perspective*, Cambridge University Press: New Delhi

Jenkins, Bonnie (2006): "Nuclear Terrorism: Addressing Non-state Actor Motivations", *The ANNALS of the American Academy of Political and Social Science*, http://www.sagepublications.com

Jetly, Rajashree, (ed.) (2009): *Pakistan in Regional and Global Politics*, Routledge: New Delhi

Jones, W. Rodney (1998): "Pakistan's Nuclear Posture: Arms Race Instabilities in South", *Asian Affairs*, 25 (2), 67-87

Kapur, Ashok (2001): *Popkhran and Beyond India's Nuclear Behaviour*, Oxford: New Delhi.

Kapur, S. Paul (2005): "India and Pakistan's Unstable Peace Why Nuclear South Asia Is Not Like Cold War Europe", *International Security*, Massachusett, 30 (2), 127–152.

Kavka, S. Gregory (1987): *Moral Paradoxes of Nuclear Deterrence*, Cambridge

University Press: U.S.

Kayathual, Kumar,Mukesh, (1999) : *South Asia and Emerging Trends in International Relations*, Pointer Publishers: Jaipur India, 1-66,134-160 and 196-234.

Kissinger, Henry, A. (1984): *Nuclear Weapons and Foreign Policy*, West view Press: Colorado

Kodikara, U. Shelton, (ed.) (1993) : *External Compulsions of South Asian Politics*, Sage: New Delhi

Kolkowicz, Roman (ed.) (1987) : *Dilemmas of Nuclear Strategy* , Frank Cass: London

Kolkowicz, Roman (ed.) (1987): *The Logic of Nuclear Terror*, Allen and Unwinilnc: London

Kondapalli, Srikanth and Santhanam K. (ed.) (2004): *Asian Security and China 2000-2010*, Shipra Publications: New Delhi

Kumar, Sushil (2003): "Power Cycle Analysis of India, China, and Pakistan in Regional and Global Politics", *International Political Science Review*, 24(1), 113–122

Kumaraswami, P.R. (ed.) (2004): *Security Beyond Survival*, Sage: New Delhi, 218-235

Lahiri, Dilip in Kesavan, K.V. and Singh, Dalgit (2010): *South and Southeast Asia: Esponding to Changing Geopolitical and Security Challenges*, K W publishers: New Delhi.

Leo, Rose, E. & Evans D. Hugh (1997): *Pakistan's Enduring Experiment,Journal of Democracy*,Johns Hopkins University Press

Makhijani, Arjun (1999): The South Asian Nuclear Crisis Peace Review,11:1,147-151

Malohtra, Vinaykumar (1997) :*TheClinton Administration and South Asia*, South Asian Publishers: New Delhi

Mehta, Maj, Gen (ed.) (2007): *International Encyclopedia on Terrorism Laws*, 1 (3), Pentagon Press, 1049-1060

Mistry, Dinshaw (2009): "Tempering Optimism about Nuclear Deterrence in South Asia", *Security Studies*, 18, 148–182,

Mitra, K. Subrata and Rothermund, Dietmar (ed.) (1998): *Legitimacy and Conflict in South Asia*, Manohar Publication: New Delhi :1-16 and 122-219

Nayak, Nihar (2009):"Nepal: New 'Strategic Partner' of China? ", IDSA Strategic comments ,www.idsa.org

Nuclear Proliferation: Darkest Cloud Over South Asia? South Asia Could Be the Next Korea, The Washington Report on Middle East Affairs. Washington: Aug 31, 1994. XIII (2), 16

P.R. Chari (2003): Nuclear Crisis, Escalation Control, and Deterrence in South Asia Washington, DC , www.stimson.org

Pandey , Savita, (2005): *Politics of Ethnic and Religious minorities in Pakistan*, Shipra Publication: Kolkata

Perkovich, George, (1993): "A Nuclear Third Way in South Asia", *Foreign Policy*, 91, 85-104

Phukon, Girin (2002) : *Ethnicity and Polity in South Asia*, South Asian Publishers: New Delhi

Prajapati ,Vishnu (ed.) (1998) : *South Asia Power and Politics*, Commonwealth Publishers: New Delhi.

"President's Visit to South Asia Building New Relationships Despite Kashmir, A Coup and Nuclear Weapons" (2003): *Foreign Policy Bulletin*, May/June;1-33

Raman, Sudha (2006): *Nuclear Strategy The Doctrine of Just War*, Manas Publications: New Delhi

Ramana, Siddharth (2011): India-Pakistan-China Nuclear Trilateral Dialogue Report of Meeting held at IIC Conference Room on 18 April 2011; www. http::/ipc.org

Reddy, Rammanohar and Raman M. V. (2003) :*Prisoners of Nuclear Dream*, Orient Long Man: New Delhi: 27-53.

Saighal, Vinod, Major General (2003): *Reconstructing South Asian Security*, Manas Publications: New Delhi , 80-84

Samuel, Cherian (2009): "Enhanced International Cooperation Through Aided Military Training Programmes: A Study of the US Experience, with Specific Reference to South Asia" ,*Strategic Analysis*

Shastri, Amit and Wilson A. Jayaratnam (2001): *The Post Colonial States of South Asia Democracy, Identity, Development and Security*, Curzon Richmond: Britain

Sing, Swaran (ed.), (2007) : China Pakistan Strategic Cooperation India perspectives, Manohar Publishers: New Delhi, 17-23,105-118 and 301-330

Singh, Gurharpal (2002): "South Asia -Afghanistan, Bangladesh, Bhutan, India, Maldives, Nepal, Pakistan, Sri Lanka : 153

Singh, Priyanka (2007): "The United States in South Asia: An Unending Quest for Stability", *Strategic Analysis*, http://www.informaworld.com

Stern, Jessica, (2000): "Pakistan's Jihad Culture" ,*Foreign Affairs*, 79(6), 115-126

Tareen, Sher, Ali (2009):*Normativity, Heresy, and the Politics of Authenticity in South Asian Islam*, Blackwell: USA.

Taylor, Trevor and Imai Ryukichi (1994) :*The Defence Trade: Demand, Supply and Control- The Security challenges for Japan and Europe in the Post Cold War*, Royal Institute of International Affairs: London

Tellis, J. Ashley (2000): *Stabilty in South Asia Prospects of Indo-Pak Nuclear Conflict*, Natraj Publishers: Dehra Dun

The number of Indian security personnel killed by militants increased from approximately 340 in 1998 to between 500 and 600 each year in 1999, 2000, and 2001.1

Tkacik, Michael (2010): "Pakistan's Nuclear Weapon Programme and Implications for US National Security", *International Relations* , 124 (2), 175-217

Travis, A. Thom (1997): *India Pakistan and The Third World In the Post Cold War System*, Har-Anand Publishers: New Delhi

V. R. Raghavan (2004): "The Double-Edged Effect in South Asia" *The Washington Quarterly*, MIT Press, 27 (4), 147-155

V. R. Raghavan (2004): "The Double-Edged Effect in South Asia", *The Washington Quarterly*, 27 (4), 147-155

Vanaik, Achin and Bidwai, Praful (1999): *South Asia on Short Fuse Nuclear politics and the Future of Global Disarmament*, Oxford: India, 109-118

Ward, Adam and Hackett, James (2003): "South Asia's nuclear navies", *Strategic*

Comments, 9 (9), Routldge, 1-2

Williamson, John and Ahliuwalia Isher, (ed.), (2003): *The South Asian Experience With Growth*, Oxford: New York

Yasmeena, Samina (2006): *South Asia after the nuclear tests: Prospects for arms control?* University of Western Australia: Australia.

Ziring, Lawrence (2005) : *Pakistan at the Crosscurrent of History* , Manas Publications: New Delhi

7 | Indo – US Nuclear Deal And India's Nuclear Policy

Rajesh Kuniyil

India became an independent nation on 15 August 1947 after a long struggle against British colonial rule that lasted well over 150 years. The freedom struggle was spearheaded by Mahatma Gandhi, who was against imitating the Western way of economic development through large-scale industrialization using machines rather than a human workforce. After Independence, India's first Prime Minister, Jawaharlal Nehru, laid the foundation of nuclear policy. Jawaharlal Nehru was a follower of Gandhi, but his education at a British public school and at Cambridge University led him to reject any opposition to modern technology. On the one hand, he strongly rejected nuclear weapons because of their capacity for great and indiscriminate destruction, and on the other, he was reluctant to close the door to them entirely, acknowledging that "there is always a built-in advantage of defence use if the need should arise." (Kapur 1976). This mix of idealism and realism set the tenor for future nuclear policy. In 1964, when China demonstrated its nuclear capability just two years after defeating India in a border war, Prime Minister Lal Bahadur Shastri approved advanced research on an underground test, but did not approve an actual test. A decade later, amidst an increasing sense of isolation as the Cold War appeared to be fading, Indira Gandhi did approve the 1974 test, but did not follow it up with a weapons programme. She did, however, initiate the Integrated Guided Missile Programme, which led to the development of India's present crop of nuclear-capable and conventional missiles.

The success of the Manhattan Project at Los Alamos in producing the atomic bomb heralded the start of the 'nuclear era'. Nehru was fully aware of the consequences of these developments, as is evidenced by a speech (Newman 1965) he gave in Mumbai in June 1946, even before

India's Independence. He said, 'As long as the world is constituted as it is, every country will have to device and use the latest scientific devices for its production. I have no doubt that India will develop its scientific research and Indian scientists will use atomic energy for constructive purposes. But if India is threatened she will inevitably try to defend herself by all means at her disposal. I hope India, in common with other countries will prevent the use of atomic bombs'. In turn Bhabha convinced Nehru that research and development in this strategic field had to be done by an independent organisation that reported directly to the prime minister. Bhabha's closeness to Nehru helped him make rapid progress in this field. The plans for producing nuclear power began to take concrete shape about fifty years ago when the administrative organisation was established. The Atomic Energy Act had already been passed by the Constituent assembly in 1948 after protracted debate and opposition to the proposed administrative structure for research and development gave Bhabha complete control and in an exceptional departure from normal practice, the atomic energy organisation was permitted to establish its headquarters in Mumbai, far from the bureaucratic complex of Delhi. These two factors helped to kick start the programme with unusual speed and efficiency. Plans for the construction of nuclear reactors began in earnest after the UN Conference on Peaceful Uses of Atomic Energy held in Geneva in 1955; Bhabha was elected the President of the conference. He utilized the opportunity to persuade Canada, France and the United Kingdom to assist India in its power programme. As a result of his efforts, Canada agreed to build a 50 MW research reactor. The United Kingdom gave India the design and the enriched uranium fuel for a swimming pool reactor, while France assisted in the design and construction of a zero energy test reactor. All three nations also offered to train scientists and engineers in this new field. (Banerjee and N. Sharma 2008)

Historical Context of India's Nuclear Policy

India ultimately went in for the deadliest instruments of unsentimental realpolitik, but a long view suggests that this policy was not so much purpose fully conceived at the outset as it was incrementally advanced by successive political and scientific leadership. Important contextual factors gradually pushed India's leadership. Important contextual factors gradually pushed India's leadership towards nuclear weapons development. Regional security considerations were crucial, but they do not fully account for India's policies, let alone the considerable pauses the country took enroute to weaponization. Each era's policy choices shaped new material possibilities for subsequent decision-makers, even as a strong norm of nuclear restraint lived on-a legacy of India's non-violent independence movement and diplomatic opposition to nuclear proliferation during the long premiership of Jawaharlal Nehru (1947-64). The final 'crossing of the Rubicon'- (Mohan 2003) when India unambiguously announced its intention to become a nuclear weapon state-occurred only in the 1990s, and even today a significant stand of elite opinion in India remains strongly anti-nuclear. (Sen 2005)

India's nuclear arming behaviour is the assumption that structural factors, defined in terms of the relative power within India's regional security environment, were permissive but not imperative to the development of India's nuclear bomb. Accordingly, it is assumed that India's foreign policy is determined by a compound of various interrelated national interests. National security is considered one of these interests but, deviating from conventional explanatory models, is not placed on the top of its preference system per se. Within the discourse of India's strategic thinkers, the proper appreciation of the prestige/security duality of nuclear weapons was largely prevented by the all dominant, polarizing debate between idealist (Nehruvian) and realist world views. The idealist/realist divide, however, fails to explain why Nehru, who was India's first Prime Minister, usually referred to as the mastermind of India's idealist approach to foreign policy, actually paved the way for the country's development of nuclear weapons by creating the necessary infrastructure. The answer to this puzzle is quite simple: no direct causality exists between the government's idealist approach to foreign policy and the extent to which it is satisfied with its position in the international system. Throughout India's post-independence history, all of its governments – 'idealists' as well as 'realists' – regarded India's position within the international system as lower than it deserved. Although the moral high ground inherent in Nehru's idealist foreign policy unquestionably prevented India's early nuclear breakthrough and protracted its nuclear programme for some years or even decades, it always considered the nuclear option as a vital instrument to ensure India's international status. Among the very few Indian scholars who appreciate this continuity in India's prestige-oriented foreign policy is Raja Menon:

The division of national interests into status quo powers and revisionist powers is too well known to merit repetition here. But it is important in one context: No matter how idealistic a government is it will find itself automatically in one or the other camp. Nehru's idealism would not prevent New Delhi from seeing the world in 1947 as an unequal place with residual colonialism, ideological imperialism and Cold War power politics. In looking at the world and assessing its political state, the idealists and realists don't disagree. They both see it as a place that needs some rearranging; the idealists may believe that the rearranging can be permanent, but this is likely to be a subjective view. Other powers who would like some more rearranging will always be a permanent phenomenon, and in that sense, the tussle between the status quo and revisionist powers is the heart and essence of power politics.... . Nuclear weapons are all about power politics, and it is most unsettling to any strategist to see the contortions that the Ministry of Defence (MOD) put itself through shortly after Pokhran II in trying to justify the tests on the basis of threats. The USA is today the only pole in a unipolar world with no country actually targeting it with nuclear weapons, but there is no talk of retaining the residual 2,500 nuclear weapons on the basis of threats, for the threats have disappeared. The arsenal is now required for influence and prestige. (Menon2000: 27, 28)

Menon defines nuclear weapons less as devices for enhancing the country's security, and more as instruments of influence and prestige aimed at enhancing the country's international status. As Karsten Frey has argued, 'structural conditions of India's regional security environment were permissive to India's nuclear development, but not sufficient to make India's nuclearization imperative for its self-preservation'. (Frey 2006) Understanding the evolution of India's nuclear policies calls for a 'levels-of-analysis' approach, which combines partial explanations at the international (systemic and regional), state (domestic politics), and individual (decision-making) levels, and above all, pays close attention to the context and conjuncture through which causal variables interact.

While a country's position in arms control and disarmament negotiations necessarily a product of its political, economic and strategic environment and its national security perceptions it is equally a product of its unique historical experiences that have determined its fundamental world view. Several political analysts, both Indian and Western, have placed India's security concerns and its approach to nuclear issues in the geographical region of South Asia, or at best, in a region including China. Yet, India's promotion of the goal of total nuclear disarmament predates the nucleariaistion of China and even the emergence of the US-USSR nuclear revelry. For example, as early as 1948, India tabled a resolution in the UN General Assembly that noted the then UN atomic Energy Commission's proposal for the control of atomic energy……. For peaceful purposes and for the elimination from national armaments of atomic weapons". The resolution recognized the grave dangers of international peace and security resulting from the absence of effective international control of atomic energy. (Narain Yadav 2009)

India's Three stage nuclear program

New Delhi's nuclear planners can never be accused of thinking small. Even at the very beginning of India's nuclear efforts, Homi Bhabha proposed an ambitious three-stage plan for India nuclear development that sought to develop original technology that would allow the country to compensate for its insufficient uranium reserves. Thermal reactors-today's typical power reactors-represented the first part of Bhabha's vision. Thermal reactors use slow or thermal energy neutrons to fission uranium-235, a naturally occurring fissile isotope of Uranium. Bhabha envisioned that, in second stage, spent fuel from these thermal reactors would be reprocessed to separate plutonium for fueling breeder reactors, which would "breed" more plutonium.

In the third and final stage, this plutonium would fuel reactors that would irradiate thorium to make uranium-233. India has about one-third of the world's known supply of thorium, which is not useful by itself but can transform into the fissile material for U-233. U -233 can power nuclear reactors and provide the fissile material for nuclear weapons. This material could therefore provide additional fuel for India's electrical power production reactors and additional material for nuclear weapons. (Ferguson2008)

The Indira Gandhi Years.

The first major blow to the nuclear programme was the death of Nehru on 27 May 1964. His successor, Lal Bahadur Shastri continued to support the policy that Nehru had initiated on atomic energy, but he was adamantly opposed to the development of a nuclear arsenal. Realism is most relevant in explaining the developments of the Indian nuclear weapon programme in the immediate aftermath of the Chinese nuclear test on 16 October 1964 and the related decision by Prime Minister Lal Bahadur Shastri to give the go-ahead to SNEP in November 1965. ('India ' country profile on the Nuclear Treat Initiative) Shastri resisted the demands for a nuclear armoury, but failed to formulate a clear policy on the issue. The Indo-Pak war that broke out in September 1965 occupied him until it was ended under pressure from the USA and Russia. The former Soviet Union brokered a cease-fire in Tashkent, but on 10 January 1966, within hours after signing the Tashkent declaration on peace, Shastri died. A fortnight later, India sustained a second and far greater loss when Bhabha died in a plane crash on Mt Blanc in Switzerland. After a brief spell of governance by a bureaucrat, the government appointed a space scientist, Vikram Sarabhai as the chairman of the Atomic energy commission, much to the chagrin of the senior scientists at the atomic energy establishment. When in December 1971, Sarabhai died suddenly, Prime Minister Indira Gandhi appointed H. N. Sethana, a senior engineer in the atomic energy centre to succeed Sarabhai. Sethna had been responsible for setting up the plutonium recovery plant, as well as a factory for refining uranium and the fabrication of reactor fuel elements in Trombay. Mindful of the success and the importance of the Manhattan Project, scientists began studies in the early 1970s on the design of nuclear explosives in great secrecy within the Trombay establishment, anticipating permission to test them sometime in the future. After some initial hesitation, Prime Minister Indira Gandhi gave the green signal for an underground test. It was conducted at Pokhran in the Rajasthan desert on May 1974. (Banerjee and N. Sharma 2008)

India conducted its first 'peaceful' nuclear test in May 1974, near Pokhran in the Rajasthan desert. The test represented the culmination of the scientists' work on an explosive device and a permissive political environment. It was not a proximate response to any deterioration in India's security situation. Ironically, in fact, India's position had somewhat improved in the period before nuclear test. A war with Pakistan in 1971 resulted in the independence of Bangladesh (formerly East Pakistan), and 'India emerged as the dominant power on the subcontinent'- (Ganguly 2002) though, over the longer run, Pakistan's devastating loss spurred it to intensify its own quest for a bomb. The Nixon-Kissinger 'tilt' in favour of Pakistan during that conflict was a new nadir in US-India relations, but India's consummation of a Treaty of Friendship with the Soviet Union 'served as a vital guarantee against possible Chinese misbehaviour' (Ibid) given the, by then, well-established enmity between Moscow and Beijing. India's victory in the 1971 war was politically advantageous to Indira Gandhi, and it encouraged in image of a determined leader that complemented her populist strategy for consolidating power. She apparently gave the political authorization for the nuclear test in 1972; the decision, like many taken by her government, was made behind closed doors in consultation with nuclear scientists and a few trusted political advisors, with even the military kept out of the loop. (Perkovich 1999)

The Indian experiment had immediate international fallout. Canada felt betrayed because it was almost certain that the plutonium for the Pokhran test was extracted from the CIRUS reactor built with Canadian help. The Canadian government immediately stopped all assistance and made further cooperation conditional on India accepting the safeguards of the International Atomic Energy Agency (IAEA) for all its nuclear installations. The USA and Canada blacklisted all research institutions and industries even remotely connected with the (DAE). Such stern reactions seriously affected the Indian nuclear power programme making it difficult to import necessary materials which stalled and almost killed the nuclear power programme. (Ibid)

India's Initiatives towards Disarmament

In 1978, India once again proposed a ban on nuclear weapons testing, this time as part of a defined programme of nuclear disarmament. The proposal was made at the Special Session of the U.N General Assembly on 9 June 1978 by then Prime Minister Morarji Desai. The first step of the proposal continued four elements: (1) A declaration that utilization of nuclear technology for military purposes, including research in weapon technology, should be outlawed; (2) Qualitative and Quantitative limitations on nuclear weapons and an immediate freeze under international inspection; (3) Formulation of a time-bound programme -not exceeding a decade-for gradual reduction of the stockpile with a view to achieving total elimination of all nuclear weapons; and (5) A Comprehensive Test-Ban Treaty. This proposal was reiterated when Mrs. Gandhi became Prime Minister for the second time. In 1982, India proposed another progeamme, which included a proposal for a convention on no use or threat of use of nuclear weapons, a freeze on the manufacture of nuclear weapons *combined* with a cut-off in the production of fissionable material for weapons purposes, arid a test-ban Treaty. (Narain Yadav 2009)

Operation Shakti 1998

Despite long-standing intelligence monitoring, India's five nuclear tests on 11 and 13 May 1998 took the world by surprise. They have been especially embarrassing for the US Central Intelligence Agency (CIA). The tests have also revealed the limitations of seismic monitoring as a source of information. Western experts have been unable to agree on exactly what the seismic results indicate about the size and nature of the devices detonated. The tests, code-named *Shakti 1998*, took place at the Pokhran desert test range south-west of New Delhi. They were organised by the Department of Atomic Energy (DAE) and the Defence Research and Development Organisation (DRDO). The DAE, which operates the Atomic Energy Commission and the Bhabha Atomic Research Centre (BARC) near Bombay, designs nuclear explosives and produces nuclear components. The DRDO makes high-explosive parts and is responsible for weaponising nuclear devices.

In the post-1998 test phase the Indian government created considerable confusion by publicly changing its position on which nation(s) nuclearization was aimed at countering. The Indian government began by stating that it sought to counter China, then backed away from that position. By June 1999 relations with China improved to the extent that the two countries entered into a security dialogue. The other nation that nuclearization was aimed at was obviously India's traditional rival Pakistan and there was talk of using India's new nuclear capability to pursue a more aggressive policy against Pakistan in Kashmir. India's Home Minister, Mr Lal Krishna Advani, suggested that the nuclear capability now gave India the ability to engage in hot pursuit of Kashmiri insurgents across the border into Pakistan. (Gupta 2000)

Arguments for weaponization

There are two thrusts to India's nuclear program: power generation and potential weapons production. From the start, alongside its quest for an autarchic industrial policy and a nonaligned foreign policy, India searched for nuclear self-sufficiency as a matter of conviction.(Thakur 1998) There are strong strategic, political, and technical incentives to maintaining a nuclear option. Advocates of the nuclear option argue that nuclear weapons would enhance India's international status, ensure its strategic autonomy, erode great-power hegemony, reinforce India's leading role in the Third World and the nonaligned movement, expand its diplomatic choices in global affairs, and stabilize relations with China and Pakistan. The Indian military believe that the production and deployment of indigenous missiles will transform the traditional battlefield by their reach and firepower and thereby help to stabilize the situation in Kashmir without a war. More importantly, India perceives the nuclear option as a cost-effective "political force multiplier" against China's nuclear-weapons status and conventional superiority. The destabilizing effects of India's nuclear option on relations with Pakistan are regarded by New Delhi as regrettable but acceptable "collateral damage." (Ibid)

The most common explanation of why India tested in May 1998 is that proliferation politics were closing "windows of opportunity" for India. (Evera 1999) this is a view that Indian government officials and senior scientists expressed at the time of tests. R. Chidambaram, the head of India atomic energy establishment, reportedly told Prime Minister Atal Behari Vajpayee, for example, that with Comprehensive Test Ban Treaty (CTBT) due for review in September 1999, "the more we delay, the more the danger grows of India losing its option altogether." (Chengappa 2000) Those who make this argument suggest that the global nonproliferation effort had reached a tipping point. India's ability to conduct tests and to move forward in terms of a credible nuclear weapons program would have been severely constrained if it had not tested in 1998. (Singh 1998) A series of developments, some of them explicitly aimed at India, were putting tremendous pressure on India. The Argentina-Brazil nuclear rapprochement; South Africa's opening up of its nuclear program; the dismantling/repatriation of Soviet nuclear remnants in Belarus, Kazakhstan, and Ukraine; the four power deal on North Korea's nuclear program; the accession of China, France, and South Africa to the Nuclear Non Proliferation Treaty (NPT); the indefinite extension of the NPT; the conclusion of the CTBT; the start of the Fissile Material Control Treaty (FMCT) talks; a tightening of nuclear proliferation export controls (both nationally and multilaterally) all these in combination presented New Delhi with a global nonproliferation regime in which it would have been diplomatically much more costly to test.

India's Nuclear Doctrine and NFU

The draft nuclear doctrine declares: 'India's strategic interests require effective, credible nuclear deterrence and adequate retaliatory capability should deterrence fail.'(The Draft Report of India's National Security Advisory Board on Indian Nuclear Doctrine 1999) The report goes on to state that India will not engage in the first-use of nuclear weapons. India's "minimum credible nuclear deterrence" doctrine and "no first use" policy are based on the concept of deterrence by denial, rather than deterrence by punishment. India's nuclear policy is underpinned by a categorical and unambiguous commitment to "no first use" of nuclear weapons against nuclear armed adversaries and the non-use of nuclear weapons against non-nuclear weapons states. The real distinguishing feature of India's nuclear doctrine is that it is anchored in India's continued commitment to global, verifiable and non-discriminating nuclear disarmament (Kanwal 2001). India also opted to develop only a credible "minimum" nuclear deterrent due to the widespread recognition that nuclear weapons are political weapons and not weapons of war fighting and their sole purpose is to deter the use and threat of use of nuclear weapons. There is a broad national consensus on the development of a credible minimum nuclear deterrent capability and the doctrine of no first use. Minimum deterrence may be defined as "a small force of survivable nuclear weapons (that) would deter an adversary from initiating military action that would threaten a nation's vital interests." (Gallucci 1991) India is not looking at establishing any capability beyond this level of deterrence.

India's May 1998 nuclear tests were followed by many policy pronouncements in rapid succession. In an interview with India Today soon after the nuclear tests, Prime Minister Atal Behari Vajpayee said that there was no need to cover the nuclear explosions "with a veil of secrecy... India now is a nuclear weapons state (The Times of India 1998) On May 27,1998, Atal Behari Vajpayee, India's Prime Minister, stated in Parliament- suo motu Statement of the Prime Minister in Parliament): "We do not intend to use these (nuclear) weapons for aggression or for mounting threats against any country; these are weapons of self-defence, to ensure that India is not subjected to nuclear threats or coercion. We do not intend to engage in an arms race." On May: 29,1998, the day following Pakistan's nuclear tests at Chagai,. Prime Minister. Vajpayee announced in Parliament that India had declared, a voluntary moratorium on further nuclear testing, was ready to engage in negotiations for an FMCT, had undertaken to exercise stringent export controls on nuclear and missile related technologies as well as those relating to other weapons of mass destruction and had offered to discuss a no first use agreement with Pakistan and other countries, bilaterally or in a multilateral forum. ("PM's reply to Discussion in Rajya Sabha on Nuclear Tests 1998) On December 15, 1998, Prime Minister Vajpayee spelt out the principal elements of India's nuclear policy in a statement in Parliament. (Bedi 1998) India's resolve to preserve its nuclear independence, minimum nuclear deterrence, no first use, non-use of nuclear weapons against non-nuclear powers, and a firm commitment to the elimination of nuclear weapons.

India's Credible Minimum Deterrence

Credible Minimum Deterrence (CMD) is one of the central pillars of India's nuclear policy. Nuclear policy makers often argue that India's nuclear weapons programme, has always been guided by the understanding of minimum deterrence avoiding largess in terms of cost, pace or posture. Credibility came upon demonstration of weapons capability. The credible minimum posture was considered apt to justify India's nuclear weapons and missile capabilities after the 1998 tests. K Subrahmanyam called it a doctrine adopted to suit India's requirements and thinking on nuclear weapons (Subrahmanyam 1999). Bharat Karnad (2008) defines it as a self-explanatory, moderate, limited, reasonable and legitimate posture. The CMD doctrine highlights that India does not seek an open-ended nuclear arsenal and pillars other postures like the second-strike capability and no first use. CMD has now become the over-arching feature of the Indian Nuclear Doctrine, advertising three aspects of a nuclear weapons-empowered India: security with a thrust on deterrence, a responsible nuclear weapons state and commitment to global nuclear disarmament. India, shall pursue a doctrine of credible minimum deterrence. In this policy of 'retaliation only', the survivability of our arsenal is critical. This is a dynamic concept' related to our strategic environment, technological imperatives and the needs of national security. The actual size, components, deployment and employment of nuclear forces will be decided in the light of these factors. India's peacetime posture aims at convincing any potential aggressor that:

- Any threat of use of nuclear weapons against India shall invoke measures to counter the threat; and

- Any- nuclear attack on India and its forces shall result in punitive retaliation with nuclear weapons to inflict damage unacceptable to the aggressor.

The fundamental purpose of Indian nuclear weapons is to deter the use and threat of use of nuclear weapons by any state or entity against India and its forces. India will not be the first to initiate a nuclear strike but will respond with punitive retaliation should deterrence fail. India will not resort to the use or threat of use of nuclear weapons against states that do not possess nuclear weapons, or are not aligned with nuclear weapons powers. India's nuclear doctrine of "credible minimum deterrence" has yet to be articulated fully, and has undergone significant changes between 1999 and 2003.

The 2003 Indian Doctrine Shift

This widespread perception of India's nuclear doctrine suggests a degree of continuity and consensus in India's nuclear doctrine since 1998 that is unwarranted. Indeed, a closer look at the evolution of Indian doctrine reveals that it has changed significantly, through contentious debates within the Indian government and between civilian authorities and the official adversary bodies and military organizations that influences doctrinal decisions. (Pant 2005) Although Indian government official claimed in January 2003 that there were no major changes in nuclear weapons doctrine, in fact significant shifts in Indian nuclear doctrine were instituted in New Delhi.

In January 2003, the New Delhi government issued its first official statement that outlined in unprecedented detail the principles and goals that would guide Indian operational nuclear doctrine and posture: (M E A 2003)

1) Building and maintaining a credible minimum deterrent;

2) A posture of "No First Use": Nuclear weapons will only be used in retaliation against a nuclear attack on Indian territory or on Indian forces anywhere;

3) Nuclear retaliation to a first strike will be massive and designed to inflict unacceptable damage;

4) Nuclear retaliatory attacks can only be authorized by the civilian

political leadership through the Nuclear Command Authority;

5) Non-use of nuclear weapons against non-nuclear weapons states;

6) However, in the event of a major attack against India, or Indian forces anywhere, by biological or chemical weapons, India will retain the option of retaliating with nuclear weapons;

7) A continuance of strict controls on export of nuclear and missile related materials and technologies, participation in the Fissile material Cutoff Treaty negotiations, and continued observance of the moratorium on nuclear tests;

8) Continued commitment to the goal of a nuclear weapons free world, through global, verifiable and non-discriminatory nuclear disarmament.

Indo-US Nuclear Deal

The Indo-US joint statement of 18 July 2005 underlined the US administration's commitment to 'full civil nuclear energy co-operation and trade with India ... [and to] seek agreement from Congress to adjust US laws and policies' towards that end. The United States also stated its intention to 'work with friends and allies to adjust international regimes to enable full civil nuclear energy cooperation and trade with India, including but not limited to expeditious consideration of fuel supplies'. (Paul and Mahesh Shankar 2007) This decision signified 'the recognition of India's growing role in enhancing regional and global security ... [and] that international institutions are going to have to adapt to reflect India's central and growing role'. ('Indo-US Joint Statement', 18 July 2005) India committed to identifying and separating civilian from military nuclear facilities, placing the former under International Atomic Energy Agency (IAEA) supervised safeguards; maintaining its unilateral moratorium on nuclear testing; working towards the conclusion of a Fissile Material Cut-Off Treaty; refraining from the transfer of nuclear technology, especially that related to enrichment and reprocessing, to states that do not possess them; and instituting strict export-control regulations with regard to nuclear materials and technology by harmonising legislation with and adhering to the Missile Technology Control Regime and Nuclear Suppliers Group guidelines. (Ibid) It is a recognition of the fact that in a world facing severe energy crisis with escalating oil prices and rampant environmental pollution due to consumption of conventional sources of energy, it is illogical to deny clean fuel to India, which though a non-signatory to the Non-Proliferation Treaty, has not violated any legal commitment and never encouraged proliferation of nuclear weapons. On 18th July 2005, in a joint statement with Prime Minister Manmohan Singh, President George W. Bush announced that he would work to achieve full civil nuclear energy cooperation with India.

The United States recognized India there in to 'be a responsible state with advanced nuclear technology'. Obfuscating the reality that it can't be recognized as a de jure nuclear weapon state. The United States also pledged that India should acquire the same benefits and advantages as other such states, for which the President will seek agreement from the congress to adjust U S laws and policies and will work with friends and allies to adjust International regimes to enable civil nuclear energy cooperation and trade with India (Gaan 2008: 54). This deal will not effect on the strategic programs, there will be no deceleration on Bhabha's three stage formula, to which the DAE and the Government of India have remained committed till now, envisaged moving from using natural uranium, then the plutonium thus obtained in fast breeder reactors, to the final stage where thorium would be utilized and there will be no effect on our advanced Research and Development Programme.

The Indo - US Civil Nuclear Accord is seen as the most significant development giving implicit formal recognition to India's nuclear weapons status and a possible opening up of opportunities for it to become a global player in the field of nuclear energy. The wording on the July 18th, 2005, joint statement between India and the US provides an essence of the deal: India with its strong commitment to preventing WMD proliferation and as a responsible state with advanced nuclear technology, should acquire the same benefits and advantages, reciprocally assuming the same responsibilities and practices as other leading nations with advanced nuclear technology, such as the P-5.

The Indo- US civil nuclear deal is an attempt to create a delicate balance between the policies pursued by India, the Nuclear Suppliers Group as well as the nuclear non-proliferation inspection body, the International Atomic Energy Agency. It is a recognition of the fact that in a world facing severe energy crisis with escalating oil prices and rampant environmental pollution due to consumption of conventional sources of energy, it is illogical to deny clean fuel to India, which though a non-signatory to the Non-Proliferation Treaty, has not violated any legal commitment and never encouraged proliferation of nuclear weapons. On 18th July 2005, in a joint statement with Prime Minister Manmohan Singh, President George W. Bush announced that he would work to achieve full civil nuclear energy cooperation with India (Joint statement between George W Bush and Prime Minister Manmohan Singh, White House Press Release 18 July 2005). While the joint statement elicited a widespread and tumultuous reaction in both the domestic and international level, the statement in and of itself, contained very little substance. Under existing US law set forth by the Atomic Energy Act of 1954 and the Nuclear Non-Proliferation Act of 1978, the President lacked the authority to sanction nuclear fuel exports of the sort, implicitly promised in his joint statement with the Prime Minister. Section 123 and 128 of the Nuclear Non-Proliferation Act (NNPA) laid out a requirement for full scope safeguards in order that the United States could proceed with significant nuclear exports to a non-nuclear weapons state safeguards that India neither had nor had promised to impose. Furthermore section 129 of the NNPA forbade the US government from exporting nuclear fuel to any country that had detonated a nuclear weapons after 1978, a criteria on that India also failed (Temple 2009: 46).

Right up to October 2008, more than three years later, the Indo-US nuclear deal had yet to become a 'done deal' (Cheri 2009 : 1). In between, the US Congress passed the Hyde Act in end-December 2006, giving a 'free pass' to India. Later in March 2007, the 123 agreement was finalized. Three further hurdles needed to be crossed: India had to negotiate an India Specific Safeguards Agreement with the International Atomic Energy Agency (IAEA); the United States had to persuade the Nuclear Suppliers Group (NSG) to amend its guidelines and make India an exception to as mandate and finally, the US Congress had to pass the 123 Agreement to incorporate the IAEA and NSG requirements.

President Bush had signed the 123 Agreement in to law, and it was also authorized by representatives of the two countries on 10th October, 2008. Some doubts persist over 'open issues' like the inter- relationship between the Hyde Act and the 123 Agreement, and whether the 123 Agreement will serve India's best interests due to some restrictions for qualifying it.

Thereafter, the 123 Agreement crossed the IAEA hurdle without much difficulty. A proposal for amending the NSG guidelines was drafted by the United States, approved by India, and placed before the NSG in mid August 2008. (Statement on Civil Nuclear Cooperation with India Text of Draft US Proposal to NSG, August 2008). Initially six NSG members Norway, New Zealand, Austria, Switzerland , Ireland and the Netherlands-professed dissatisfaction with the US proposal, and wanted to incorporate several conditions into the 123 Agreement, notably that NSG cooperation would automatically cease if India conducted a nuclear test in the future. This stand was supported by China (Global Security Newswire 2008). The NSG met again in the beginning of September 2008 when the US presented a revised draft as amendment to the NSG guidelines in consultation with India. The additional liabilities accepted were that the NSG members pledged to notify each other of approved transfers to India, and were' invited' to exchange information about their bilateral agreements with India. Should any member consider that circumstances have arisen which require consultations, they will act in accordance with paragraph 16 of the NSG guidelines, which envisage consultations to determine and assess the reality and extent of the alleged violation (Statement on Civil Nuclear Cooperation with India, Revised Draft of US Proposal to NSG September 2008).

The Indo-US nuclear deal exempts India from the operations of the International nuclear regime which has ostracized India since its first Pokharan test in 1974 and made it ineligible to receive nuclear technology, materials and equipment from abroad. No doubt, the sanctions imposed upon India by restrictive technology control regimes, like the NSG and national legislation like the US Nuclear Non- Proliferation Act (1978), forced India to develop its atomic energy programme all by itself, overcoming great difficulties over the last three decades. Much success has been achieved in indigenizing India's programme but the need for nuclear materials and technology from abroad is apparent (Chari 2009: 9).

In 1974, India conducted a 'peaceful' nuclear explosion at Pokharan (Vishwanathan 2009:103). The real justification lies in these circumstances, although scientific and development progress also provided some rational. Triggered by this development, the US Congress passed a series of constraining laws culminating in the Nuclear Non-Proliferation Act in 1978. This not only sharply curbed nuclear cooperation, but also sought to impose stringent sanctions on any country which might be considered a proliferator. Wider international sanctions were also put in place in statutes of the IAEA and by the establishment of NSG which expanded subsequently to delivery systems in the Missile Technology Control Regime (MTCR), consequently the access to dual - use technology for all users in India, whether in the public or private sector, was gradual cut off Export controls and conditional aid and credits were used as sanctions the Indo - US nuclear accord provides a vital and probably enduring access to dual use technology, the best course is to operationalize it as fast as possible. After the arrangements with the IAEA and NSG it will be possible to do business with willing nuclear suppliers anyhow. The Civil Liability for Nuclear Damage Act, 2010 or Nuclear Liability Act is a highly debated and controversial Act which was passed by both houses of Indian parliament. The bill was the last hurdle for the government in opening up India's nuclear power industry to private investors in the USA, and proposed that financial liability for foreign suppliers – in the event of an accident – be capped at Rs. 500 crore. This amount was far lower than demanded by other countries, and even lower than levels of damages sometimes claimed in weather storms. Much of the liability was also transferred to the operator – in this case the Indian government – meaning that compensation would be covered by the taxpayer. It indicated the government's disregard for the safety and wellbeing of Indian citizens in preference of foreign investment.

References

"Indian Nuclear Doctrine", a Draft Paper proposed by the NSAB.(Publicly released by the Ministry of External Affairs in New Delhi on August 17, 1999.)

"PM's reply to Discussion in Rajya Sabha on Nuclear Tests (May 29, 1998)" (1998): *Strategic Digest,* 1583-1585.

'India' country profile on the Nuclear Treat Initiative website, available at:ttp://www.nti.org/e_research/profiles/India/Nuclear/ 2103_2603.html.

'Indo-US Joint Statement', 18 July 2005, available at http://www. indianembassy.org/press_release/2005/ July/21.htm.

"The Cabinet Committee on Security Reviews Operationalization of India's Nuclear Doctrine," Press Release, Ministry of External Affairs, Government of India, January 4, 2003 < http://meadev.nic.in/news/official/20030104/official.htm> (accessed on February 19, 2003).

Ahmar, Moonis (ed.) (2001): *The Challenge of Confidence Building in South Asia*, Har-Anand: New Delhi.

Banerjee, B. and N. Sharma (2008): *Nuclear Power in India: A Critical History*, New Delhi: RUPA and Co.

Bedi, Rahul (1998): "India Confirms Nuclear Policy", *Jane's Defence Weekly*, London, December 23.

Bhatia, Shyam (1979): *India's Nuclear Bomb*, Vikas: Ghaziabad.

Bundy, McGeorge (1984): 'Existential Deterrence and Its Consequences', in Douglas Maclean (end.), *The Security Gamble: Deterrence Dilemmas in the Nuclear Age* Totowa, NJ: Rowman and Allan Held.

Buzan, Barry (1987): *Introduction to Strategic Studies: Military Technology and International Relations*, The Macmillan Press Ltd: London.

Chari, P. R. (2009): "Introduction: The Indo-US Nuclear Deal", in Chari P. R.(ed) (2009): *Indo – US Nuclear Deal Seeking Synergy inBilateralism*, Routledge: New Delhi.

Chengappa, Raja (2003): *Weapons of Peace: The Secret Story of India's Quest to Be a Nuclear Power*, Harper Collins Publishers India: New Delhi.

Cohen, Stephen, Philip (1984): *The Pakistan Army*, University of California Press: Berkeley.

Constituent Assembly of India (1948): Legislative Debates, ref.3, p.18.

Durrani, M. A. (2004): "Pakistan's Strategic Thinking and the Role of Nuclear Weapons," CMC Occasional Paper, Albuquerque, NM: Sandia National Laboratory.

Evera, Stephen, Van (1999): *CausesofWar*, Cornell University Press: Ithaca, NY.

Ferguson, Charles D. (2008): "Reshaping the U.S.-Indian Nuclear Deal to Lessen the Nonproliferation Losses", *Arms Control Today;* 38 (3).

Frey, Karsten (2006): *India's Nuclear Bomb and National Security*, Routledge: Oxon, UK.

Gaan, Narottam (2008): "India and United States in Seesaw on the Nuclear Partnership", *Indian Foreign Affairs Journal*, 3 (3), July-Sept, 53-67.

Gallucci, Robert L. (1991): "Limiting US Policy Options to Prevent Nuclear Weapons Proliferation: The Relevance of Minimum Deterrence", in James C. Gaston (ed.), *Grand Strategy and the Decision-making Process,* National Defence University Press: Washington D.C.

Ganguly, Sumit (2002): *Conflict Unending: India-Pakistan Tensions Since 1947,* Oxford University Press: New Delhi.

Gizewski, Peter (1994): *Minimum Nuclear Deterrence in A New World Order,* Aurora Papers, 24, Ottawa: Canadian Centre for Global Security.

Global Security News Wire (NTI) 'Questions Persist on Indian Nuclear Trade Exemption', 5 Sept-2008.

Goldstein, Avery (2000): *Deterrence and Security in the 21st Century: china, Britain, France, and the Enduring Legacy of the Nuclear revolution,* Stanford, CA: Stanford University Press, 2000, See Alastair Iain Johnston, 'China's New "Old" Thinking: The Concept of Limited Deterrence', *International Security,* 20 (3), Winter 1995-6, pp. 5-42.

Government of India, Ministry of External Affairs, *Draft Report of National Security Advisory Board on Indian Nuclear Doctrine,* August 17, 1999<http://meadev.nic.in/govt/indnucld.htm>.

Gupta, Amit (2000): "India's draft nuclear doctrine, The Round Table: The Commonwealth", *Journal of International Affairs,* 89 (355), 353-364

Hindu (2005): "We Share concern of Nuclear Scientists, Says Vajpayee", global News Wire-Asia Africa intelligence Wire, July 22, available at LexisNexis *Academic,* http://web.lexis-nexis.com/universe.

Informal Group on Prime Minister Rajiv Gandhi's Action Plan for a Nuclear Weapons-Free and Nonviolent World Order 1988 (RGAP 88), www.pugwashindia.org/images/uploads/Report.pdf (accessed on 12-3 2013.

Joint statement between George W. Bush and Prime Minister Manmohan Singh, White House Press Release, 18 July 2005.Washington D.C, Available at http://www.whitehouse.gov/news/release/2005|07/2005 0718-6-html.

Kanwal, Gurmeet (2001): "India's nuclear doctrine and policy", *Strategic Analysis,* 24 (11), 1951 — 1972.

Kapur, Ashok (1976): *India's Nuclear Option: Atomic Diplomacy and Decision Making*, Praeger: New York.

Karnad, Bharat (2008): *India's Nuclear Policy*, Westport, Connecticut: Praeger Security International Series.

Kirk, Jason A. (2010): "The Evolution of India's Nuclear Policies", in India's Foreign Policy Retrospect and Prospect (Ed) Sumit Ganguly, Oxford University Press: New Delhi.

Mazari, Shireen (1999): "Kashmir: Looking for Viable Options," *Defence Journal*, 3, (2).

Mazarr, Michael J. (ed) (1997): *Nuclear Weapons in a Transformed World: The Challenge of Virtual Nuclear Arsenals*, New York: St. Martin's Press and *Virtual Nuclear Arsenals: A second Look* (Washington DC: Center for Strategic and International Studies, 1999)

Menon, Raja (2000): *A Nuclear Strategy for India*, Sage Publications: New Delhi.

Ministry of External Affairs, India, website, http://meaindia.nic.in/pressrelease/2003/01/04P01.htm

Mohan, C. Raja (2003): *Crossing the Rubicon: The Shaping of India's New Foreign Policy*, Palgrave Macmillan: New York.

Nanda, Harbaksh, Singh and Anwar Iqbal (2003): "India Rejects Pakistan's Offer to Cut Nukes," *United Press international*, available at LexisNexis *Academic*, http://web.lexis-nexis.com/universe.

Nanda, Prakash (1998): "PM Unveils Doctrine of Minimum Credible Deterrence," *Times of India*, August 5.

Narain, Yadav, Surya (2009): *Nuclear Weapons and National Security: Emerging Challenges for Asia*, Global Vision Publishing House: New Delhi.

Newman, Dorothy (ed) (1965): *Nehru: The First Sixty Years*, vol. 2, John Day: New York.

Pant, Harsh V. (2005): "India's Nuclear Doctrine and Command Structure: Implications for India and the World," *Comparative Strategy*, 24 (3) 277-293.

Paul, T.V. and Mahesh, Shankar (2007): "Why the US–India Nuclear Accord is a

Good Deal", *Survival*: Global Politics and Strategy, 49(4), 111-122.

Perkovich, George (1999): *India's Nuclear Bomb: The impact on Global Proliferation*, University of California Press: Berkeley.

Perkovich, George (2002): "What Makes the Indian Bomb Tick" in D.R. Sar Desai and Raju G.C. Thomas eds., *Nuclear India in the 21 st Century*, Palgrave: New York.

Rajagopalan, Rajesh, (2005): *Second Strike: Arguments about Nuclear War in South Asia*, Viking: New Delhi.

Sen, Amartya (2005): *The Argumentative Indian: Writing on Indian History, Culture, and Identity*, Farrar, Straus, and Giroux: New York.

Singh, Jasjit (1998): "Why Nuclear Weapons?" in Jasjit Singh, ed., *Nuclear India*, New Delhi: Knowledge World in association with the institute for Defence Studies and Analysis.

Snow, Donald M. (1989): 'Stability and Soviet American Relations: The Influence of Nuclear Weapons', in Donald M. Snow (ed.), *Soviet-American Relations in the 1990s*, Lexington Book: Lexington, MA, and Toronto.

Statement on Civil Nuclear Cooperation with India (Text of Draft US proposal to NSG, August 2008) Available at http://www.armscontrol.org/node/3274.

Statement on Civil Nuclear Cooperation with India, (Revised Draft of US Proposal to NSG, September 2008), Availableat http://www.armscontrol.org/ ystem/file/Revised+NSG+Draft+For+Sept+4-5+mfg.pdf.

Subrahmanyam, K. (1998): "No First Use Stand", *The Economic Times*, August 6.

Subrahmanyam, K. (1999): "A Credible Deterrent – Logic of the Nuclear Doctrine", *The Times of India*, New Delhi.

Sundram, C. V., L. V. Krishnan and T. S.Iyengar (1998): *Atomic Energy in India 50 years*, Government of India, Department of Atomic Energy.

Temple, David (2009): "Politics and Lobbyists: The International Politics Dynamics Influencing U S Congressional Approval of the Nuclear Deal", in Chari P. R. (ed) (2009): *Indo – US Nuclear Deal Seeking Synergy inBilateralism*, Routledge: New Delhi.

Thakur, Ramesh (1998): "The nuclear option in India's security policy", *Asia-Pacific Review*, 5(1), 39-60.

The Draft Report of India's National Security Advisory Board on Indian Nuclear Doctrine is available at http://www.indianembassy.org/policy/CTBT/nuclear_doctrine aug 17 1999.html.)

The Times of India (1998): "India is Now an N-weapons State: PM"May 16.

To cite this article: (1998) "India and Pakistan's nuclear tests", *Strategic Comments*, 4(5), 1-2.

Vishwanathan, Arun (2009): "India and the NSG from Estrangement to Engagement", in Gupta, Aravind (ed) (2009): *India in a changing GlobalNuclear Order*, Acadamic Foundation: New Delhi.

Waltz, Kenneth N. (1990): 'Nuclear Myths and Political Realities', *American Political Science Review*, 83 (3).

8 | Sino – Indian Relations in The Era of Globalisation

Devender Sharma & Ved Prakash Sharma

Abstract

India and China–the world's two oldest civilization-states, once great powers and now the most populous countries–are back as claimants to preeminence in Asia and the world. Both are heavily engaged in the global economy and possess nuclear powers with expanding military capabilities to match their growing ambitions. They also have a long history of bitter rivalry and an unresolved border dispute that erupted in war. Only during the last three years have India and China begun to shed their wariness toward each other by initiating measures to stabilize their relationship, including regular high-level visits. The rapprochement is based on a mutual need to focus on social and political stability, and strong economic growth and a sense of security, so each can avoid the perils of stagnation or decline. The incipient Sino-Indian entente has prompted some to argue that it has the potential to radically alter India's and China's security environment and restructure Asian geopolitics. Long-time observers of India-China relations, however, maintain that India- China ties remain fragile and as vulnerable as ever to sudden deterioration as a result of misperceptions, unrealistic expectations, accidents, and eruption of unresolved issues. Internal issues of stability and the external overlapping spheres of influence forestall the chances for a genuine Sino-Indian rapprochement. Indeed, the issues that bind the two countries are also the issues that divide them and fuel their rivalry. With their ever-expanding economies and widening geopolitical horizons, the bilateral relationship between the two rising Asian giants could be characterized more by competition than cooperation. As India and China proceed simultaneously on their relative power trajectories, geopolitical equations and power relations in Asia are bound to undergo significant realignment. This paper is an attempt to analyze the Sino-Indian relations in Post-cold war Globalized era.

The dawn of twenty-first century coincided with an unusual phenomena in the arena of international relations and that is the emergence of China and India as global powers. The steadily rising rate of economic growth in India has recently been around 8 percent per year and there is much speculation about whether and when India may catch up with and may even surpass China's over 10 percent growth rate. India and China understand the concept of co-existence and the growth very well. This engagement has elements of both rivalry and cooperation. However the pattern of engagement is still limited and will remain secondary to relationship with other global players, especially the US.[1]

The post-cold war external environment of a globalizing world, without rival political alliances, gave India the opportunity to improve relations with all the major powers the risk of a direct conflict between two or major powers, had also diminished due to interdependence created by globalization. Looking at the world from India, it often seems that we are witnessing to the collapse of the so called 'Westphalian nation-State System' and redistribution in the global balance of power learning to the rise of major new powers and forces.

The twin processes of the world economic crisis and economic interdependence have resulted in a situation where cold war concepts such as containment have very little relevance, and where no power is insulted from global developments. The interdependence brought about by globalization is helping to reduce the tensions among the major powers of the world. But simultaneously, no one power is capable to solve issues by itself, as we are seeing in Iraq, Afghanistan, Palestine or elsewhere. The major powers are coming closer to form conditions to deal with the issues, ranging from political to social, economic to environmental, despite of differences on various issues. We are witnessing the emergence of a world order marked by preponderance of several major powers, where each major power is engaging with as well as competing with all the others.

The former cold war system has been replaced by a system of 'Cold Peace' between competing powerful countries such as 'India and China or the US and China the salient feature of the era of 'Cold Peace' is that both have clearly opted for a path of friend by or formal methods of resolving their bilateral disputes.[2]

In this light of changing international scenario a little effort is being made to understand the Sino-Indian or China-India relations in the post-cold war era, where economics is playing more important role than the politics. As India and China are the two major Asian powers and are all set to become next superpowers in the near future, their relations occupies as significant place in the world politics.

India and China are the two most populated countries of the world. According to the human development report, 2011, the population of China in 2010 was 1329.1 millions; whereas the population of India was 1164.7 million.[3] The two nations have 35 percent population of the world community and 9 percent of the total geography of the world. These two Asian nations shares approximately 4,000km boundary between them.

India and China are one of the world's oldest surviving civilizations with the history of their civilizations dating back to more than five and four thousand years respectively. India and China are the most expansive landmasses as that dominate the physical map of Asia for time immemorial. Geographically, China is India's biggest Asian neighbour separated by the great Himalayas. "It is certainly correct see religions", says Amartya Sen, "as a major reason for the historical closeness of China and India, and to appreciate the central role of Buddhism in initiating the movement of people and ideas between the two countries". Beyond Buddhism, the non-religions consequences of Sino-Indian relations stretched well into medicine and music. According to elaborate accounts left by a number of Chinese visitors to India-Faian in the 5th century and yijing in the 7th century it was evident that their interest was by no means restricted to religious theory and practice only.

Beside religious and intellectual interactions, Indian traders were engaged in importing goods from China for re-exports to central Asia more than 2,000 years ago. Kautilya's Arthashastra, gives a special place to 'silk' and cloth from the land of China' among precision articles and objects of value. There are references in the Mahabharta to Chinese fabric or silk are similar references to the ancient Laws of Manu.

Sino-Indian cultural exchange continued into the 13th and 14th centuries, as Islam penetrated ever more deeply into China thanks partly to direct Sino-Arab links, and partly to the fact that Islam had become the state religion in the Delhi Sultanate and was making great stride in India as a whole. One example of Chinese influence on the Delhi Sultanate was the attempt made by Mohammad Tughlaq to introduce paper money, which had been current in China since the end of the 13th century.[4]

During the British colonial period an agreement was signed between the British India Government and Tibet, which led to the foundation of famous McMahon line between India and Tibet in 1914. China had not recognized this agreement as it believed that it was not a party of the agreement. The border issues since then has become a major irritant in the Sino-India relations.

On 1 April 1950, India became the first country among non-socialist countries to establish diplomatic relations with New China, thus leaving behind a thick stroke of writing in the annals of friendly relations between China and India. Since then, relations between China and India, the two large countries in Asia, have entered a new era. From 1950 to 1958, China-India relations witnessed a friendly 'honey-moon' phase, with the slogan of 'Hindi-Chini Bhai Bhai' resounding across the land of both countries. However, it was indeed very unfortunate that China-India relations sharply deteriorated after 1959 owing to their differences on the Tibet question and China-India boundary question and under the influence of a number of complicated factors, both international and internal, leading to the border conflict in 1962 and confrontation between the two countries for more than ten years. Since 1976, China-India relations were gradually restored and improved. In 1988, the visit of Indian Prime Minister Rajiv Gandhi to China became a major turning point for China-India relations, which entered a new period of overall restoration and development after that, with only a short setback in 1998 after India's nuclear tests. With the beginning of the new century, a rapid development of China-India relations was achieved and a Strategic and Cooperative Partnership was established in 2005.

In general, India is one of China's neighbours with whom China's relationship has witnessed big ups and downs after the founding of New China. It will be very beneficial to sum up some experiences and enlightenments from the tortuous course of China-India relations. At present, though the general trend of China-India relations is good, there exist some unstable factors in the relations, due to the fact that the China-India boundary question remains unresolved and mutual trust between the two countries is insufficient. Therefore, it is important to sum up and reflect on the past in order for both countries to march towards the future in a better way.

It can be seen from the history of international relations that it is somewhat of a rule that differences of one kind or another would emerge between countries especially between major powers. In order to safeguard relations between the two sides, it would be of the utmost importance to handle these differences in a correct way. Since the differences between China and India have been related to questions such as Tibet and China-India boundary, which involve sovereignty and territorial integrity, the above point has become even more conspicuous.

India-China relations were amicable during the first ten years of existence of the People's Republic of China-India was the second non Communist Country after Burma to recognise Communist China. It was hoped that this would further strengthen the immemorial friendship between India and China and be conducive to the stability of Asia and the peace of the world.[5]

The decade of 1950's was the phase of *'Hindi-Chini-Bhai-Bhai'*. There was bonhomie in Sino-Indian relations. The famous Panchsheel agreement (1954) became the guiding principles of their relations. Even in the famous Bandung Conference (1955) the then Chinese Premier Chou-en-lai declared that "China would not transgress the territorial integrity of any country, not even by one inch". He further said, "if by mistake, the Chinese people crossed the frontier of neighbours, the government of China will bring them back".[6]

But in the last years of 1950's, the Sino-Indian relations got deteriorated. The Tibet issue and border skirmishes created tensions in the Sino-Indian relations. The asylum of Dalai Lama by India enraged China the issue of Tibet has been a big irritant in the Sino-Indian relations. Tibet loans large in Sino-India relations and politics, even after 60 years of Chinese occupation, because of its intimate connection with the strategic interests of both parties. It is a manifestation of continuing Sino-Indian strategic rivalry in inner Asia and the Himalayas. Mao's strategists considered Tibet as China's back door, and some of India's elite still consider it as a buffer zone between India and China. Tibet, thus present itself, even today, as a strategic dilemma for both the countries.[7]

The 1962 war which was the result of increasing tensions in the Sino-Indian relations in the late years of 1950's and initial years of 1960's had significant impact on Sino-Indian relations. India was defeated in this limited but long term effective war. It collapsed the 'Hindi-Chini-Bai-Bhai' framework. And this war created mutual suspicion and trust deficit in the relations of India and China.

The worsening Sino-Indian relations had facilitated a Sino-Pak rapprochement, which according to India, was a product of shared hostility towards Indian by the former countries in 1963 Pakistan had signed a border agreement with China and Pakistan ceded some disputed territory of India and Pakistan to China. Further in the 1965 and 1971 Indo-Pak wars China supported Pakistan and favoured Pakistan on the issue of Pakistan. Ever since then, the China-Pakistan nexus had been a major irritant in the relationship between India and China.

The process of normalization of India-China relations had started in the late years of 1970's by the visit of the then Foreign Minister of India Atal Bihari Vajpayee in 1979. The 1988 visit of China by India's then Prime Minister Rajiv Gandhi has been as the greatest such breakthrough in facilitating, and underlining their critical as well as also symbolic turn towards building rapprochement.[8]

In the post-cold War era, there is great change in the world politics. The post-cold war era appears to be characterized by shifting alignments, changing interests and a more integrative approach to strategic concerns. The forces of globalisation and the dominance of capitalist world economy, a new set of forces are bearing down on old notion of power and sovereignty. In the post-cold war scenario, there is increase in greater partnership between the countries in the international affairs economically as well as politically. The process of globalisation and the end of the political economic ideological divide were paralleled by a transformation in international relations. They also imparted a greater momentum to the far reaching domestic reforms in the People's Republic of China since the late 1970's and substantially boosted its policy of opening up to the outside world. Simultaneously it has made its policy to resort peaceful relations with its neighbours.

After the end of cold war there has been multi-level exchanges and discussion between India and China. Various agreements of mutual interests in all the fields such as science and technology, education, culture, trade and on LAC (Line of Actual Control) have been signed. The agreements on LAC signed in 1993 and 1996 have helped to ease the tension along the India-China boundary.

Pokhran-II nuclear explosions by India cited China as a threat proved a stumbling block in the bilateral relationship of the two countries. But in the 21st century both the Asian Countries are looking forward for better cooperation and engagement to solve various disputed issues.

China and India are emerging as pivotal components of the evolving balance of power in Asia. The economic rise of these two Asian powers implies that the next few decades will witness a massive redistribution of global wealth towards the Eastern hemisphere. The gradual structural change in the international system has been a part of an ongoing process for the past three decades, one that first emerged in 1978 opening of China and followed by a decade later with India's seminal reforms in 1991. China has been growing at near double digit growth rates, and has now emerged as the second largest economy of the world. India's growth after a somewhat slower start has picked up momentum and has been averaging a growth of close to 9%. Experts now predict that by 2050 India and China along with the USA will be the dominant trinity among the world's economics.[9]

Besides the economic achievement both the Asian giants are playing a greater role in the global affairs and management of global economy both are the leading members of the G-20 grouping, which is emerging as a global economic management group and is poised to replace rich nations club G-8. As members of BRICS, both are set to achieve the status of leading economics of the world in few decades.

The relations of India and China are important not only for these two Asian countries but also for the Asian continent and the world as well. India and China are the leading powers of Asia and the experts are of the view that if 21st century would be the Asian century then India and China has to play crucial roles in realizing it. Both India and China along with Japan occupy central place in the ongoing debate, on the notion of 'Rise of Asia' or 'Asian Century'.

If India and China are able to have cordial relations then it will not only be good for these two nations rather it will be good for the development of their neighbouring countries and peace in Asia as well because the much of the development and peace in this region depends upon the nature of relations of these two countries.

These two Asian countries despite of growing very fast in terms of economic growth still have millions of people who are striving in poverty. But these two countries are spending too much on military expenditure. According to the Stockholm International Peace Research Institute (SIPRI) in 2009 China spent US $ 114 billion which was 2.2 percent of its GDP whereas India spent US$ 36 billion of which was 1.8 percent of its GDP.[10] If India and China have peaceful and cordial relations then this huge amount of money, which is being spent on military can be utilize in the social and economic development of the two nations.

While facing differences, it is necessary, first of all, for both sides to deal with the relationship between the partial interest and the overall interest very carefully.

Reviewing the developments since the establishment of diplomatic relations between China and India, one can see that relations were quite smooth when both sides could handle their differences calmly, attaching importance to the overall interest. For instance, both sides dealt with the Tibet question quite well in the initial period after the establishment of diplomatic relations between them, with the result that this question did not affect the development of their friendly relations in the 1950s.

However, after the Tibet rebellion in 1959, both sides over-estimated the seriousness of their differences on the Tibet question and later on the China-India boundary question failed to give first priority to the overall interest of safeguarding their friendly relations, leading to the conflict and confrontation between the two sides.

Today, when people re-examine China- India relations in that period, it is not difficult for them to see that despite the fact that differences between China and India involved core interest of both sites, they constituted only questions of partial interest after all, while safeguarding China-India friendly relations were related to their fundamental and overall interest on the question whether a peaceful environment could be maintained for both countries. So it is not difficult to differentiate what is primary from what is secondary. Again, the situation from 1988 up to now has indicated that despite the fact that differences between both sides on the China-India boundary question have not been resolved yet, both sides have reached a common understanding that while seeking ways and means to settle the boundary question, both sides should develop relations in other fields and make efforts to create atmosphere and conditions conducive to the final settlement of the boundary question in a fair and reasonable way. Due to this understanding reached by both sides with the overall interest of China-India relations in view, in recent years, India's diplomatic strategy has shown a certain degree of inclination towards the United States. However, India has still adhered to its policy of friendship with China, with the result that a general balance has been maintained in the trilateral relations between China, India and the United States.

The above are some important aspects of the policy of good neighbourliness and friendship adopted by both China and India towards each other. These are achievements obtained by the two countries through their summing up of both positive and negative experiences in the past and constitute forceful guarantees for the future development of China-India relations. It has not been easy to gain these fruits and they therefore need to be highly cherished by both governments and peoples.[11]

The situation in recent years has indicated that both sides have taken a number of steps in this respect with favourable consequences. The main steps taken by the Indian side in support of China are: recognizing Tibet as part of China's territory; taking resolute measures so that the Olympic torch passed through New Delhi successfully in April 2008. The main steps taken by the Chinese side in support of India are: recognizing Sikkim as part of India's territory; making positive remarks on India's desire to become a permanent member of the United Nations Security Council; adopting a flexible attitude so that the resolution to lift nuclear embargo against India could be passed by the Nuclear Suppliers Group. On the major question of climate change which involves fundamental national interest of both nations, China and India have cooperated very closely to make a joint approach, which has won the attention of the international community. Since both China and India are large countries and are very active in the international arena, both sides could find a number of problems on which mutual support is needed in the future. If both sides could give more support to each other, the mutual trust between the two sides would certainly be greatly enhanced.

In general, China-India relations have matured gradually, after passing through a tortuous course in the past sixty years and this is very significant. In the future, with the continuous development of friendly relations between the two countries, it can be expected that those unstable factors in their relations would be further removed so that mutual trust between the two countries would be steadily enhanced.

Notes

1. Mahendra Kumar Das, *Sino- Indian Relations; Threat Perception,* http://www.sspconline.org/opinion/SinoIndian_Relations_Threat Perceptions_03-11-2011

2. C.P. Bhambri, "India-China: Cold Peace", *The Economic Times,* Editorial, New Delhi, Nov. 21, 2009.

3. Human Development Report, 2011, p.124.

4. Dr. Amrita Dey "India-China Economic Relations: Time to Look Beyond Problems, "World *Focus,* Delhi, Volume XXXI, No. 5, May 2010, p.197.

5. A.A. Bokshchanin, "Sino-Indian Relations from Ancient Times to the Sixteenth Century" Edited by S.L. Tikhivinskis, *China and Her Neighbour,* (Mos Cow Progress Publishers, 1981), pp. 120-121.

6. A. Appadoria, M.S. Rajan, *India's Foreign Policy and Relations,* (New Delhi: Allied Publishers, 1971) pp. 40-42.

7. Dalijit Sen Adel, *China and Her Neighbours* (New Delhi: Deep and Deep Publications 1981), p. 91.

8. Dr. Satish Kumar, "Tibet Factor in India-China Relation", World Focus, New Delhi, Volume XXXI, No. 9, Sep. 2010, p.425.

9. B.R. Deepak, *India and China: 1904-2004,* (New Delhi: Manak Publications, 2005) p.24.

10. Mohan Guruswamy and Zoraur Daulat Singh, *India China Relations : The Border Issue and Beyond,* (New Delhi : Viva Books Private Limited 2009), p.1.

11. http://q=sino+indian+relations&hl=en&safe=active&gbv=2&rlz=1W1GG LL_en&prmd=ivnsu&ei=7yJfT8SuH8jHrQex7_CTBg&start=10&sa=N

9 | Pakistan's Afghan Policy Post 2014 Scenario: Options for India

Sudhir Singh

Abstract

Pakistan and Afghanistan relations have always been turbulent due to gamut of factors. Pakhtunistan is top among them. After 1979 Soviet intervention, Pakistan has adopted the policy to keep Afghanistan volatile to achieve strategic depth against India. In the backdrop of 9/11 terror attack the NATO led attack was commenced against Taliban in 2001. Since last 13 years despite part of coalition against terror, Pakistan has been supporting terror elements preciously to score points against India. Despite civilian regime in Islamabad, military has to sustain old Afghan policy which is bound to inflict collateral damage to India therefore we must reformulate our strategy to cope up with the impending dangers.

Since millennia, Afghanistan remains at the junction between Asia and Europe. It has kept the country in the chessboard of each and every global power game. The Greco-Bactrian (250-150 BCE), Kushan (30-375 AD) and Sassanid (224-651 AD) empires derived much of their wealth from the Silk Road, a series of interlinked trading networks criss-crossing the Eurasian land mass and centred around what is known as Afghanistan. Despite the decline of the importance of the Silk routes, Afghanistan's ability to act as a regional conduit never entirely faded from collective perception. Only a century ago, the modern father of geostrategy, Halford Mackinder, described the area as 'the heartland of Eurasia' and the 'geographical pivot of history.'[1] The country's location between four potentially wealthy but volatile and conflict ridden regions- Central Asia, the Middle East, South Asia and the Far East – endows it with extremely important geostrategic assets. But the Afghan instability which remains sustainable since 1979 Soviet intervention has prevented it to garner the benefits out of this geographical situation. Although there are gamuts of players in Afghanistan but Pakistan has been one of the most important due to its variety of proximity and divergences with Afghanistan. It has become extraordinary important in the backdrop of NATO withdrawal by the end 2014. This paper is intended to analyze these issues in detail.

By the end of 2014, NATO forces are intended to withdraw. NATO may leave some trainer to impart military training to the Afghan National Army (ANA) but final decision will take place when the post Karzai elected President will take over by August 2014. In the later part of 2013 the ANA had 1,87,000 soldiers and combined with Afghan police etc their strength is around 3,50,000. Till date no security agreement has been inked between Afghan government and the NATO forces about sustainability of NATO forces to play supportive role for the ANA after 2014. Since June 2013, the ANA however has taken over the security operations in all 34 provinces and NATO forces are supporting the ANA to contain the Taliban.

Pakistan never had a peace with Afghanistan right from its inception till 1979 Soviet intervention. Pakhtunistan remains an apple of discord between both countries. Although the Afghan rulers accepted Durand Line (1893), that cuts through the Pastun homeland, they never really have given up their claims on 'Pashtunistan', the area right of the Indus.[2] The tribal areas along the Afghan border had retained a semi- independent status and were administrated by political agents.[3] These areas are called as Federal Administrated Tribal Areas (FATA) and remain turbulent even today. The leftover fighters after the withdrawal of the Soviet army in 1990 are holed up here and even today due to strategic and tough terrain of the area, they remain there. Since October 2001 the NATO forces have launched 'Operation Enduring Freedom' against the Taliban and Al-Qaeda and these fighters recruited throughout Afghan Jihad (1979-1990) and their next generation fought bitterly against the NATO forces and undermined NATO initiative for a peaceful and prosperous Afghanistan. Although Pakistan government kept promising to the NATO forces that it is serious to erase these safe heavens of the breeding ground of international terror from this area but till recently it remains merely lip services. In fact Pakistan has extended sanctuary to the Haqqani group and used them as an asset to target Indian installations. This group has been involved into the many attacks on Indian establishments in Afghanistan. In his swearing in ceremony Indian PM, Narendra Modi had invited all

SAARC leaders in May 2014 and after initial opposition from the army Pakistani PM, Nawaz Sharif arrival was announced. But in the meanwhile Indian consulate at Heart near the Iran border was attacked. Later on international intelligence agencies have identified Pakistani connectivity to this attack. After Mumbai carnage it was one of the worst attacks on Indian establishment outside India. Fortunately nominal casualty was made in this attack. Why Herat attack was planned when Pakistani PM, Nawaz Sharif had already announced his New Delhi visit? We could recall Kargil in this regard to understand this tango. It did happened because our PM, A.B. Vajpayee visited Lahore and inked 'Lahore Declaration'. It was the first instrument after 1971 Shimla, which talks about the bilateral mechanism to resolve bilateral issues including the core issue of Kashmir. Pakistani army was apprehensive that if Vajpayee visit will goes well, it could have losing its leverage from the corridor of power in Islamabad. In her recent book 'The Wrong Enemy; America in Afghanistan 2001-2004,' senior American journalist Carlotta Gall who has spent ten years in Afghanistan has concluded that "The embassy bombing was on operation by rouge ISI agents acting on their own. It was sanctioned and monitored by the most senior officials in Pakistani intelligence." The evidence was so damming that the Bush administration dispatched the deputy chief of the CIA, Stephen Kappes, to Islamabad to remonstrate with Pakistanis. The bomber struck before Kappes reached Islamabad. Gall writes "Investigators found the bomber's cell phone in the wreckage of his exploded car. They tracked down his collaborators in Kabul, the man who had provided the logistics for the attack. The facilitator, an Afghan, had been in direct contact with Pakistan by telephone."[4] According to Gall, as the Afghan government investigated the attack, they became convinced that "the ISI was working with al Qaeda, the Taliban, the Haqqanis, and Pakistani groups such as Lashkar-e-Taiba" for this attack. Gall concludes "At the core of Pakistan's thinking was an obsessive desire to dominate Afghanistan in order to protect its own rear flank from India. In that way of thinking, the Taliban were guarantors of Pakistan's national strategic interests."[5] Haqqani group is most favorites among them for the Pakistani army. During last 13 years India has been actively extended all round support to the reconstruction process of Afghanistan. Pakistani army has been jealous from Indian presence and has engineered terror attacks on Indian establishments through Haqqani group and other state sympathetic groups like LET in Afghanistan. Haqqani group have been detrimental for the NATO forces also and inflicted collateral damage to it. Speaking at a security forum in

Colorado in the last week of July 2014, John Allen, the retired four-star general who led US and NATO forces in Afghanistan, voiced skepticism about Islamabad's past willingness to go after the Haqqanis, even as he acknowledged the opportunity presented by the ongoing offensive going on in North Waziristan.

"When I was commander there, the Haqqani killed or wounded over 500 of my troops. And the operations in Waziristan somehow missed them every time they conducted ops on the eastern side of the border".⁶ Within this conference Afghan Ambassador Eklil Hakimi, said his information suggested that Haqqani militants had safe passage inside Pakistan and were going elsewhere inside Pakistan.⁷ United States urged Pakistan not to allow Haqqani fighters to escape otherwise it is bound to lose US assistance if they will not targeted during ongoing military operation in the North Waziristan.

Since last 13 years India has been among top five contributors in the reconstruction of Afghanistan. Between 2002 to 2010 New Delhi pledged $ 1.2 billion dollor in reconstruction and humanitarian assistance to the country, of which $ 759 million has since been disbursed on highly visible projects.⁸ It has built many infrastructure and provided transportation and key power assistance. India has also constructed Zaranj –Delaram road in western Afghanistan which connects Irani port of Chabahar to Central Asia through Afghanistan. Through this route, Afghanistan has another outlet for the sea and in addition it has reduced its dependence for the same over Pakistan. Other scheme includes the construction of electricity lines from Uzbekistan to eastern Afghanistan under the NEPS scheme, the new Afghan parliament and additional roads. In November 2011, an Indian consortium led by the state owned SAIL secured a mining contract for the Hajigak iron ore deposit, the largest such deposits in Asia, in the central Afghan province of Bamiyan. India is expected to invest $ 10 billion in Afghanistan over the next 30 years, and this has significant implications for the strengthening of relations between the two states.⁹ Such cooperation was foreshadowed by Karzai's recent overtures to the Indian government for military aid under 2011 Afghan-India strategic partnership agreement, a move that has further piqued Islamabad.¹⁰ This has been accepted by the eminent Pakistani Afghan expert, Ahmed Rashid also. Pakistan is apprehensive that growing Indian presence in Afghanistan is intended to pursue anti-Pakistani activities. But somewhere it is miscalculation as well.

In November 2011 CBS poll, a majority of Americans said that Pakistan is either unfriendly (39%) or an enemy (24%).Only 2% called it an ally.[11] For their part, Pakistanis don't see the relationship healthy. The June 2011 Pew Research poll showed that most Pakistanis see the United States as an enemy and a potential threat to their country's security.[12] On the one hand, since joining hands in late 2001, Washington has been praising Islamabad for its commitment and sacrifice of more than 4,500 military personnel and as many as 45,000 Pakistani civilians in the "war on terror." In 2011, soon after the killing of Osama bin Laden inside Pakistan, President Barack Obama said, "We have been able to kill more terrorists on Pakistani soil than just about anyplace else. We could not have done that without Pakistani cooperation."[13] On the other hand, American officials have suspected and often accused the Pakistani military of supporting militant groups, particularly the Afghan Taliban. Although Washington and Islamabad have never been on the same page since 9/11, both sides have always made an effort to maintain their ties. This scenario has developed a status which could be termed as 'trust deficit' between both US and Pakistan. In its one decade experience the US has realized that Pakistan is part of the problem and not the part of the solution in Afghanistan. The parochial prism of the Pakistani army about Afghanistan is still dominant in the power corridor despite 7 years of post-military democratic governance. The military has been jealously guarded its stance on Afghanistan. It is the holy cow for the sustainability of the dominance of the army over the ruling civilian oligarchy. Former Pakistani PM, Yusuf Raza Gillani once stated when he was the PM (2008-2012) that Pakistani army is not within the Pakistani state but Pakistani state is within the Pakistani army. This tendency remains a bone of contention between civilian- military trust deficits. Former secretary General of the United Nations, Boutros Boutros Ghali has carried out a comprehensive study on the interlinking between democracy and the military. The central argument of his findings is that in those societies military is powerful, democracy could not sustain for a long time. Pakistan is perhaps classic country suited for his thesis.

Pakistani military therefore not allow Afghanistan to stabilize. In the scenario of the backdrop of NATO forces the Afghan people and the international community is anxious about the post withdrawal security situation. Nawaz Sharif is in power and his past nature has given anxiety to Afghan people. Interestingly, many Afghans are also uncomfortable with the return of Nawaz Sharif as Pakistan's premier. One of Nawaz Sharif's

1993 election campaign slogans (targeting the Pakistan People's Party at the time) was 'you gave up Dhaka, we took Kabul'. Till today, these words are recalled with equal dismay and aghast by Afghans.[14] Nawaz Sharif was basically planted as a stooge by military dictator, General Zia-Ul-Haq to contain the might of then PM, Mohhamad Khan Junejo. Later on military extended covert support to him to contain Pakistan People's Party and its leader, Benazir Bhutto particularly during the civilian interlude between 1988 -1999.

Modi government has also pledged to work hard for the reconstruction of Afghanistan. Pakistan feels insecure with the deepening Indian interests in Afghanistan. Herat attack was a continuation of that mindset. These kinds of attack will be occurring in future as well. It was basically a provocative attack engineered by the military to derail any initial bonhomie between PM Modi and Nawaz Sharif.

The Pakistan government has launched a military operation called 'Zerb-A- Herb' in North Waziristan in FATA in June 2014 to remove these terror groups in the aftermath of terror attack on Karachi airport in June 2014. The NATO forces have already announced that they will withdraw by the end of 2014. In this backdrop an operation to remove terror elements in one of the most suitable place for the Jihad factory is not going to yield any purpose.

As I have already stated that Afghanistan never accepted Durand Line as legitimate border line between both countries. Even the Taliban regime, which was promoted by Pakistan (1996-2001) refused to accept it and taken the line that a Muslim does not require to obtain visa to visit another Islamic country. Right from the independence, Pakistan has perceived Afghanistan as their courtyard which is providing it 'strategic depth' vis-à-vis India, while India supports Afghanistan in order to sandwich Pakistan from the western side. It is also an open secret that this prevailing proxy war in Afghanistan has been a biggest stumbling block on the way to more intense economic relations between South and Central Asia. Network of gas pipelines are also not established yet despite hectic efforts between South and Central Asia due to prevailing anarchy in Pakistan and Afghanistan. The connectivity by road and rail between South and Central Asia would have been yielding enormous economic dividends for both India and Pakistan. It is well argued by Hussian Haqaani, former Pakistani Ambassador to the United States,

"The Policy tripod I wrote about has become less sustainable. Among the factors that have changed is the stress within Pakistan. The issue of India as an eternal enemy has come under a lot of strain. Before the Bin Laden raid, Pakistan was a subject discussed only among American foreign policy experts. Now Pakistan has become part of the American pop culture. Pakistan's elite should embrace a new liberal paradigm. There is no eternal enemy of Pakistan, there is no existential threat to Pakistan, it should maintain an effective military, it should maintain a minimum nuclear deterrent, and after that it should focus on educating its people. Put our 48 per cent children who do not go to school into schools, open up the economy, organize agriculture, create jobs, take advantage of being at the centre of trade ties from India to Central Asia, from Iran to India, from the Middle East to India and China. For the last 66 years, the elite have thought that Pakistan is strategically important because it sits at the crossroads of conflict. I say that Pakistan should now look at itself as sitting at the crossroads of opportunity."[15]

It seems that the sagacious advice of Ambassador Haqqani is not duly taken care of by the Pakistani security establishment. Pakistan must understand that a weak Afghanistan will be detrimental for its stability and prosperity.

The sustainability of NATO operation since last 13 years in Afghanistan has further exposed Pakistan. In the meanwhile due to this operation terror factory shifted to Pakistan and created huge loss to people and economy. But To contain this threat, Pakistan promoted political Islam in Afghanistan and thus tried to remain an important player. It is also an open secret that 2014 Pakistan is not 1979 Pakistan. It has become not only weak by losing 55,000 people and 6,500 soldiers in their home grown insurgency but by all counts it is a crumbling state. The United States has poured $ 30 billion[16] since Operation Enduring Freedom till date to Pakistan but it is not cooperating adequately. Few of America's bilateral ties have been as fraught as those with Pakistan.[17] Despite all rounds support by the United States, it has provided safe heavens to the Taliban shura at Quetta and Haqqani's in FATA. The elimination of Osama Bin Laden in May 2011 at Abbotabad vindicates the fact.

According to a book 'Duty; Memories of a Secretary at War' written by former US defence secretary Robert Gates,

"I gave him a list of specific actions we wanted Pakistan to take. The US also instructed Musharraf to disrupt certain major infiltration routes across the border; enhance intelligence cooperation and streamline Pakistani decision making on targeting. Musharraf kept a straight face and pretended to take all this seriously."[18]

Pakistan has used all negative means to keep Afghanistan turbulent despite international community consistent request to contribute positively. Today Pakistan is one of the most hated countries in Afghanistan.[19] This hostility is no longer confined to the Northern Alliance or elements in the Afghan government, but now runs so deep that most Afghans have stopped differentiating between Pakistan's military and the general population.[20]

Since last many decades Pakistan has used terror as an instrument of its foreign policy and intended to sustain it. Destabilization in Afghanistan is must for the pursuance of this project. Given the situation it seems that Pakistan will not cooperating to stabilizing Afghanistan because it's all powerful Army feels that it could convert Afghanistan again its courtyard and thus achieving the doctrine of strategic depth against India. In 1988 November, Benazir Bhutto elected PM of Pakistan after a general election in the aftermath of the General Zia-Ul-Haq's plane crash in August 1988. But the army first took three assurances from her then only she was allowed to enter into the corridor of power. These three were Kashmir, Afghanistan and Nuclear policy. Since March 2008, civilian regimes are ruling over Pakistan but still they are not autonomous to take their own decision on Afghan front. Army has always considered Afghanistan as an instrument to sustain their monopoly over the power. Of course Kashmir is also connected with the project because their dominance over Afghanistan is intended to create anarchy in Kashmir. Despite 7 years of present democratic rule there are certain limitations of elected regimes in Pakistan and they could not bypass army's role while formulating any policies about Afghanistan and Kashmir.[21] Therefore, a trust deficit is prevailing between the army and the civilian dispensation on these critical issues. Civil-military trust deficit in Pakistan on Afghan affairs also cut the space for positive role for Pakistan. It is intended to sustain the Hobbesian state of nature in Afghanistan. For this particular project of the military a stable and peaceful Afghanistan could be detrimental therefore they are compelled to keep Afghanistan volatile.

It may be safely said that despite all round destruction by home grown Jihad factory, Pakistan perhaps not change its old Afghan policy. To cope up with the situation the Modi government has to reformulate its polices to ensure national interests.

Policy Options for India

Afghan society has already witnessed rampant violence since last 3 and half decades. There is hardly any Afghan family today which is not either led by a widow or a disable. It is high time to establish peace and stability. Afghan people are ready. Only Pakistan needs to be prevented both by persuasion and arm twisting to destabilize Afghanistan. International community needs to be present in Afghanistan with all rounds of reconstruction efforts. It could stretch to decades. Since last 3.5 decades it has been shaky due to the power game of the great powers. For a stabilization process, right from withdrawal of the NATO forces another decade is required. Since 2001 the NATO forces had engaged in "Operation Enduring Freedom" and somehow security situation has improved comparatively. With all round reconstruction efforts, Afghanistan may stabilize in next decade. If it will happen then it will a great help to peace and prosperity to not only South, Central and South West Asia but in the entire globe.

Since last 3.5 decades Afghanistan has remained a den of international terror. It could be a heaven of peace and stability through consistent and collective international efforts. Due to geographical proximity the support of Pakistan would be crucial for the stabilization of this war torn and devastated country. Bypassing Pakistan may be possible if India will reformulate its strategy to cope up the post 2014 NATO withdrawal situation. India has to understand in clear terms that in case of Taliban take over or dominance over Afghanistan, Pakistan will be in dominating situation which has been denied by the 13 years long NATO operation. In this scenario it is possible that new wave of terror will prevail particularly in Kashmir because leftover of the Afghan jihad may be diverted towards Kashmir. Pakistan is struggling with the civil-military cold war. In the backdrop of the NATO withdrawal the military will wish to dominate power structure of Pakistan either by covertly or overtly. For that project, Kashmir needs to boil. Despite relative peace in Kashmir since last one decade the seed of unrest is prevailing and it could ignite with any contemporary provocations. Needless to say that it will have an imprint on rest parts of the country as well. Therefore peace and prosperity in Afghanistan is must for the sustainable development in India.

Since the end of the cold war, India has done well by all counts and has been considered as a force to be reckoned with. NDA-1 regime denoted atomic weapons and demonstrated its power to the entire globe. This event proved positive for Indian strategic calculations because traditionally India is considered as a shying emerging global power. Today India's status as a rising power is taken as a given. It has a GDP of $ 1.8 trillion,[22] a projected GDP growth rate of seven percent in the fiscal year of 2014-15,[23] a 46.8 billion dollar defence budget, a nuclear stockpile of more than 80 warheads and ballistic missiles,[24] a newly built aircraft carrier,[25] and expectations that by 2020 it will overtake Japan, France and Britain to become the world's fourth largest military spender.[26]

As Kautilaya has stated that a country must demonstrate its capability to secure its border, India must secure its border from the incoming terror onslaughts. For that besides strengthening its external and internal security system it also requires to solicit the support of the like minded countries. China has all weather relationship status with Pakistan but the Chinese western province of Xinjiang is also infested with terror and it has also its linkage with the Afghan Jihad. We needs to garner Chinese support as well because beside security threats from terror network based in AF-PAK, it has commercial interests as well in this area. Russia is one of the worst sufferers from terror therefore we must solicit Russian support as well. Russia was part and parcel along with Iran and India to extend all rounds support to the Northern Alliance against the Taliban during Taliban regime in Afghanistan. In the backdrop of the ISIS advances in Syria and Iraq, the threat on Iran is knocking the door. The Central Asian Republics are also extremely vulnerable because of weak governance and presence of IMU and drug trafficking. The Taliban have been connected with the IMU and in June 2014 attack on Karcahi's Jinnah airport, Pakistani authorities have identified both Uighurs and the IMU terrorists among attackers.

The western power led by the United States is equally concerned for peace and prosperity in Afghanistan. They have learnt a lesson that till Afghanistan will not stabilize they will also not remain in peace. By early 2012, Pakistan's repeated, deliberate efforts to undercut U.S. policies had clearly prompted U.S. officials to reconsider the value of the overall security partnership with Islamabad. This became clear when Secretary of Defence Leon Panetta, during a June 2012 trip to Afghanistan and India, issued Washington's starkest criticism yet of Pakistan, pointedly stating that Washington was "reaching the limits of [its] patience" with Islamabad's refusal to crack down on terrorist safe havens operating in its territory.[27]

Panetta further noted India's positive contributions to Afghanistan's economic and commercial development and, arguably more significantly, expressed support for Delhi's training of the country's nascent armed forces and encouraged it to continue with this security assistance mission. Panetta's implicit nod to Indian military engagement in Afghanistan represented a significant shift in U.S. policy away from Pakistan and an acknowledgment that Delhi had more to offer in terms of promoting Afghanistan's internal stability. The United States has already delinked its Pakistan policy from India policy and it was vindicated by 2010 visit of President Obama, when he visited New Delhi but avoided Islamabad. The tendency is sustainable due to wider convergences of interests between India and the United States on the larger canvass of the Asia-Pacific. Foreign secretary, John Kerry has visited New Delhi in the last week of July 2014 and expressed his desire to sustain the process. Prime Minister, Narendra Modi has planned to visit Washington in September 2014 and President Obama has indicated enough to sustain the process. It is a new beginning because of a small thaw in bilateral relations of both countries in last few years of UPA-2. (2009-2014).

We need to solicit the support of all concerned to stabilize Afghanistan and prevent Iraq type situation there. Eminent Indian security analyst, Raja Mohan has rightly stated in November 2013 " Any nuclear deal between Washington and Tehran will immediately bring down oil prices, relieve the current macroeconomic pressures on India , and improve Delhi's energy security calculus over the longer term . US. – Iran rapprochement will help to strengthen Afghanistan against the Taliban and Pakistan and expand India's room for regional maneuver after 2014."[28] The interim deal between Washington and Tehran has already been concluded and it is time when Indian diplomacy must act and bring Iran and United States on the same page to ensure peace and stability in Afghanistan. Iran has also contributed huge resources in the reconstruction of Afghanistan. During 2002-2010, Tehran pledged $ 673 million most of which has been has been spent on infrastructural development in western Afghanistan.[29] Iran is an important player and it had been part and parcel of Indian efforts along with Russia and Central Asian Republics to contain Taliban during its rule over

Afghanistan. (1996-2001). Although Pakistan has been increasing jealous by growing Indian and Iranian involvement in Afghanistan, it is nowhere in the position to contribute to match these contributions by India and Iran.

Global balance of power have played and still playing its devastating role in this war torn country since centuries. But the regional rivalry has also spoiled the situation. Pakistan is an important neighbour of Afghanistan but despite part and parcel of global war against terror it has not collaborated properly and instead worked with tacit understanding of Haqqani networks and others to keep Afghanistan volatile. As part of this approach, Pakistan has been more eager to see that regional cooperation processes and projects are shaped in ways that make Kabul economically and strategically dependent on Islamabad than to enable Afghanistan to emerge as a regional player in its own right.[30] While seeking to secure strong leverage in Afghanistan in order to control the nation's politics after the withdrawal of the NATO, Pakistan has also sought to deprive its regional rival, India , of any significant foothold in the country, and to check what it perceives as Iran's regional ambitions. The victory of Nawaz Sharif's PML-N in May 2013 election has been a window of opportunity. PM, Sharif has expressed his desire for domestic and foreign policy reforms in order to save Pakistan, signaling major changes in Islamabad's approach to Afghanistan and the US. In his first major foreign policy statement after the election on 6th June 2013, Sharif called for neighbourly relations with Afghanistan and India, stressing 'the importance of developing regional consensus on supporting a stable government and peace in Afghanistan, the resolution of all disputes including those with India over Jammu and Kashmir.[31] However, substantial progress on these fronts will depend on the extent to which Sharif is able to diminish the entrenched and structural role of the Pakistani army in domestic policies and foreign policy. From 15th August 2014, Islamabad is under seize by Imran Khan' party PTI and cleric Kadri's PAT. Both are seeking removal of 2013 elected Nawaz Sharif government. According to Husain Haqqani, former Pakistani Ambassador for United States "Sharif could have handled the problem better …but I have no doubt that Imran Khan and Quadri have been egged on by the military covertly to clip Sharif's wings. Pakistani democracy remains fragile and subject to the military's manipulations. The Sharif government is too weak to move forward with serious talks with India. There will be definitely be an attempt by the Taliban and their backers to grab power as they did in the chaos following the Soviet withdrawal."[32] Elements within the Pakistani military have been sympathetic for the Taliban resurgence in Afghanistan and turbulence in Kashmir, both as a means of self-preservation and to increase Pakistan's leverage in a complex and unpredictable region. Sharif seems to have recognized that Pakistan's stability and security are critically linked with Afghanistan and India. But as vindicated from Ambassador Haqqani statement he is unable to convince the army that a stable Afghanistan is in the larger interests of Pakistan too. Therefore it is crystal clear that Pakistani army and their stooge will try their level best to capture the power in Kabul. Pakistani military however has become weak due to the sustainable volatile domestic situation but as an institution it is unlikely to accept Sharif's wish over both critical issues. Military has also protested Sharif's participation in the swearing in ceremony of Indian PM, Nareandra Modi.

Pakistan's Afghan policy is decided by the military. Given the prevailing security architecture of South and South West Asia, it seems unlikely that military will allow any stabilization in Afghanistan. Needless to say those situations in Afghanistan will determine security architecture of India, South, and Central Asia and will also make an imprint on global peace. India must take all possible steps to ensure peace and stability with the tacit understanding with like-minded countries in Afghanistan.

Notes

1. H.J. Mackinder, (1904) 'The Geographical Pivot of History', *Geographical Journal*, Vol-23, No-4, April-1904.

2. The last British governor of the NWFP sees it differently, referring to documents from 1893 to 1956 concerning the Durand. Caroe, Olf Kirkpatrick (1976) *The Pathans 550 B.C-A.D 1957*, Karachi, Oxford. P-466.

3. The rulers of the Princely states of Swat, Dir, Chitral, and Amb joined Pakistan shortly after independence but not the Khan of Kalat, who wanted to remain independent , Baloch, Inayatullah (1987) *The Problem of Greater Baluchistan, A Study of Baluch Nationalism.*

4. Lalit K. Jha,(24 March, 2014) ISI executed Kabul Indian Embassy attack, US couldn't stop it, *The Indian Express,* New Delhi.

5. Ibid.

6. Do not let Haqqani fighters resettle, (26 July 2014) US tells Pakistan, *Reuters*.

7. Ibid.

8. Afghan Minsitry of Finance, (2010) *Developmnet Cooperation Report*, Kabul, P-95.

9. Etlaf Najafizada, (6 December 2011) 'Indian Group Wins Rights to Mine in Afghanistan's Hajigak, *Bloomberg Businessweek*.

10. Hamid Shalizi,' (19 May 2013) Afghanistan's Karzai seeks Indian Military Aid Amid Tensions with Pakistan, *Reuters*.

11. "Poll: Americans' views on foreign policy,"(11 November 2011) *CBS News*.

12. "U.S. Image in Pakistan Falls No Further Following bin Laden Killing,"

13. "Obama: (8 May 2011) U.S., Pakistan Can Find Ways To Improve Cooperation."

14. Hina Baloch, (28 January 2014) Afghans and Pakistanis; friends turned foes?, *Dawn*, Karachi.

15. The Idea Exchange, (20 October 2013) *Indian Express*, New Delhi.

16. C. Fair, (27 July 2014) *Times of India*, New Delhi.

17. Sumit Ganguly, (April 2014) "The Pathological Alliance, *Current History*, P-165.

18. Mushraaf refused to act Against Al-Qaeda, (12 January 2014) Taliban; US ex-defence secretary, PTI, *The Indian Express*, New Delhi, P-12.

19. Dr. Pervez Hoodbhoy, (18 March 2012) "What Pakistan should do in Afghanistan?" *Express Tribune*, Lahore.

20. "Helmand despatch: (1 August 2010) 'Pakistan is the true enemy," *Daily Telegraph*, London.

21. Singh, Sudhir, (2013) Limits of Electoral Mandate in Pakistan, *Politico*, Vol-1, P-67.

22. World Bank, India, http;//data.worldbank.org/country/india

23. India's GDP growth Forecast to 6 percent for FY 14; (13 August 2013) Credit Suisse, "The *Financial Express*, New Delhi.

24. India as a Great Power; (30 March 2013) Know Your Strength, *The Economist.*

25. Indian-Built Aircraft Carrier INS Vikrant Launched, (12 August 2013) *BBC.*

26. The Idea Exchange, (20 October 2013) *Indian Express,* New Delhi.

27. Jim Garamone, (7 June 2012) "U.S. Reaching Limit of Patience with Pakistan on Safe Havens," *American Forces Press Service.*

28. C. Raja Mohan, (20 November 2013) The Great Game Folio, *The Indian Express,* New Delhi.

29. Op, Cit, No. 6.

30. Mary Anne Weaver, (2002) Pakistan; *In the Shadow of Jihad and Afghanistan,* Farrar, New York.

31. Op, Cit, No-6.

32. Military pushing Imran Khan-Nawaz govt. too weak for talks, (22 August 2014) *Times of India,* New Delhi.

PART III

MARITIME SECURITY OF INDIA: THE CHALLENGES AND OPTIONS

10 | Challenges And Options For A Maritime India In The 21St Century

R S Vasan

Abstract

The transformation of the global maritime security landscape has been quite dramatic with the unfolding of events in different oceans of the world. On a global scale, it is do with the recalibration of the US pivot to Asia and the impact of the withdrawal of US and allied forces from Afghanistan. At the regional level, it is piracy that took centre stage in the West Indian Ocean and the Gulf of Guinea that brought the international community together to contain this scourge. The capture of a floating armoury off Tuticorin by the ICG recently brings out that not all the anti-piracy measures have been carefully thought out. In another region, it was the declaration of the ADIZ over disputed Islands in the East China Sea with potential to affect the maritime balance not only in the region but also elsewhere with the downstream effects. It is in the backdrop of such events that India needs to work on the options for its maritime forces to take on the challenges of this century. The growth of the maritime forces in India has been steady and is poised for greater role in the Indian Ocean and beyond. The recent commissioning of the Aircraft Carrier INS Vikramaditya in November 2013 and the ongoing sea trials of the INS Arihant, the restoration of the control of the strategically important A&N Islands to the Navy and the addition of new platforms, weapons and sensors are equipping the nation with a formidable strategic and diplomatic option for using the Navy as an instrument of foreign policy to serve national objectives. The paper seeks to examine the full import of recent developments in the maritime arena in areas of concern to India's both long term and short term challenges.

There is a greater focus today in the maritime domain with the changing contours of maritime seascape. The oceans continue to be the bridge between nations, civilisations and other stake holders. The cost of sea transportation remains the cheapest and with technology aiding sea transportation with huge volumes, modernisation of ports and harbours, building of mammoth ships in a big way, the dependence on the Sea Lines of Communication (SLOCs) will continue to increase manifold. While there is clamour for unfettered use of the seas as enshrined in UNCLOS which promotes the concept of the freedom of the high seas and navigation, large tracts of seas and also the arteries of the world have also come under pressure from pirates and non-state actors. The picture below is indicative of the global movement of sea traffic. The figures of the ships that ply the oceans annually amply demonstrate the increased dependence on the sea routes on one hand and also an increased vulnerability at sea for pirates and Viloent Non State Actors (VNSAs) or even state supported terrorist acts as in the case of Mumbai terror attack.

Sea Lines of Communication (SLOCs). The importance of the SLOCs for promoting trade between nations for safe movement of energy and other products has never been felt so acutely as in the recent years. It is not just the two Asian energy hungry nations that are dependent on the energy products from other parts of the world but also most other maritime nations who are dependent on the seas for similar imports and exports. China and India the two growing economies in particular are critically aware of the importance of the SLOCs and the concept of the freedom of navigation. The number of ships that ply the Indian Ocean and the straits as indicated below makes it clear that the number of ships will go up and so will be the need to protect them from acts of piracy and also from non-state actors. It must also be noted that the SLOCs lead up to the choke points of the world. In the Indian context, the Straits of Hormuz on the west and the Straits of Malacca on the East or the most important choke points through which energy products are moved. The disruption either along the SLOCS or due to hostile situation in the choke point would disrupt the smooth flow of traffic and also will seriously impact the economy of the nations who are dependent on the free and smooth flow of merchandise through the sea routes.

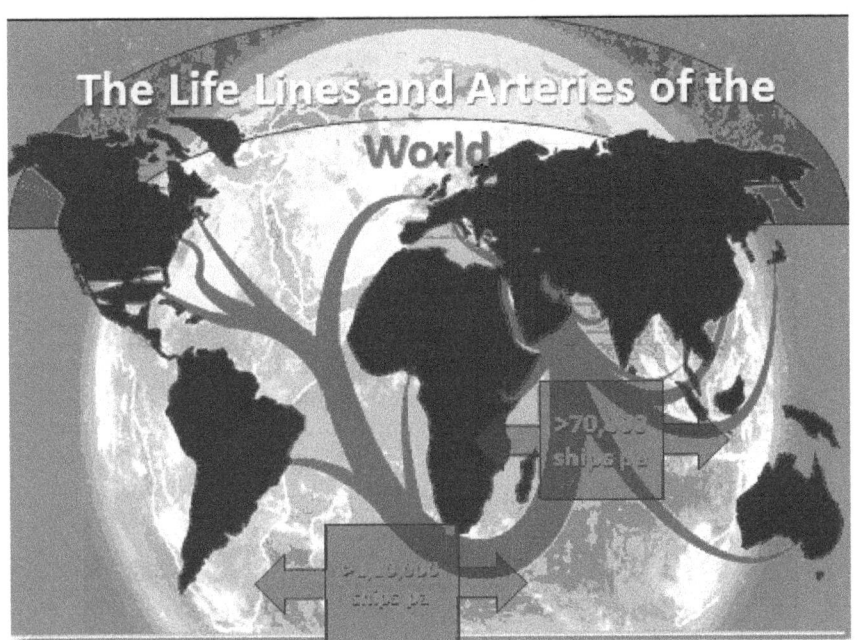

The Indian Reach and Responsibility. In the backdrop of the global traffic, particularly in the Indian Ocean it is important to note that India has a huge responsibility. If the Exclusive Economic Zone (EEZ) confers the advantage of ownership of over 2 million square kilometers for harnessing the ocean living and non-living resources, the Search and Rescue Region requires the ability to provide Search and Rescue in an area that is nearly double the EEZ.

The map[1] on the next page indicates the extent of the EEZ and the SRR respectively.

The Exclusive Economic Zone in the Arabian Sea and the Bay of Bengal as well as around the A&N Islands and the L&M Islands while enhancing the area for harnessing also increase the challenges of C4ISR (Command Control Communication, Computers Intelligence Surveillance and Reconnaissance) for the Indian Maritime agencies. The Island groups in the Bay of Bengal and the Arabian Sea respectively have provided an excellent opportunity for India to monitor the exit /entry points from Malacca Straits and also the Sea Lines of Communication around peninsular India. The setting up of the Tri Services command therefore Port Blair has added punch to the capability of the Indian Defence Forces

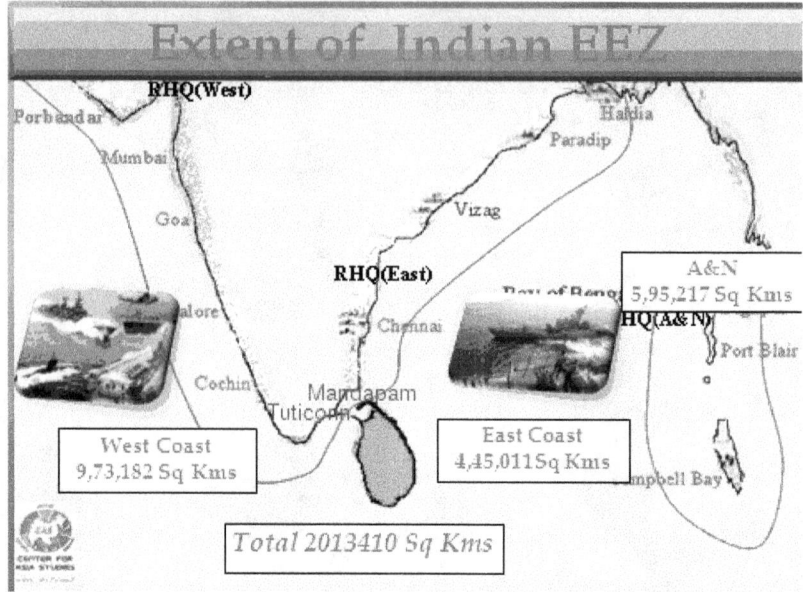

who now are functioning under a unified command. From the strategic point of view, this is also a great advantage vis-a-vis China which is dependent on the Malacca Straits for transit of all its products in general and the energy products in particular on which the nation Is dependent for its economic progress and prosperity. Termed as the Malacca Dilemma, China is examining various options to overcome this dependency. The options include over land connectivity, cutting through a land mass in the Isthamus, Strategic Petroleum reserve (SPR) etc.

Likewise, the Search and Rescue Region which is now administered by the Indian Coast Guard as a nodal agency demands that the responsibilities for saving lives at sea and for maintaining a credible SAR structure are maintained on a 24x7 basis. It also requires close coordination with the other Maritime Rescue and Coordination Centres of other neighbouring nations who maintain similar structures. The Coast Guard is also the nodal agency for combating marine pollution and the Director General of the Coast Guard is responsible for the National Oil Spill Disaster Contingency Plan(NOSDCP).

What needs to be borne in mind is the fact that there is phenomenal legal and illegal activity that goes in the area of responsibility and there has to be very close coordination with the Navy, the Coastal police, intelligence agencies, shipping agencies, State authorities who regulate fishing and

Challenges And Options For A Maritime India in The 21St Century

leisure activity along the shores and such like. So by no means is it an easy task. The map below[2] is indicative of the areas in which India has agreed to provide the Search and Rescue structure. In fact the western limits of the Search and Rescue region are close to the areas where pirates have ventured out in the past far from the Somalia coast. The traffic from the Straits of Hormuz to the Malacca Straits which passes under the watchful eyes of the Indian agencies is intense and it would be always a challenge to separate the innocent traffic from the mischievous ones. Some of the concerns of China are also due to this geographical advantage that provides plenty of options for the Indian Maritime Forces to keep the areas under surveillance and also intervene as and when required be it in times of war or in Military Operations Other Than War (MOOTW) as required both in the EEZ and also the Search and Rescue Region .

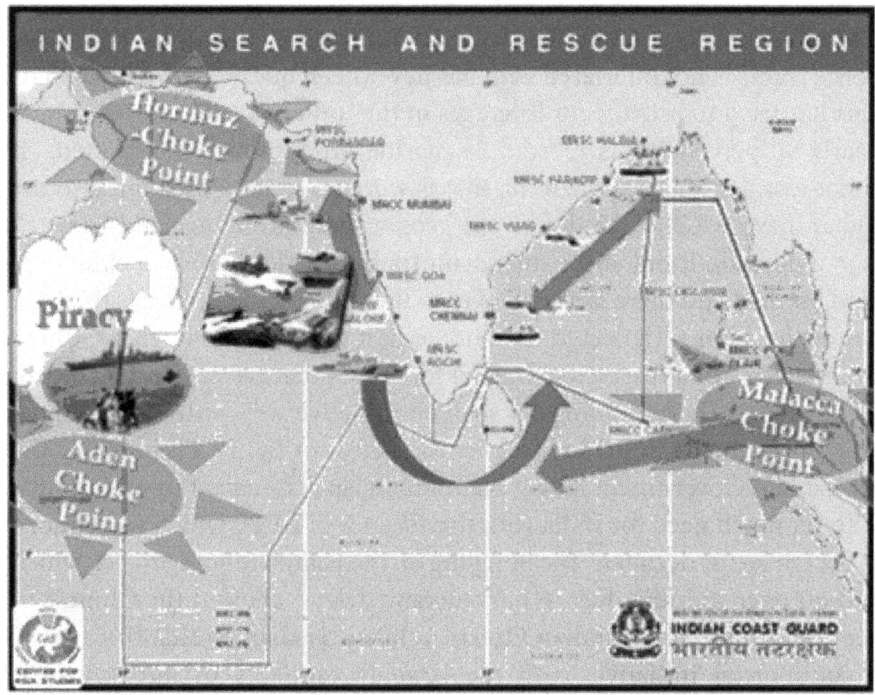

Some of the incidents in the recent past in our areas of interest have caused great concern to the Indian security agencies. The apprehending of a floating armoury MV Sunguard Ohio off Tuticorin has thrown up many questions about the legitimacy of such vessels which claim to provide the required armed security guards for the transit of the merchant vessels through the High Risk Area. The related aspects of the case are covered by this author and the paper is available on Academia.edu.[3] The shooting of two fishermen resulting in death of the innocent fishermen by the Italian marines from the vessel Enrica Lexie again has brought to fore issues related to use of armed guards and the jurisdiction of Flag States in the EEZ. The legal and associated issues are covered in a detailed analysis of the author.[4] The interception and subsequent destruction of a Pakistani boat with suspect intentions on the night of 31st December 2014 by a well coordinated operation between the intelligentsia agencies and the Coast Guard indicates that there is a need to ensure that there is seemless C4ISR architecture both in the SRR and also in the EEZ where there is phenomenal activity of all kinds including fishing, smuggling, movement of ships and crafts of all description, commercial activity, off shore drilling and other activities that are happening on a 24x7 basis.

China Factor. That China has legitimate interest in ensuring that its sea borne traffic is not interfered with has never been questioned. China on its part has tried to provide for leverages in the Indian Ocean through which nearly 90 percent of its mercantile marine products are transported. It is not just the Malacca dilemma that is worrisome for China but also the Indian navy which both due to the geographical advantage and its reach is in a position to hit at the merchant traffic should there be a clash over land borders and there is a spill over to the Indian Ocean. Just as the USA has deployed its fifth fleet in the Middle East to protect its interests, China would in the long run be looking out for bases that can support its Indian Ocean Fleet. The beginnings of such an initiative were witnessed with its huge investments in Sri Lanka post the defeat of the LTTE in 2009. The Sri Lankan Government led by Mahinda Rajapaksa leaned towards China without much need for India with the absence of LTTE which was a thorn in Sri Lanka for decades. The bungling of the Hambanthota project which was on offer to India due to bureaucratic delays allowed the Chinese to get a foot hold in the Indian Ocean. While it is claimed that this is only a commercial initiative, with the large investments in infrastructure, ports and air ports, Sri Lanka would have not been in a position to negate any request for facilities in any of the ports of Sri Lanka. This was amply demonstrated during the visit of Xi Jinping to Delhi. Just as the Premier of China was meeting the PM of India, the PLA Navy submarines were berthed in Colombo along with a support ship indicating the shape of things to come. However, all that has temporarily changed with the change of leadership in Sri Lanka with the new dispensation lead by Maithripala Siri Sena favourably inclined towards India. The situation in Maldives likewise is no different as Chinese have invested heavily in Maldives and the new political dispensation is favourably inclined towards China much to the chagrin of India which also faced the embarrassment of one of its prime private company being shown the door from a prestigious airport project. In addition to the traditional all weather friend Pakistan, China obviously is wooing the nations in the maritime neighbourhood of India to insure its future and protect its strategic interests. The commitment of China to build the China Pakistan Economic Corridor (CPEC) by investing about 50 billion dollars indicates both vision and commitment even though the corridor passes through the disputed area claimed by India. The CPEC is a strategic option being exercised with multiple objectives. This will also provide a gate way to the Arabian sea through the port of Gwadar which China has taken over from Singapore for operating the port. So it is both an alternative route for transporting the energy goods and also a corridor that would promote connectivity and trade along the entire CPEC. If that is the initiative along the land routes, the Maritime Silk Route is another major initiative that aims to provide China an opportunity to invest heavily in the countries from SE Asia, to South Asia to Africa and even extend it to Europe. The contours of the MSR are covered subsequently.

Maritime Silk Route. The Chinese leadership in October 2013 made grand announcement about the Maritime Silk Route (MSR) with aim to have maritime constituencies in all of Asia, Africa and right up to Europe. Something like 43 billion US dollars has already been earmarked and it is the intention to provide for developing of the ports and infrastructure in various ports and destinations of strategic importance. The region surrounding New Silk Road Economic Belt and the Maritime Silk Road contains 4.4 billion people (63 per cent of the world's population), with an aggregate GDP of USD 2.1 trillion (29 per cent of the world's aggregate wealth).[5]

It must be remembered that the idea is more to revisit the past where trading nations used the land and sea routes for transporting silk and spice.[6] If it was spices for India it was silk for China which zealously guarded the secret of making silk. Both India and China were prosperous till about the 15th century with the optimum harnessing of the resources. Both were wealthy nations and great civilizations which flourished till the cycle of ups and downs caught up with them both. Both India and China started losing their top slots to western powers with the advent of colonialism and technology which aided the west to subjugate other countries around the world.

There are references to the glory of the past centuries particularly 14-15th century where China's Navy sailed the oceans from the South China Sea right up to the African shores and beyond. It is a different matter that the South China Sea is today an arena of great and small power conflicts. The reclamation of the land areas in SCS by building artificial Islands and runways to enable air operations [7] has vitiated the atmosphere and the smaller neighbours are not exactly in a position to take on the might of China. In a recent case, China even ordered the Philippines to keep its military planes off form the disputed areas.[8] It has also been impatient[9] with any remarks made by even the ASEAN block which has the maximum number of disputants to the territorial claims in the SCS.

Rewinding to the past, The PLA Navy even commemorated the five hundred years of this event in a big way by an encore performance by its modern naval units. The map below is illustrative of the silk routes both over land and over the sea. By investing a large sum of 43 billion US dollars, China is indeed thinking big to ensure that its future is secured by economic investments and connectivity from Africa to Asia

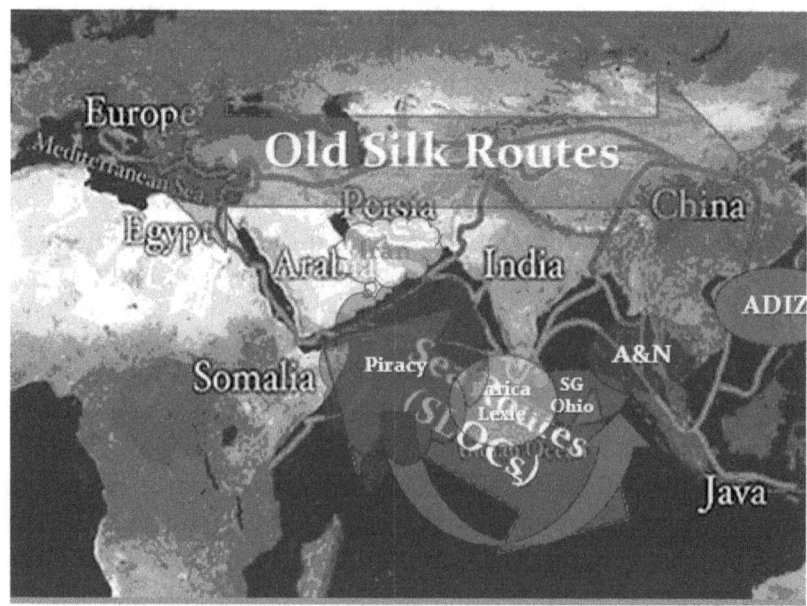

to Europe. The large investments in the countries in Asia and Africa would go towards augmenting infrastructure and also building of related facilities for promoting trade and commerce of greater proportions. These investments in the assessment of the Chinese would provide the leverages and strategic flexibility as China wants to insure its future that would be heavily dependent on the sea routes.

The destination countries in India's maritime neighbourhood have evinced keen interest in the project and have also agreed to be part of this Chinese initiative as it brings in direct investments in the blue economy. It is not that every country is enthused about the project. Even Indonesia as part of the ASEAN grouping seems to have reservations[10] about the Chinese initiative as it fears that its own dependence on China will increase manifold. India as an Indian Ocean Power likewise seems concerned about this initiative that is virtually in its traditional areas of influence in its backyard. India has been cautious and has requested for more details about the nature and intent and is not in a hurry to join the initiative.[11] The view from New Delhi is that they will examine each case based on its merit and will take a call on the need to join hands with China.

Anti Piracy Measures- While piracy is as old as the sea faring traditions of nations, there was a phenomenal increase in the number of incidents particularly off Somalia. While there are many reasons attributed to the increase, it is agreed that it is the lack of employment, governance, poaching by foreign fishing vessels and indiscriminate dumping of toxic waste in the waters off Somalia that led to increased incidents of piracy as it became a means of livelihood. In addition, with the lure of easy money, there were many syndicates with powerful leaders who controlled the acts of piracy. It had established itself as a great economic enterprise. The handlers ashore had access to modern technology and the pirates were just unemployed youth who were paid their daily wages and incentives when they took over a vessel. The detailed study undertaken by One Earth Foundation clearly brings out the kind of money that is involved in running this enterprise.

The alarming rise of such incidents and the large number of seafarers who were held hostage for claiming huge sums as ransom brought together the international community. While the International Maritime Organisation (IMO) issued various guidelines for ships passing through the High Risk Areas, the owners and the crew were all part of the anti-piracy measures which were aimed at bringing the success rate of pirates.

The Changing Dimensions of Security: India's Security Policy Options

The psychological trauma faced by the sea farers in captivity and the families ashore did not bring any confidence in the measures adopted. However after peaking in mid-2000, the presence of the navies around the world, the Best Management Practices (BMP) and other hard and soft measures ensured that the incidents were brought down to single digits. The picture below depicts the global presence of naval forces from different parts of the world that participated either collectively or individually in sustaining the momentum against such violent acts at sea. It is clear from the diagram below that the areas in which the pirates were successful were quite close to India's EEZ or the SRR and hence, India required robust action to ensure that the threat did not reach Indian shores.

Commencing 2008, China also has ensured that an anti-Piracy patrol was sustained by deploying PLA-N units on a regular basis. Most of the nations which felt threatened by the escalating nature of piracy off the African coast ensured that they deployed naval units in the area. The end of the year report of the Piracy Reporting Centre specifically acknowledges the role played by the navies of the world in combating this menace. The picture below indicates the kind of effort that went in to containing this scourge. While there were many combined forces including the Combined Maritime Force, EU Naval Force, CGPCS and SHADE, India with its central position in the Indian Ocean had to take many proactive measures to ensure that the threat did not reach the Indian shores.

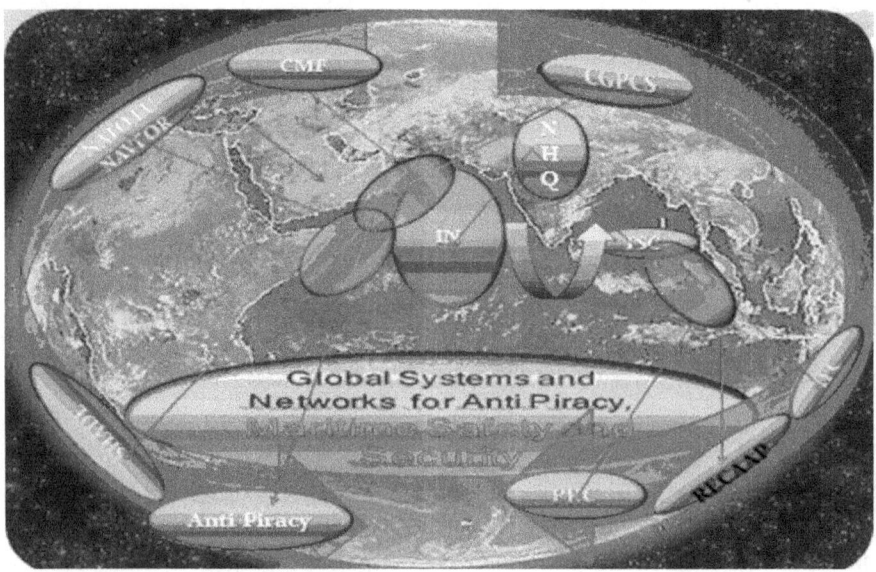

The deployment of the vessels in the area has indirectly benefited the Chinese navy which was able to put the concept of out of area operations to test and refine their operating procedures for such extended operations. China not being a Indian Ocean Power just as the other Extra Regional Players are, was able to fine tune its procedures for working on the extended line of logistic support all the way from the South China Sea through the Malacca Straits sailing around India to reach the areas of interest.

Challenges in the Indo Pacific Century. A lot has been said and debated about the impact of the recalibration of the American Strategic new thrust in the Indo Pacific area. A large tract of the Indo Pacific area is indeed part of the area earlier referred to as the Asia Pacific. The resignation of the area of interest bring a sharper focus to the Indian Ocean which connects the African ports and shores to the Australian coasts and ports with India in a dominant position. So what are the challenges in the Indo Pacific? While discussing the challenges it must be borne in mind that the traditional challenges to sea farers, navies, law enforcement agencies, Flag States have not changed. However, there is an element of technology availability to both sides that change the rules of the game. The terrorists, pirates and any other VNSAs have access to the same levels of sophisticated technology as others in the oceans and it does complicate the envelope out at sea. Some of the important challenges are discussed in the succeeding paragraphs.

Presence of Extra Regional Powers. Though during the Galle conference in Sri Lanka the National Security Advisor of India Mr Ajit Doval gave a clarion call for keeping the Indian Ocean as a Zone of Peace, the ground reality is illustrative of no such thing happening with the increased importance of Indian Ocean to the growing economies not just in Asia but also to the rest of the world. The energy security requirements both in the past and the present will ensure that those who need to protect their interests on the SLOCS and along the energy routes will ensure that there navies are present. The classic example is that of the US which has been in the Indian Ocean and also has deployed its fifth fleet from the Middle East with ships deployed from friendly bases such as Bahrain. With the discovery of shale gas and the increased production of domestic energy products, the USA is expected to depend less and less on the traditional energy sources in the Middle East. Based on this factor, there were expectations that the energy independence will perhaps bring down the number of deployed units of USA. However, the decision of the USA to increase the number of units in the Middle East to about forty (up by 25%) is indicative of the factor that US will continue to be interested in the region due to not just the energy needs but also due to the changing dynamics of geo politics in the Middle East.

The cold war in any case ensured that both US and the Soviet Union were competing with each other in the Indian ocean region by trying to keep tabs on the movement of naval units in general and nuclear submarines in particular who found the warm waters of Indian Ocean as safe sanctuaries for prowling the oceans and also for being in state of readiness should there be a nuclear war.

When one moves fast forward to the present, it is clear that the scene is being replayed not just with the old player but the new players such as China. China is a dominant power of this century and has been increasing its naval presence in the Indian Ocean while simultaneously seeking to increase its foot prints in this area of great interest. India was very concerned with the Chinese thrust in the Indian Ocean. Having lost out on the offer to invest in Hambanthota more by inaction, lack of strategic vision and lethargy of the decision making system, it was worried about the gains made by China in the maritime neighbourhood. Maldives, Sri Lanka, Bangladesh and of course Pakistan who are all members of the SAARC were wooed by the Chinese leaders with heavy investments and offer of technical/material/monetary assistance. India also suffered from a policy paralysis during the UPA rule and slowly conceded strategic space to China which has deep rooted interests in the Indian Ocean and in the maritime neighbourhood of India.

According to the Ministry of Defence report *"Naval Diplomacy entails the use of naval (Maritime) forces in support of foreign policy objectives to build 'bridges of friendship' and strengthen international cooperation on one hand, and to signal capability and intent to deter potential adversaries on the other. The larger purpose of the Navy's diplomatic role is to favourably shape the maritime environment in the furtherance of national interests, in consonance of the foreign policy and national security objectives."-*

From the point of view of India a growing maritime power it has to take cognizance of the developments in the areas of interest. The Chinese interest and thrust in the Indian Ocean Region is of particular interest to India which has elected a new Government that promises to deliver.

Under the new leadership, the expectations are that a multi-dimensional maritime prowess would be developed in a time bound manner. While some of the components of this development are evident, there is still a lot of scope for renewed thrust on developing a modern maritime power that protects national interests in any part of the world. The list includes:-

1. Two fleets that are centered around a Carrier Battle Group

2. A net centric operations capable force that has robust and fail proof capability.

3. Indigenous potent surface forces that compliment naval missions and objectives

4. Credible underwater force including modern conventional submarines with missiles and AIP

5. Fleet of nuclear submarines as components of the Strategic Force of the nation which can deliver devastating blows on any adversary who chooses the nuclear route to attack India first.

6. An efficient and sufficient amphibious capability that provides the options to the planners and also puts the enemy on the defensive.

7. The Coast Guard, the Coastal Security Group and special forces that complement the efforts of the mainstream forces in pursuit of national objectives both during peace and war.

8. A dynamic indigenous ship building and repair capability that can be competitive in defence sales.

To sum up, the challenges in the century of the seas and also the required actions for India could be listed as :-

1. Maintaining the sanctity of the sea lines by ensuring that there is uninterrupted flow of traffic for trade, commerce and any other legitimate activity. This definitely involves having effective anti-piracy measures, a credible C4ISR architecture along with a technology aided decision making ability.

2. Stabilising the maritime neighbourhood which has been the focus of Chinese interests. While it may be quite a challenge to match the economic prowess and clout of China, India will need to pull

out all stops to ensure that it retains the traditional influence and strategic space in the Indian Ocean.

3. To prevent the kind of attacks as witnessed during the Mumbai terror attack in November 2008 that brought about a paradigm shift in the handling of the maritime terrorism from across the border.

4. Protecting the interests of the fishermen and regulating the issues related to livelihood and security. The case in example is the frequent crossing over of the Indian Tamil fishermen to Sri Lankan waters in pursuit of fishing. However, a strong mechanism has to evolve to ensure that this does not affect bilateral relations. Also, the declaration of the High Risk Areas unilaterally has affected fishermen. The case of Enrica Lexie in which the two serving Italian marines shot dead two fishermen off the Kerala coast mistaking them for pirates throws up many legal, operational and interstate challenges that need to be managed in a better manner. Likewise, the operation of floating armouries under the excuse of providing armed sentries to ships in the HRA has thrown up many legal questions and the validity of such concepts without the sanction of international bodies.

5. The revitalising of the Indian Ocean Region Association should be of prime importance to all stake holders and member states. The scope of its activity needs to be enhanced to bring about greater cohesion amongst the member states and also to ensure that they are able to present a common front to protect and promote the common interests.

6. From the point of view of India, The thrust on indigenization needs to be even more vigorous if India aims big and wishes to play a greater regional and global role.

Notes

1. The map is courtesy Indian Coast Guard which has indicated the extent of EEZ in Bay of Bengal and the Arabian Sea

2. Map developed using the Coast Guard map that designates the Search and

Rescue Region (courtesy Indian Coast Guard)

3. http://www.academia.edu/4834074/The_curious_case_of_MV_Seaman_Guard_Ohio

4. http://www.asiastudies.org/index.php?option=com_content&view=article&id=262&Itemid=262

5. H.E. Ambassador Yang Yanyi, "China to revive ancient Silk Road", euobserver, 12 May, 2015. https://euobserver.com/euchina/128666

6. "Trade History of the Silk Road, Spice & Incense Routes", Silk Routes.Net, http://www.silkroutes.net/SilkSpiceIncenseRoutes.htm

7. IHS Jane's 360. "China Building Airstrip- Capable Island on Fiery Cross Reef" by James Hardy and Sean o' Connor, 20th November, 2014, http://www.janes.com/article/46083/china-building-airstrip-capable-island-on-fiery-cross-reef

8. "China is ordering Philippine military planes to get away from disputed areas of the South China Sea", May 7th, 20015, http://www.businessinsider.com/china-orders-philippine-military-to-leave-disputed-areas-of-south-china-sea-2015-5?IR=T

9. Reuters. "China slams ASEAN chief for South China Sea comments" by Ben Blanchard, March 11th, 2015, http://in.reuters.com/article/2015/03/11/china-southchinasea-idINL4N0WD2Z620150311

10. "Indonesia must reject Chinese maritime Silk Road offer: Sultan", ANTARANEWS.com, 11 May, 2015. http://www.antaranews.com/en/news/98895/indonesia-must-reject-chinese-maritime-silk-road-offer-sultan

11. Mrunal, "China's Maritime Silk Road initiative, Purpose, Salient Features, India's stand", http://mrunal.org/2014/10/diplomacy-china-maritime-silk-road-initiative-purpose-salient-features-india-stand.html

11 | Terror on High Seas

Vibhuti Singh Shekhawat

Antonio Gramsci Once Said, "I am a pessimist because of intelligence but an optimist because of will."[1] What is the Indian response and reaction to this saying? The Indian situation is the absolute reverse of it. We are pessimist because of will and optimist because of intelligence. We have intelligence enough to know a problem but lack the will to solve it in time. The reason: to quote Shakespearean, we cannot stoop to conquer. The impression we are giving to the outside world is that India is a big country - too big to be taken care of administratively. We are infested with terrorists of many descriptions such as Indian Mujahidins, Maoists, Naxalites, secessionists in Jammu and Kashmir and the northeastern India including the seven sisters and terrorists coming from across the border from Pakistan. But we lack the will to tackle them and are only wasting the resources in the illusive mission to eliminate them. The more we try to eliminate them, the more we inadvertently strengthen and promote them by our ad hoc policies and simplistic solutions. We efface the symptoms but do not reach the bottom to identify the causes of malaise. Small wonder, there is a continuity of terror which manifests itself with intermittent intermissions. Blasts continue to occur in a sequence or periodically and these acts of unremitting terror show no signs of abating. While acts of serial bombings in several cities of India are still fresh in our memory, new forms of terrorist attacks occur that continue to baffle our security personnel. One can identify and explain one new addition to the existing forms of terror viz., the maritime terror which we did not visualize till the Mumbai 9/11 attack that was sea borne. For the first time it awakened us to a danger from across the high seas. One may turn to it now.

Maritime Terror: Terror today is no longer an imaginary ghost; it is a ground reality. In its new incarnation, it is showing up from the deep blue see. Some of the narrow creeks in the Indian ocean, particularly in a place about fifteen hundred kilometers, from Mumbai there is a narrow channel which is navigable by small boats and it leads to a point which is not too far away from the heights of Trombay. Once this point is reached, the maritime operators of terror can come dangerously close to three vital installations viz., Bhabha Atomic Research Centre, the BPCL Oil refinery and a container port. These landmark installations become vulnerable to firing by maritime terrorists. The huge unguarded coastal line of India is the new route for terrorists to infiltrate in India and create mayhem.

It may be remembered that India has a vast coastline, stretching to more than 5400 kilometers. In addition, 2100 kilometers of shores are on more than 1900 islands. To add to it, there are 13 major seaports and about 185 minor ones around which are located high security vital installations such as space centers, missile testing sites, nuclear research facilities and their bases.[2] The entire stretch is unprotected except for some notified areas. A.K. Antony, the Defence Minister told the parliament in the budget session of 2007 that the terrorists were planning attacks through the sea route.[3] M.K. Dhar, the former Joint Director of Intelligence Bureau once said, "The sea is dark area of India's intelligence gathering system. It did not get a priority as our bread-and-butter was something else. You can't make sense of coastal security when the logistics are almost non-existent."[4] It shows that the government is aware of the danger of terrorist attack from the high seas.

It may be remembered that the terrorists often camouflage their deadly operations though what are called the "flags of convenience"[5] which are the ships registered in Panama or Liberia. Vice Admiral K.K. Nayar, the Chairman of National Maritime Foundation explains the nature of this threat by saying that "If terrorists blow a hole in an oil tanker passing through the Straits of Hormuz or Malacca, a direct fall out would be steep increase in oil prices and ship insurance."[6]

What adds to our difficulties are logistics, the labyrinthine creeks through which boats can operate in stealth. Since the positioning of creek is what it is, they are beyond even satellite mapping. The satellite images cannot tell and differentiate between normal maritime boats and those driven by suspected terror elements. In 2002, the Bangladesh government made a major haul of illegal arms stocked in a ferry at the Chittagong port. It was meant for the militants of the northeast according to Hormis Tharakan, the retired chief of Research and Analysis Wing (RAW).[7] The

Al Queda terrorists too are not far behind in the technology of maritime attacks though their plans received a jolt when their chief maritime operative Al-Masiri was arrested. But this has not dampened their spirits and determination to renew their nefarious activities. Their journal known as Mu'askar al-Battar makes a pointed reference to their intended maritime attacks in this region which is a cause for great concern. The Institute for Analysis of Global Safety, Washington predicted that the terrorist were training their guns on oil gas installations and Bombay High. India's largest offshore oil field falls clearly in their range. Says Admiral Arun Kumar "If operatives of a terror group are on a kamikaze mission, the oil field will be history."[8] This is not a dreadful hypothesis or a figment of imagination. B. Raman, former additional secretary, RAW narrates a confession from a Babbar Khalsa militant of how he was directed by his Pakistani trainers to join the Mumbai Flying Club, take a solo flight and crash it into Bombay High.[9] Sam Bataman of the Institute of Defence and Strategic Studies, Singapore conjures up the dreadful vision of nuclear installation being attacked by the terrorists and suggests that "in the longer term, presumably there would more nuclear installation requiring security."[10]

The worse affected are the containers that alone account for about ninety per cent of world trade and if they are attacked on the high seas, it will choke all international business. Keeping in view this, the USA has launched an ambitious Container Security Initiative which involves a cumbrous procedure of scanning all foreign containers at US ports in order to detect possible mischief by terrorist on the way. India should emulate USA and this checking should be done at the Indian ports also. What makes it of greater concern to us is that these maritime vessels are operating in the open sea and getting at them is not all that difficult. In view of this new threat in the Indian Ocean, there can be only fragile peace. The NDA government was toying with the idea of providing state of art detection equipment and big vessels to the maritime states of India in order to set up coastal police stations. States of Gujarat and Kerala were earmarked for implementing this scheme but the project remained on paper only and never took off. Nor did UPA do substantially in this direction. The Coastal Security Scheme revived by the UPA government in 2005 also met a similar fate. Of the sanctioned amount of Rs. 372 crores for this project only 13 crores was released and in 2007 only 10 crores was released. Critical areas like Andaman and Nicobar, Lakshadweep, Pondicherry and Daman and Diu got no money at all. This is the sad story of our concern for the security of maritime boundary, though lip service continues to be paid to maritime security. Pompous declarations in this regard are not matched by actual acts. The Mumbai attack of November 26, 2008 has emphasized the urgency of taking suitable steps in these directions.

Some other steps are being taken in this direction. India is seeking port facility at the Sittwe estuary in Myanmar for better surveillance. The presence of existing Coast Guards is being increased and the radar surveillance too is being strengthened. India has also signed a treaty with 13 country of Asia to fight piracy on the high seas. All this will indeed we very useful but India must move quickly in this direction and act fast to fight the maritime terrorist threat. The Mumbai fiasco should not be repeated. Any recurrence of 26/11 would be hazardous.

India's main strategic challenge comes from its prosperous northern neighbour; China. Without entering into a detailed discussion about respective capabilities and intentions, it can be said that China and India, are going to make uneasy neighbours. For the two nuclear-armed nations to rise, almost simultaneously, without conflict will require either adroit diplomacy or a miracle; possibly both. The all-weather Sino-Pakistan alliance, with its strong anti-Indian slant, further complicates our security problems.

Within the Sino-Indian strategic equation, the maritime dimension is a relatively new factor. The rapid growth of both economies has led to increasing reliance on energy and raw materials, which are transported by sea. This has focused sharp attention on the criticality, for both economies, of uninterrupted use of the sea-lanes for trade and energy transportation. Thus, while the PLA Navy makes forays into the Indian Ocean, the IN has newfound commitments in the South China Sea.

The navy's biggest challenge is going to be the timely replacement of ageing platforms and obsolescent equipment. The envisaged order of battle of about 150-170 ships and submarines, and possibly 250-300 aircraft assumes certain delivery rates from shipyards and aircraft factories; which they seem incapable of meeting. At the same time, our other major source, of hardware, the Russians, have brazenly reneged on costs as well as delivery schedules, in violation of solemn agreements. One of the more serious challenges before the navy's leadership will be to persuade the Russians as well as Indian DPSUs to deliver on time and within cost.

The failure to acquire even a reasonable level of self-reliance in major weapon systems in the past 66 years has made India the biggest importer of arms world-wide; and this must count as a failure of the DRDO and DPSUs. Crafting a viable and time-bound strategy which will persuade the DRDO to develop, reverse-engineer or import the technology for weapons and sensors for our indigenously built warships will constitute another major challenge for the IN.

China's pursuit of a, so called, 'string of pearls' strategy tends to draw considerable attention in strategic circles due to its high-profile economic connotations. While India may not be able to match China's financial munificence, the navy's 'foreign cooperation' initiatives have ensured creation of a favourable maritime environment in the region. Apart from activities such as exercises, joint-patrolling, port calls and flag-showing deployments, the navy's out-reach also includes provision of maritime security on request by neighbours.

Intense maritime activity in the Indian Ocean and the huge area that has to be kept under surveillance requires substantial reconnaissance and anti-submarine capabilities. The expected advent of the PLA Navy, especially its nuclear submarines, into the Indian Ocean will lend urgency to the maritime domain awareness (MDA) task. The Indian Navy has evolved a multi layered surveillance capability with deployment of task-optimized aircraft, as well as unmanned aerial vehicles for each layer. The 'icing on the cake' is the recently launched GSAT-7 communication satellite, meant exclusively for IN use, which will facilitate the networking of sensor and weapon data across its vast footprint.

The arrival of INS Vikramaditya, with its complement of MiG-29K fighters and Kamov-28/31 helicopters, will boost the navy's capability to exercise sea-control and to project power over the shore. Current plans envisage a second (and perhaps third) indigenously-built carrier joining the fleet in the 10-15 years. Given the wealth of carrier operating experience available in the IN, these ships are capable of tilting the balance of power in our region.

Operationalisation of the Ship, Submersible, Ballistic, Nuclear (SSBN) 'Arihant' will ensure that India has an invulnerable 2nd strike capability; thus enhancing the effectiveness and credibility of its nuclear deterrent vis-à-vis adversaries; China and Pakistan. As the Service responsible for safe and efficient conduct of SSBN operations, the IN will also be the custodian of their nuclear-tipped ballistic missiles, thus enhancing its status and importance in the national security totem-pole.

The induction of the nuclear-powered attack-submarine (SSBN) INS Chakra has placed a powerful weapon of offence and sea-denial in the hands of the Indian Navy. Unlike warships which remain vulnerable to detection and attack from all three dimensions, a SSN on patrol vanishes from sight; to reappear as the deadly nemesis of ships and submarines. Apart from the anti-shipping role it can also undertake, with virtual impunity, tasks as varied as surveillance, special-operations, intelligence-gathering and land-attack.

The recent visit of Indian Prime Minister Narendra Modi to Japan has also upgraded the relationship between New Delhi and Tokyo to a more "special strategic and global partnership". This visit has indeed been very "special" for India. Japan has committed to increase its investment in Indian economy and defence sector. Thus, to conclude, it can be said that a strong and balanced navy along with the powerful coastal forces are very crucial for India in order to deal with the rising quantum of marine and coastal terror.

Notes

1. Times of India, March 17, 2007, P.11.
2. Neelesh Mishra and Rahul Singh, Terror from the Deep Blue, in Hindustan Times, Chandigarh March 18, 2007, P.12.
3. Ibid.
4. Ibid.
5. Ibid.
6. Ibid.
7. Ibid.
8. Ibid.
9. Ibid.
10. Ibid.

References

Dr. Amrita Dey "India-China Economic Relations: Time to Look Beyond Problems, "World *Focus,* Delhi, Volume XXXI, No. 5, May 2010, p.197.

12. Emerging Maritime Threats and Challenges In India's Marine Domain: Post 26/11

Mukund Narvekar

Introduction to India's Maritime Domain and challenges

India's marine domain is vast and it stretches from Persian Gulf in the west, to as far as Malacca strait in the east, and to the down south in the Indian Ocean. The marine domain of India is defined by its interest, which stretches out in the respective maritime region with its various maritime installations, economic area of interest, and to the security and protection of the major assets around the maritime borders.

India's influence in the Indian Ocean can be seen with its rich glorious maritime history. Its active exploration and command over the ocean, which later forced and attracted numerous empires and traders to its zenith in Indian Ocean. Its glorious mercantile history and its effective commanding and controlling role in promoting mercantile trade since the time in memorial gave the very name to this mighty ocean 'The Indian ocean'. Naturally the lasting impact of India in Indian Ocean comes with its long coast line of 7516 kms and the two island chains of Andaman and Nicobar in Bay of Bengal and Lakshadweep Island in Arabian Sea. This island on both the side has given India an extra space into the marine world to dominate both sides of the region, reasonably effectively. These islands are also can be considered as the windows of opportunities in terms of economic engagement and strategically 'floating permanent forties' like aircraft carrier.

India's topography and its geo-political position in the Indian Ocean have unleashed its strength and weakness. Out of 28 Union States of India, 9 Union States (Gujarat, Maharashtra, Goa, Karnataka, Kerala, Tamil Nadu, Andhra Pradesh, Odisha and West Bengal.), 2 Union Territories

(Puducherry, Daman and Diu) and in addition are the two island groups: Lakshadweep and Minicoy in Arabia Sea, and the Andaman and Nicobar in the Bay of Bengal, share maritime boundary, which add to 2.172 million km2 of Exclusive Economic Zone.

India's coasts are characterised by a diverse range of topography such as creeks, small bays, back waters, rivulets, lagoons, estuaries, swamps, mudflats, as well as hills, rocky outcrops, sandbars, beaches and small islands (inhabited as well as uninhabited). Some of these water bodies and channels run deep into the main land, which most of are still remained unguarded against any threats. For instances the maritime border with Pakistan at Sir Creek line and in west Bengal delta area remain most volatile for criminals and anti-national activities. Numerous cases of the smuggling of goods, gold, narcotics, explosives, arms and ammunition as well as the infiltration of terrorists into the country through these coasts have been reported over the years.

Significantly these 9 union states, 2 union territories and two island chain of India harbour 13 major ports and 187 minor ports, which are vital for India's economic growth. Some of these major and minor ports of India are in the close proximity to the rogue states, which possess a big challenge. This rogue states are the breeding ground for such growing threats like maritime terrorism, piracy and the non-state actors.

In Indian maritime Domain, India still faces the maritime boundary issues with Pakistan, Bangladesh and of fishermen issues with Sri Lanka. As far as maritime border issue with Pakistan over its riverine border along the Sir Creek, This disputes dates back to the colonial time. "In 1908, the rulers of Kutch and Sindh fought over a pile of wood lying on the banks of Sir Creek, which divided the two provinces. The dispute was resolved in the years 1914 and 1924 but was resurrected in 1965 when Pakistan claimed half of the Rann of Kutch. The dispute was referred to an international tribunal for arbitration. The tribunal pronounced its judgment in 1968, upholding 90 per cent of India's claim in the Rann of Kutch. The tribunal did not take into consideration the issue of the delimitation of the boundary along Sir Creek as it deemed the issue as already resolved." The dispute over this is still on with respective claims and over claims from both the sides.

With Bangladesh "India insists on the 'equidistant/'median-line' principle i.e. 'low water' sea baseline; Bangladesh prefers an 'equitable' principle i.e. 'straight baseline' based on 10-fathom depth criteria to offset the concavity of its coastline. The appearance of a small island near the confluence of Ichhamati and Rai Mangal rivers in the aftermath of cyclone Bhola in 1970 further complicated the dispute as the island was claimed by both India and Bangladesh. The 3-kilometres long and 3.5 kilometres wide island was called the New Moore in India and Talpatti in Bangladesh. Negotiations to resolve the dispute between India and Bangladesh first started in 1982, but were not successful. The talks were revived again in 2008, but no solution came forth." Meanwhile, "in 2009, the New Moore Island disappeared." This incident, however, did not contribute to the resolution of the dispute. "On October 6, 2009, Bangladesh instituted arbitral proceedings for the delimitation of the maritime boundary with India under Annex VII of UNCLOS," the verdict of which has given in Bangladesh favour, which india has welcomed positively in 2014.

As far as maritime issue with Sri Lanka is concerned, "the maritime boundary has been settled with the signing of three agreements in June 1974, March 1976 and November 1976." But issue over alleged Indian fishermen killing by Sri Lankan forces has surfaced a hot debate between India and Sri Lanka. These unresolved maritime borders issue with these nations still haunt India's safety and security in the region. Most of the time the prey during such conflicts between the governments executive machinery are the local fishermen, who has to get into the trouble water for their daily catch.

Indeed, water at south is full of trouble with issues like maritime border disputes, fishermen are getting catch for sailing or fishing in wrong side. At times the situation just goes out of control as it involved killing of fishermen at sea. To add this, around the corner of Indian Ocean the intrusion by pirates and act of piracy has again lead to the apprehension for the safety of cargoes and sea lines of communications. And last the instability in the region, example in Yemen and Pakistan is another added recipe for instability in Indian Ocean.

The ongoing maritime tussle and build-up by China and USA in Indian Ocean is another advanced prospects as well as challenges to India and obstacle to its aspiration to become maritime masters of Indian Ocean. The threats and challenges to these aspirations are numerous and vary from the perspective from the non-traditional, political – military and socio-economic domain. This chapter will try and understand the Emerging maritime threats and challenges in India's marine domain: Post 26/11.

The emerging maritime threats and challenges in India's maritime domain: Post 26/11 can be broadly categories into two sections, namely conventional and non conventional.

Conventional Maritime Security threats to India

The emerging conventional maritime threats are in the form of unauthorized maritime entry or Arrivals in Indian water; Illegal activity in the protected areas; Illegal exploitation of natural resources; Prohibited import and Export; Maritime disputes and Maritime war.

Having understood the importance and complexity of India's maritime domain, it is equally vital space for economic boost. The stability, peace and prosperity lies on the safety of this domain from possible conventional threats. Therefore it is vital to understand and analyse the growing of conventional maritime security threats to India in India's maritime domain.

1) Unauthorized Maritime Entry or Arrivals

Ocean and seas are very complex entity in itself. Geographically it is very difficult to mark state control border in the ocean and seas. But conventionally it has been accepted under the UNCLOS that state posse's legal authority and suzerainty till 200 nautical miles in the sea and ocean from its land territory. Beyond 200 NM starts the international water, where anybody can sail or fish. India's geo-political position in south Asia and its proximity with neighbouring states is alarming, which has developed challenges and threats to Indian maritime security. These threats are primarily because of porous borders which facilitates illegal migration in India. Such migrations, traditionally has witness across the land borders from north-eastern states and from Sri Lanka through Palk Strait.

Migration of such nature highlights the loopholes in the security. Recent 26/11 terror attack in Mumbai is classic example of unauthorised maritime entry and loopholes in India's maritime security. Even though the Mumbai carnage is recent event, there have been a lot of illegal migrations in India. The major area of concerned has been between India and Sri Lanka and to the north- eastern states of India and Bangladesh. Since the end of civil war in Sri Lanka the flow of illegal migrants are under control but it cannot be neglected nor accepted the total suppression of LTTE movement, because India has a major nuclear installation in the south. Similarly in the Bay of Bengal, India and Bangladesh need to work out on setting up of institution to monitor influx of unauthorised human migration in India.

Apart from unauthorised human influx, Indian coast has become a landing zone of choice for runaway vessels. MV Wisdom and MV Pavit is a classic example of unauthorised maritime entry in Indian water. MV Wisdom a 26-year-old container ship, which in the course of its lifecycle has been blessed with 14 name changes, was on its actual course on a voyage from Colombo to Alang for scrapping. It broke its tow and she inland off the oil rigs, around the security establishments in and around Bombay High.

The drifting of MV Pavit off Mumbai coast still remains a mystery. According to reports, the ship sunk after it was abandoned off the Oman coast on June 29 before drifting and getting grounded off Juhu Versova beach on July 31. The crew members of the abandoned ship were rescued by US Naval ship and brought to Kandla by Indian merchant vessel MV Jag Pushpa.

Veeresh Malik, shipping and marine security expert, said, "The winds and current during this time of the year would not push the ship southwards down from Omani coast towards India. It should have drifted towards the Gulf of Kutch. The fact that it moved towards Mumbai leads to the suspicion that it did get some assistance to reach Mumbai."

On the evening of July 30, alarmed fishermen from Versova village apparently spotted a huge tanker drifting towards Mumbai. Some of them reportedly called the Santa Cruz Police Station and alerted the cops. If that to be true, then it means no action was taken for 14 long hours. For 840 minutes, nothing was done to apprehend an unwanted visitor *(MV Pavit)* - an abject failure of those in charge of keeping Mumbai secure. Now the question arise is, what if this ships were carrying nuclear waste or highjack by terrorist with weapons of mass destructions?

The bigger issue is, the MV Wisdom and MV Pavit brings out with shocking precision that despite all the fuss after the 26/11 attack by boat from Karachi, Indian coastline is as open as it was. Never mind small fishing boats, but huge ships like the MV Wisdom and MV Pavit can sail through, without being stopped or challenged.

2) Illegal activity in the protected areas

Given the extent of India's exclusive economic zone of 2013410 sq km, India has to covers a very large area to protect its highly securitised agents and also for search and rescue operations. There are various agents and maritime installations across Indian maritime borders. These installations are very vital for India's national security and therefore the security and protections of these installations are paramount. The installations within EEZ and off the coast are strategic in nature such as major and minor ports of India, nuclear installations and plants, various major maritime training and research institutes, shipbuilding and shipyards of the nation, energy security and the safety of natural resources like fishing. Indeed these installations demands round the clock monitoring and security as they are the wealth of India.

Considering the very large area of India's Exclusive economic zone, there are various instances of illegal activities, which go unnoticed in the areas mentioned above. The vitality of this marine installations and its proximity to the urban setup has witness many intrusion activities, especially at ports areas. Such intrusion are very dangerous for the safety of ports, as it might give a way for non state actor or sleeping cells to get hold of vital intelligence.

Apart from intrusion on the shore, there have been several instances of intrusion off the shore in Indian water by Pakistani, Sri Lankan and Bangladeshi fishermen. The illegal fishing activity in the Indian water by these fishermen has been serious issue. The bilateral talks and agreement seems to be remained on the paper and on the ground, these fishermen continue to intrude in the Indian water. This has been more kind of give and take relations as an Indian fisherman does do the same. As a result fishing community suffers the most in the exchange of law and order. Either they have been arrested or in the Sri Lankan case they resort of direct action of opening of fire.

At proximity of energy requirement, India does harbour a small percentage of energy production basins in its water. "The Mumbai offshore basin has the largest oil and gas producing field which includes the fields of Mumbai High, Heera, Neelam and Bassein." "The basin produced an average 348,740 barrels of crude oil per day, and 48.19 million standard cubic metres of gas per day in the fiscal year ending March 2011."

At eastern seaboard, "huge off-shore oil and gas reserves have been discovered in the Cauvery and Krishna-Godavari (K-G) basins. For example, in 2002, the Reliance Company discovered 40 trillion cubic feet in block D6 in the K-G basin. The Oil and Natural Gas Corporation (ONGC) has 24 blocks in the K-G basin, which currently produces approximately 800 tonnes of oil per day, and 3.2 million metric standard cubic meters of gas per day."

These installations are in grave areas of Indian water. Their proximity towards urban settlements and illegal fishing in these areas may attract possible site for observation. In such complex security environment, guarding these installations from 'Trozen horse' or possible highjack trawlers or boat by terrorist cannot be neglected.

3) Illegal exploitation of natural resources

Another area of conventional threat to India's maritime security has evolved through the Illegal exploitation of natural resources in Indian exclusive economic zone, namely Fish. Apart from fish there are various other types of marine minerals, which have great potential once deep sea mining technology is procured.

The oceans indeed hold a veritable treasure trove of valuable resources. Since time Sand and gravel, oil and gas have been extracted from the sea. In addition to this, minerals transported by erosion from the continents to the coastal areas are mined from the shallow shelf and beach areas. For instance these include diamonds off the coasts of South Africa and Namibia as well as deposits of tin, titanium and gold along the shores of Africa, Asia and South America.

As far as India and its deep ocean mining are concerned, it needs more deep understanding of importance of these resources. Even though India lacks the technological availability, it does have great potential once it develops the technology by itself or get the transfer of technology from US. Meanwhile, around the world the efforts to expand ocean mining into deep-sea waters have recently begun and the demand for ocean deep sea minerals such as manganese, gas hydrates, cobalt crusts and sulphides has increased.

These minerals have already made its way into the market, thus growing more demand to explore. This has led to major scope for deep sea mining, which has already started at different places. "the major focus is on manganese nodules, which are usually located at depths below 4000 metres, gas hydrates (located between 350 and 5000 metres), and cobalt crusts along the flanks of undersea mountain ranges (between 1000 and 3000 metres), as well as massive sulphides and the sulphide muds that form in areas of volcanic activity near the plate boundaries, at depths of 500 to 4000 metres."

Contemporary there may not be a direct threat to these minerals in Indian EEZ, but one cannot negate about the future. But definitely the exploitation of fish resources by Indian neighbour in Indian EEZ and vice-versa has always been on the tale for discussion. In the exchange of maintaining law and order at sea, it's the fishermen from both the side who are affected the most. It may be between India /Sri Lanka, India / Pakistan or India /Bangladesh.

It has been more in news especially between India and Sri Lanka. It has taken a toll largely on Indian fishermen. According to the recent PIL (public interest litigation) filed by DMK MP, AKS Vijayan , "more than 400 Tamil Nadu fishermen have been killed after 1983, including as many as 118 between 1991 to 2008." The killing of fishermen at sea has raised serious doubt and question on the credibility of Indian navy and coast guard. Advocate General Navaneethakrishnan in the Madras High court, also submitted that "it was the duty of the coast guard to give protection to fishermen from Tamil Nadu. They should liaise with the Lankan navy to ensure protection and the question of deploying vessels near the International Maritime Boundary Line (IMBL) was the responsibility of the Central government." Further Assistant Solicitor General Ravindran said that "there had not been any attack in the Indian territory. The clashes occurred when Indian fishermen ventured into Sri Lankan waters." These indeed need a mechanism to facilitate better understanding in recognition of each other maritime binderies in complex environment.

Between India and Pakistan the issue is more over intelligence gathering. Hundreds of Indian fishermen and Pakistani fishermen have been arrested under the charges of spying. "According to Indian government authorities there are 535 Indian prisoners, including 483 fishermen, imprisoned in Pakistani jails, while 272 Pakistani prisoners remain in Indian jails." There are no official numbers available on how many of them are classified as spies.

MOU between India and Bangladesh on co-operation in the field of fisheries, aquaculture and allied activities has largely taken into consideration for the development. The issues related to fishermen or illegal exploitation of resources are met by the memorandum of understanding between the Government of the Republic of India and the Government of the People's Republic of Bangladesh on co-operation in the field of fishers. In the MOU the article I exclusively talks about that both the "Contracting Parties as they shall promote development of co-operation in fisheries and aquaculture and allied activities between the two countries through joint activities, programmes, exchange of scientific materials, information and personnel."

4) Prohibited Imports/Exports

The threats perception through import and export through containers are very high. Given the complexity of container ships getting into Indian port, the chances of snooping of WMD (Weapons of Mass Destructions) or any other volatile or explosive cargoes in Indian ports can't be denied. The vast stretch of Indian coastal line and availability of Indian ports at easy access makes it more vulnerable. The appropriate example would be 1993 Mumbai bomb blast. The RDX was unloaded at Raigad and then transferred at Mumbai to carry out the terror attack. The landing of RDX at Raigad area was very strategic move as it is the small ports and lacks the security set up. The matter of the fact is that anywhere in Indian ports; there is a lack of technological advancement to scan the incoming ship or container.

Comparatively, post 9/11 terror attack in US and its effectiveness to deal with such menace in future is notable; they have come up with several mechanisms to tackle with such incident in future. One of the important initiatives to counter any terror threats from sea or ocean is though CSI (Container Security Initiative). The Container Security Initiative (CSI) was established in response to the September 11, 2001 terrorist attacks as part of the U.S. Customs and Border Protection's

(CBP) layered cargo security strategy. "CSI addresses the threat to border security and global trade posed by the potential for terrorist use of a maritime container to deliver a weapon. CSI proposes a security regime to ensure all containers that pose a potential risk for terrorism are identified and inspected at foreign ports before they are placed on vessels destined for the United States."

Announced in January 2002, CSI was first implemented in ports shipping the highest volume of containers to the United States; later expanding to include strategic ports. In contemporary CSI operates in 58 ports worldwide: North, Central, and South America, the Caribbean, Europe, Africa, the Middle East, and throughout Asia.

Currently, over 80 percent of all maritime cargo imported into the United States is subject to pre-screening. The World Customs Organization (WCO), the European Union (EU), and the G8 support CSI expansion and have adopted resolutions implementing CSI security measures introduced at ports throughout the world.

Given the strategic position of India in Indian Ocean, it demands equally importance to build a mechanism to counter such threats from incoming containers in India. CSI has made great strides since its inception. A significant number of customs administrations have committed to joining CSI and operate at various stages of implementation. India indeed needs to think about getting in aligned to share information and intelligence to subdue any future threats to Indian maritime security.

5) Maritime disputes and wars

Since the evolutions of the nation states, its power struggle to control territory – land and sea have continued in many manifestations such as war, strategy or diplomacy. The nation's states struggle to have absolute control have has lead to waged the wars for years and the struggle still continues. Meanwhile the modern political orders have somehow limited the conflicts, merely at the level of diplomacy. Having said that, history is the mirror to understand the battles and wars fought by kingdoms and nations states, merely to preserve its own independence and sovereignty over the space (land & water) of dominions.

Post WW-II, and declaration of UNCLOS has brought the limitations on the conflict over the dominion of sea. Equally giving the opportunity for all the littoral states to use and dominate its sovereignty over 200 NM and free access to all in the International water. The motto of UNCLOS, freedom of navigation had bridge the gap of conflicts. But one cannot negate any future naval battles.

Naval battles are the classical approach to all maritime power to dominate the sea and use it as a tool to achieve national interest. National interest has pursued the very notion of defending the land and protecting its sovereignty from any kind of external aggression by land, sea or by air. For littoral nations states during war time, whose national interest are at sea, must possess strong and effective naval force to maintain deterrence to subdue any incoming hostility and during peace time must command heavy cargo ships to pursue extensive maritime trade. This is the very paramount rationale for the existence of navy all around the world.

In Indian Ocean, India lives in a transit phase of security environment, with additional understanding of its geo-political position and existing maritime threats. Since its commencement of independence, India has got obsessed with its land frontier. As conventionally the threats and invading forces has appeared from the Khyber Pass. This frame of mind became reality with 1947-48 conflict, 1962, 1965, 1971 and 1999 Kargil conflict. 1971 was the exception where Indian Navy played a decisive role in blocking the Pakistan navy and maintain the command over the sea during the conflict.

Since then it has been a transformation phase for the Indian navy. 1999 Kargil conflict saw the huge build-up of Indian navy and evolved as one of the strongest navy in the world. In contemporary the conventional maritime threats are alarming as India has maritime border disputes with Pakistan, Sri Lanka and Bangladesh. The levels of conflict over these disputes are not totally subdued. The threat continues to exist as India share very volatile relations with Pakistan and mild over Bangladesh and Sri Lanka.

With adding to this, the growing muscles of China in Indian Ocean are disturbing. Its naval build up around India and its 'Containment theory' has force India to modernise its naval forces. In coming future the conflict between India and China will reshape the entire maritime environment in Indian Ocean. Chinas aggressive and assertive role in South China Sea is the beginning of flexing its muscles, which has entered in the Indian Ocean. Therefore India must build and equipped its maritime forces in Indian Ocean to maintain its deterrence as India faces conventional maritime war at its both fronts.

It is quite obvious that these strategic installations are vital for the security, development and prosperity of the country, but they are also high value targets for the terrorists because an attack on any of these sites would not only cause enormous loss of life and property and adversely impact the Indian economy but would also give a lot of publicity to terrorists groups. Therefore it is very important to highlight the measures taken by the coastal security authority of India to protect and secure these installations.

Coastal Security Measure pre 26/11

India has understood these conventional maritime threats and has been managing it effectively over the period of time. India's long coastline, its important installations and security of assets has led to undergo dramatic change in its security parameters. The effective role played by Navy has always been acknowledged. In fact, early years of navy being the only security institution, caught up at two different front; coastal water and in deep water. Hence there was its presence and gradually increased its role more in deep sea in the wake of 1965 and later 1971 war. Hence, Navies presence in deep sea became more mandatory, which has eventually lead to the neglect of the coastal security.

The enormous gap between the territorial water and exclusive economic Zone had lead to the promotion of illegal activity in territorial water, which hosts the major maritime installations. Their security demands, proper observation and surveillance around the clock became additional priority. The breakthrough in guarding major installations in territorial water and in contiguous zone came in 1978 with formation of the Indian coast guards as the fourth armed Union of Indian on "19th August 1978, under the Coast Guard Act."

Indian coast guard shared the responsibility with specific objectives like: "Enforcing the provision of enactment in force in the maritime zones; Assisting the customs and other authorities in anti-smuggling operations;

To preserve and protect the marine environment and control marine pollution; Measures for safety of life and property at sea including aid to mariners in distress; Ensuring the safety and protection of artificial islands, offshore terminals and other installations in MR zones."

The Indian coast guard came at very handy in protecting enormous 7,516 km coastline, 1197 islands and an exclusive economic zone spanning 2.02 million sq km, which is expected to go up to almost 3 million sq km after the delimitation of the continental shelf.

Indian coast guard effectively got engaged in various security operations in territorial waters. Over the period of time efforts has been made to bridge these gaps with effective coordination between Indian navy and coast guard. Operation Tasha and Operation Swan were one of the successful operations between Indian navy and coast guard in area of surveillance and protection of Indian coastal security.

Operation Tasha was instituted soon after the Operation Pawan. It was more of a coastal security operation on the Tamil Nadu coast to foil operations and activities of the LTTE. The concise objective was "Prevent illegal immigration and infiltration of LTTE militants to and from Sri Lanka; prevent smuggling of arms, ammunition and contraband from the Indian mainland to Sri Lanka and vice versa; enforce air surveillance and seaborne patrol to curb activities of Sri Lankan Tamil militants in the Palk Bay."

Operation Swan was instituted after the December 1993 Mumbai blast. This operation was a joint exercise between Indian navy and Indian coast guard off the coast of Mumbai and Gujarat, wherein the MARCOS – Marine commandos were used for patrolling the entire stretch.

The next set of challenges and reference to Indian coastal security were highlighted in the 2000 by the Task Force on Border Management as a part of the Kargil Review Committee. The recommendations on the coastal security included: "(a) Setting up of a specialised marine police force in the form of coastal police stations; (b) Augmentation of the strength of the ICG; (c) Formation of fishermen watch groups and (d) Establishment of an apex body for the management of maritime affairs."

Since then there has been delay in understanding the changing contour of India's maritime security. The delay in the implementation of the recommendations by the Task Force on Border Management on coastal security has resulted in the systemic failures, which eventually lead to 26/11 terror attack in Mumbai. The systemic failure and delays failed to curb down maritime threats.

Non - Conventional Maritime Security threats to India post 26/11

The physical proximity of India's coasts to politically volatile, economically depressed and unfriendly countries such as Sri Lanka, Bangladesh, Pakistan and Gulf countries adds to its vulnerability. India has been facing Pakistan sponsored cross-border terrorism for decades. Terrorists with arms and explosives has been infiltrating into the country from Pakistan through the land borders. However, over the years, with the increased deployment of security forces and surveillance equipment as well as the construction of fences, security along the land borders has been sufficiently tightened. On the other hand, security over the ocean domain has been extremely lax, with the sea routes remaining poorly guarded. The heavy fencing at border has forced non state actors to explore new routes for infiltration. Terrorists started looking towards the sea as an alternate route to slip into India undetected. This change in tactics leads to a formulations of new non-conventional maritime security threats.

26/11 Mumbai terror is one of the deadliest non-conventional maritime terror attacks on Indian soil after 1993 Mumbai blast. This carnage witness and proved systemic failure of Indian security preparedness and its lack of intelligence to counter such terror act. This attack highlighted the loopholes in the coastal security which was wide open for considerable moment of time. Terrorist successfully snooped into Indian water and carried out this horrendous act and held coastal city of Mumbai hostage for 68 hours. Thus begins a new era of non-conventional maritime security threats to India.

The emerging non-conventional maritime security threats to India are maritime terrorism and Piracy/ robbery or violence at sea.

1) Maritime Terrorism

Terrorism in India takes two forms: one is of domestic origin; the other is terrorism that is sponsored by external agencies. The domestic terrorist threats in India basically arise from separatist tendencies, ethnic and linguistic demands, religious radicalism, socioeconomic deprivation, and, at times, because of bad governance. Domestic and localized terrorism attains dangerous proportions only when they are backed by external powers or agencies that provide arms, explosives, and base for training facilities to the insurgents. Transnational Jihadi terrorism, sponsored by another country or a religious group to achieve geostrategic objectives, currently poses the main threat to India's national integrity and socioeconomic cohesion.

The long struggle against terrorism has taken a toll across India. Therefore terrorism in India is not anymore a new phenomenon. India has been facing it since last two decades. Although earlier, it was more concentrated across from land frontier, but recent 26/11 terror attack on Mumbai by sea lanes has opened up new ways of security threats. Mumbai terror attack has left a serious debate over the possibility of such maritime terrorism in coming time.

The long coastline and its proximity with rogue states have left loopholes in the India's maritime security. Over the period of time Indian Ocean has remained the zone of peace. Nevertheless, Mumbai terror attack has highlighted the strategic importance of guarding the coastline and major installations from maritime terrorism.

Before 26/11 Mumbai terror attack, the sea was seen as merely a means of communication, trade and space for international cooperation. Although it has a great potential in terms of military role, it was only explored during wartime situation. However, the 26/11 had raised eyeballs on making sea as source of new maritime terrorism and definitely has raised many questions about the credibility, readiness and effectiveness of maritime forces to deal with such menace.

The Council for Security Cooperation in the Asia Pacific (CSCAP) working group has offered an extensive definition for maritime terrorism: "…the undertaking of terrorist acts and activities within the maritime environment, using or against vessels or fixed platforms at sea or in port or against anyone of their passengers or personal, against coastal facilities or settlement, including tourist resorts, port areas and port towns or cities."

At a distance from 26/11, Mumbai terror attack, there has been a maritime terror attack around the world. For instance "terrorist hijacked an Italian cruise liner in 1985 and militants damaged USS Cole, an American warship in 2004." Terrorism has spread its web across India and it should be viewed very important because of its easy access to major ports. Apart from this, there are also possibilities that terrorist organisation may use small craft as a 'suicide-craft' for blowing up of the huge transport as well as military cargoes. For instance, Al Qaeda websites revealed that maritime attacks could also involve the use of small underwater crafts, such as mini-submarines or submerged diver delivery vessels (SDV). Some terrorist groups are known to have experimented with such methods. Intelligence report point out that radicals from Jemmah Islamiah (JI), a group linked to the Al- Qaeda network, have been trained in sea – born guerrilla tactics, such as suicide scuba diving and ramming, by the Sri Lankan Liberation Tiger of Tamil Elam.

Therefore, one cannot ignore or negate another maritime terror attack on Indian maritime installations or establishment in its exclusive economic zone. In fact the world has witness terrorist attack on economic hub. For instance "the explosion carried out by the Irish republican army (IRA) in London financial district in the 1980s, the explosion in the new York world trade centre in February, 1993, the simultaneous explosion outside economic targets in Mumbai (Bombay) in March, 1993, the Bali and Mombasa explosion of 2002." And 26/11 terror attack was one of the high scale assaults in India and there could be many such incidents on economic facilities and hub.

The deep understanding and analysis of 26/11 terror attack highlights the loopholes in Indian maritime security. It also highlighted new trends of terrorist targets, that terrorist would target economic installations to achieve maximum damage and to spread fear in public sphere. Such high value economic installations are maritime trade and sea lines of communications, Ports, Islands, Nuclear installation, various major maritime training and research institutes, Shipbuilding and shipyards of the nation and energy security.

a) Security of Maritime Trade and Sea Lines of Communications:

India's economic sea trade route has been laid down in the history. The sea line of communication has been an important highway in human history since time in memorial. Centuries ago, it has been the route and medium for spread of culture, goods and news. Sea helped to spread belief, and intercourse of thoughts and idea. As time changed and civilisation started flourishing, the importance of sea has increased in paramount. Today "some 70% of the world's population lives within 100 miles of a coastline."

All the treasures of the ancient world to the modern world were borne across the Arabian Sea, the Indian Ocean and the Bay of Bengal. Today's treasures include oil, rubber, uranium raw material and various different types of industrial cargo; have been dragged from the seas to its final destinations.

The security threats to these cargo ships cannot be neglected. In fact these cargo ships are sitting ducks in the water when they pass through the most volatile areas. The major concern for India's maritime trade is from uncertainties prevailing in its environment. As India's major import comes from the Persian Gulf – crude oil. This continuous flow of the tankers helps India to lubricate its industrial machinery and domestic consumption. Therefore any hijack or obstacles to this trade by terrorist would hamper the maritime trade and sea lines of communications of India.

In the 21st century, sea lines of communication encompass the umbilical string of the state economy and arteries of a regions economic healthiness. It may be any part of the world, sea line of communication has always been at strategic importance in the globalised world. In the present day, "ships are the primary mode of transportation of the world trade, carrying approximately 80% of the global trade by value." Moreover, "According to world bank estimate, in 1999, the world sea-borne trade was pegged at 21,480 billion ton – miles in 2010 and 41,800 billion ton – miles in 2014."

Therefore, the growth and development of 21st century is depending on the sea and its economic usage. The threat from maritime terrorism does exist because most of the Indian trade are channelized through narrow straights and passages, which does fall under the wings of non-state actors and rogue state. Although the efficient means of transportation has full-grown and resulted in greater concern for the safety of the sea lines of communications (SLOCs) but India cannot expect to negate the threats to its maritime trade and sea lines of communications. Therefore any act that is unfavourable to the safety will challenge the very existence of SLOC security; primarily oil, which is vital aspect of the daily lives of most people of the world.

In this extremely globalised world, therefore the importance of sea line of communication is paramount for the economic development and stability of the region. India's entire economy development is depended on the smooth flow of the energy resources which get dragged from the Persian Gulf. It is indeed a 'blue economy' with extensive of maritime trade across its shores and ports. The waterways have been used as a medium of trade and provided the momentum for the growth of maritime enterprise.

b) Threats to Port Security:

Ports are very important assets of the nation; its infrastructure helps to caters incoming and outgoing cargos, which contribute in a large to economy of the state. In times of globalisation ports are the facilitator for coordination gesture, hence its safety and security is paramount. As port is a facility for receiving and transferring cargo, they are usually situated at the edge of an ocean or river.

The attack of September 11, 2001 tuned awareness about the vulnerability to terrorist attack from all modes of transportations and 26/11 was such new method. Since then, Port security has emerged as a significant part of the overall debate on coastal security. Ports areas and ships in the port have much vulnerability to possible terrorist attack, because a port area has very large perimeters to secure, which might give terrorist many potential landside point of entry and exit.

Some ports are located right away adjacent to build-up of urban area, giving terrorist places to hide while approaching or escaping from the port area. Another area of concerned is when large number of truck move in and out of the ports, making it possible for terrorist to use a truck to bring themselves and their weapons into a port. Many ports harbour fishing and entertaining boats, which could be handy for terrorist to make best use to mask their approach, to a target ship.

In this complex set of global environment, India stands with the prospects and challenges. Prospects to facilitate global pattern of free movement of trade and commerce and challenges are with the existing in nature of diverse set of uncertainties around its maritime borders. Having said this India has many vital major, medium, minor and private ports around its maritime boundary. Most of this ports are very vulnerable to such terrorist attack as they are in close proximity with the human settlement, which increase the chance of terrorist snooping in and out with effective cover of adjacent build –up of urban areas.

Table 1: Major and Minor Ports of India

Region/State/UT	Major Ports	Minor Ports
West Coast		
Gujarat	a) Kandla	40
Diu & Daman	-	2
Maharashtra	a) Mumbai b) Jawaharlal Nehru	53
Goa	a) Marmugao	5
Karnataka	a) New Mangalore	10
Kerala	a) Cochin	13
East Coast		
Tamil Nadu	a) Tuticorin b) Chennai c) Ennore	15
Pondicherry	-	1
Andhra Pradesh	a) Visakhapatnam	12
Orissa	a) Paradip	2
West Bengal	a) Kolkata, Haldia	1
Lakshadweep Islands	-	10
Anadman & Nicobar Islands	-	23
Total	12	187

Source: http://www.marinebuzz.com/2009/01/26/major-and-minor-ports-in-india/

These major and minor ports are the life line and bloodline of India's economic growth. Apart from its importance from economic point of view for the country some of them are equally fragile because of its close proximity to the urban settlements as well as in proximity of rogue states. This proximity makes them more vulnerable for snooping inside the ports and to carry out terror attack. It needs to be protected from all illegal activities, as these ports are directly connected with the generating of economic hubs in India. The smooth flow of commodities and trade across India depends on the safe docking and unloading of good at these ports. The strategic geo-political importance of India in Indian Ocean boosts its port facilities as intermediary between the western market and the eastern.

The economic growth of India undoubtedly lies in the facilities and infrastructure which it offers to the world traders. Ports are therefore the nerves of Indian economy. The nature of Indian export and import has extended at very wide distances as India has its trade with over 200 countries around the world, of which the major share of trades are sailed from sea's and ocean from across the world to Indian ports and vice versa.

The positive fallout of globalisation on Indian mercantile trade has equally boosted tremendously. The growing intake of industrial input and its generating market space has grown since economic liberalisation. The consumption alongside has created a huge market for international investor. Reshaping this market availability and continuous supplies of raw material has added to its charm and has boost in India's container volumes. The robust growth in India's container volumes has come to an edge is because of global shift of mercantile trade in India. As rightly observed by Anil Singh, (senior Vice President and Managing Director, DP World subcontinent region) "Most global shipping lines believe that India is one of the most promising container markets that is emerging today, and many of them are developing products that focus on the Indian market."

At parallel lines of global shipping, growth of India's infrastructural development has taking its pace with creation of SEZ to facilitate the truly global shift of mercantile trade in India. Its "Access to the sea through the major and non-major ports has facilitated the setting up of Special Economic Zones (SEZs) which have resulted in the growth of a number of industrial cities such as: Kandla SEZ in Gujarat; Santacruz Electronics Export Processing Zone SEZ in Maharashtra; Madras Export Processing Zone SEZ in Tamil Nadu; Cochin SEZ in Kerala; Falta SEZ in West Bengal; and Vishakhapatnam SEZ in Andhra Pradesh."

Post economic liberalisation has certainly observes the tremendous economic growth in India, "about 95 per cent of her foreign trade by volume and 70 per cent by value is transported through sea. Major Ports account for 75 per cent of the total cargo by volume handled at Indian ports. Significantly, Indian exporters have set a target of attaining the export target of more than 500 billion dollars by 2014-15. Questions remain on whether it is achievable, in view of the existing port infrastructure and hinterland connectivity." Apart from the existing constrain space at ports, Department of Commerce, Government of India, were of opinion that there has been gradual increase in India's total export as well as increase in import with rest part of the world. The following table would highlight the total value in US $ million of Indian trade.

Table 2: India's total export and import with rest of the world

	India's total export with rest of the world	India's total import with rest of the world
Years	Total export (Values in US$ Million)	Total import (Values in US$ Million)
2008-2009	1,85,295.36	3,03,696.31
2009-2010	1,78,751.43	2,88,372.88
2010-2011	2,51,136.19	3,69,769.13
2011-2012	3,05,963.92	4,89,319.49
2012-2013	3,00,274.12	4,91,945.05

Source: Department of Commerce, Government of India.

These million dollars of trade make its way to the market and consumer by the safety and infrastructure offered by the Indian ports across the peninsular. The constant supply of resources to the consumer and industries, determined by the effective role played by the port authority of India and the unseen hero's of security agencies which are protecting these numerous ports day and night.

In globalised world, India cannot negate the threats which it perceives from the rough states and from the non-state actors. The 26/11 Mumbai terror attack is the fine example of non-state actor's tactics, strategy and their identification of soft target. Therefore, Ports are much in the lime light of any future terror attack. Thus it needs to be protected at all the cost with effective security, intelligence network and with proper framework of institution in place.

c) Security of the Islands:

India is fortunate to have an island territory in the Arabian Sea and Bay of Bengal region. Islands are very vital for enhancing national interest in exploiting natural resources and in adding more exclusive economic zone. However, strategic positions of island are more vital in terms of military point of view. Island plays a very vital role in putting forward strategic base or block during national emergency like wars and natural calamities.

The Indian islands are of both strategic and economic importance to the country; their location is near to the vital major sea –lanes, and they provide an advance site from which the country can project its military power (if it's required) well beyond the shores of the Indian subcontinent. In addition, the coral reefs adjacent to the Indian island chain contain fertile fishing grounds, which satisfy domestic food needs, while serving as a valuable source for foreign income. Both the oilfields and the fishing ground lies well inside India's EEZ, as do the other rich mineral deposits.

"Lakshadweep chain in the Arabian sea has 474 islands of which 358 are island and 116 are rocks, where it covers an area of 232 sq.km. The Lakshadweep coral chain is located at a distance of 230 -245 km from the Kerala coast of its 36 islands as many as 26 are uninhabited." The strategic importance of this island is that, these islands are in the close proximity to the Persian Gulf and piracy effected area. Thus these islands are very vital in military point of view. In the conflict time these islands will function as permanent aircraft carrier and even can be used as second strike capability launch pad.

Looking at the eastern sector is the Andaman and Nicobar islands. These islands are the windows of the Indian foreign policy in the eastern world. The Andaman and Nicobar, is a chain of 572 islands and islets in the Bay of Bengal. Of which only 38 islands are inhabited, and are close to Indonesia's Aceh region, which is emerging as an Islamic separatist movement hub.

An Indian intelligence official believes the separatist could move into the uninhabited islands in Andaman and Nicobar chain to establish their bases. Although the joint Andaman and Nicobar command was established by the end of the September 2001, the new command, which comprise the Army, Air force and the Navy, has given deep penetrating strategic depth to India in the Indian Ocean.

d) Threats to Nuclear Installation:

The immediate threat from maritime terrorism for Indian nuclear installation cannot be negated. The major nuclear installations at various Indian peninsulas are in fact sitting ducks. The 26/11 terror attack on Mumbai had widened the aspect of securitising the importance of these installations, especially when the region is highly armed with nuclear weapons.

Given the fact in globalised world were the easy accesses to the information and technology have sophisticated the operations of terrorist outfits. At the same moment it increases the very fact of vitality of these installations, and the proximity of these nuclear installations to the urban areas makes them more vulnerable. Any such events like 26/11 on these installations will hamper the national security and assets. Therefore one cannot negate the vulnerability of any terror attack on these installations in coming time.

Since the success of 9/11 terror attack on WTC and later 26/11 Mumbai terror attack, has opened up a new areas of possible methods to terrorist at given specific targets. 9/11 terror attack was big breakthrough for terrorist using airliner as a cruise missile. The security loopholes in the US air defence left many questions unanswered. The exceptionally success of terror attack has manifested a new trend of using air and water ways as new phenomenon of terror tactics. 26/11 Mumbai terror attack was the next in line, wherein terrorist penetrated through sea.

The potential of future terrorist attack on major installations and targets cannot be negated. The loophole in India's maritime security setup across the board has highlighted in the failure to control or to react at given time. Officially it might be a systemic failure but in real time span its failure of entire machinery. It failed to detect and understand the changing nature of terrorist targets in India.

After 9/11 terror attack, US had identified all the probabilities of any kind of terror attacks from air, land and sea on all major installations including US nuclear power plants around the country and they have briefed the security set up to deal with such terror acts. In his January 2002 State of the Union speech, President Bush said that "U.S. forces 'found diagrams of American nuclear power plants' in al-Qaeda materials in Afghanistan. An al-Qaeda training manual lists nuclear plants as among the best targets for spreading fear in the United States. The government is taking the threat seriously: in February 2002, the Nuclear Regulatory Commission (NRC) issued an advisory to the nation's 103 nuclear power plants that terrorists might try to fly hijacked planes into some of them. And eight governors have independently ordered the National Guard to protect nuclear reactors in their states."

Considering the scale of 26/11 terrorist attack and its close proximity to Bhabha Atomic Research Centre (BARC) at Trombay, The Department of Atomic Energy and the Central Industrial Security Force have reviewed security of the major nuclear power plants considering constant threats to the country's sensitive installations. Post 26/11, these installations underwent maximum security and decided to strengthen the water front security –both sea and river of all nuclear installations and fortified these areas with the help of additional security personnel and deployment of security gadgets.

Given the space and area, India's nuclear installation is very large and spread across many places. Despite a high level of security and inherent safety features, there are several security risks for Indian nuclear power plants (NPPs) and infrastructure from terrorists, such as:

- A small team of trained saboteurs gains access to an NPP, possibly with an insider's assistance, and detonates explosives at sensitive points to cause a release of radioactivity; or

- A convoy of suicide truck bombers crashes through the weakest point of entry of an NPP (usually the entry gate for transport), with the surviving truck(s) attacking vital installations of the NPP; or

- A suicide commando hijacks a fully fuelled large civilian aircraft and crashes it into the spent fuel storage pool of the NPP."

Apart from the direct attack on these installations, there might be possibilities or scenario of carrying out nuclear terror strike in India by the non-state actors. The possibility of such act is high because it's fairly easy enough for non-states actors to get hold on both Illegal Acquisition of Nuclear and Other Radioactive Material from India and Abroad, or may be through strategic political sources through inter-state conflict

Indeed, the scenario in which India coexist with two nuclear powered nations and rogue states around, the understanding of falling these weapons in wrong hands cannot be ruled out. If not directly then dismantling India's nuclear programme and spreading fear in Indian minds seems to be the only operational idea for non-state actors.

e) Threats to Various major maritime training and research institutes

In the modern era of information, the wealth of the nation lies in its Research and training institutes as it harbour the knowledge and best brains of nation. The ideas and knowledge get converted into innovation and innovations lead to development. The constant research in the maritime security is must, as to understand various elements and players involved into the wide perspective of maritime world.

Today the dependency of human on ocean and sea has grown in many ways. The conventional understanding of a man towards ocean has changed as ocean has a lot to offer to the mankind. Men since time in memorial has explored the ocean and it shall continue to do so in future. The advancement of technology and research on aquatic life with more precise information and studies has helped to discover more. The continuous research and its precise use have helped to explore the scientific studies of aquatic life and different types of minerals which has remained underneath for centuries.

Therefore, these institutions are very vital for the existence and continue flow of idea, information and data. Such institutions are the think tank to understand maritime security, its complex aquatic life and to deal with challenges with better policies in place. Some of the very important institutions are as follows: Marine engineering and research institute – Kolkata; Marine engineering and research institute

– Mumbai; Lal Bahadur Shastri College of advanced Maritime Studies and Research – Mumbai; T.S.Chanakya – Mumbai; National Maritime Academy – Chennai; Indian Institute of Port Management – Kolkata; Indian Maritime University – Visakhapatnam campus. These are the real assets of understanding India's maritime environment and the knowledge hub of India.

Apart from these major training and research institutes, India host its vital Satellite launches and missile testing facilities such as the Satish Dhawan Space Centre and the Wheeler Islands which harbour missile facility for India's space programme and military utilisations along the coast.

f) Shipbuilding and shipyards of the nation

The access of nation to the deep sea and its contribution to the world marine trade in terms of value and volume depends on the total number of merchant ships carries or uphold its flag. Equally to make them sea worthy and effective in the service of the nation depends on the facilities and hard work put by various shipbuilding companies and shipyards around the Indian peninsula. "The Indian shipbuilding industry has around 28 shipyards comprising of 8 public sectors, 6 yards under central and 2 under state governments with around 20 private shipyards."

The key government players in the Indian shipbuilding industry are Cochin Shipyard, Hindustan Shipyard, Mazgaon Docks, Goa Shipyards, Garden Reach Shipyard, and Hooghly Docks. And Key private players in the Indian shipbuilding industry are ABG Shipyard – private, Bharati Shipyard, Pipavav Shipyard, Chowgule & Company Limited, L&T Shipyard and Tebma Shipyard. "The Indian shipbuilding turnover for both the private and public shipyard sector reached 1.6 billion dollars in 2010." Further "the Indian shipbuilding industry is estimated to double from its 2010 revenue of $1.6 billion in the next five years." Having mentioned the advanced prospects of Indian shipyards and companies contribution to the nation, some of the shipyards are still volatile because of its proximity to the big cities, which attracts major population influx and sleeping cells.

Importance of shipyards and shipbuilding in nation building is enormous. These shipyards are the back office which design and build ship for national service, such as for Indian navy, coast guards and merchant vessels. "Its first indigenous aircraft carrier, eight stealth frigates, six diesel submarines and thirty other warships currently under construction in shipyards constitute definitive steps towards the Indian Navy's quest for becoming a blue water force."

Apart from building ships and platform for the needs of the national security units, Indian PSU shipyards has "emerge as an exporter of smaller to medium sized platforms in the South Asian and West Asian region, a trend signified by GSL's exploration of markets like Oman and Sri Lanka for Offshore Patrol Vessels. Capacity constraints in leading global manufacturers Japan and Korea have gradually redirected orders to emerging locations such as India. Out of a 199 ships currently on the order books on Indian shipyards, 124 are reported to be meant for export."

Shipyards indeed are the back office and the major suppliers of hardware to Indian navy. It is the enable force, which design the crafts and carriers for the security and safety of India's maritime security. Their continuous hard work, determination, advancement in technology and expertise make India a sea farer country. Therefore their safety needs to be guarded from offshore as well as from onshore terrorist threats.

g) Energy security

India is deficit country when it comes to hydrocarbon energy. The major chunk of economy is invested in meeting the energy needs from international market. This energy, crude oil is dragged in cargoes from corners of the world. The major amount of crude comes from Persian Gulf countries, which has been facing a menace of piracy and growing maritime terrorism. Therefore the safety of the sea line of communication has become paramount importance for India beyond its EEZ.

The presence of task force for combing piracy and maritime threats in international water has help to assist and escort international cargoes away from the piracy, which has for some extend has minimised the threats from non-state actors . This effort has worked brilliantly to maintain the smooth flow of international maritime trade and India is equally a major player, who has been there to provide and assist its services since 2009.

India being the most important and fastest growing economy, it is also a net importer of oil and gas. It harbours more demand for energy from its domestic market. Therefore, fulfilling this demand is paramount. It needs utmost dedication, commitment, care and foresight to protect its sea lines of communication in Indian water as well as beyond EEZ. The threats are numerous from rogue states as well as from the non-state actors. The menace of piracy and nexus of it's with terrorist organisation makes this region more volatile. The deficit nature of domestic production of its own energy resources from Bombay high made India a net importer of energy.

Even though the production at Bombay high is very small, it is equally vital for national needs and security. Therefore, the growth of Indian economy is correlated to the energy security of India. India's active foreign policy in the Persian Gulf region, its perception in the changing political and strategic environment demand more hawkish vision.

The Basic Statistics on Indian Petroleum and Natural Gas has released by the Ministry of Petroleum and Natural Gas, Government of India, New Delhi (Economic Division) of 2011 – 2012 highlights the India's energy market, which is soaring at very gradual pace.

- India has total reserves (proved and indicated) of 760 million metric tonnes of crude oil and 1330 billion cubic metres of natural gas as on 1.4.2012.
- The total number of exploratory and development wells and metreage drilled in onshore and offshore areas during 2011-12 was 756 and 1631 thousand metres respectively.
- Crude oil production during 2011-12 at 38.09 million metric tonnes is 1.08% higher than 37.68 million metric tonnes produced during 2010-11.
- Gross Production of Natural Gas in the country at 47.56 billion cubic metres during 2011-12 is -8.92% lower than the production of 52.22 billion cubic metres during 2010.11
- The flaring of Natural Gas in 2011-12 at 2.26% of gross production is higher than at 1.86% in 2010-11.

- The refining capacity in the country increased about 14% to 213.066 million metric tonnes per annum (MMTPA) as on 1.4.2012 from 187.386 MMTPA as on 1.4.2011.
- The total refinery crude throughput during 2011-12 at 211.42 million metric tonnes is higher about 2.63% than 206 million metric tonnes crude processed in 2010-11 (including RIL, SEZ Refinery.)
- The production of petroleum products during 2011-12 was 196.707 million metric tonnes (excluding 2.213 million metric tonnes of LPG production from natural gas) against the last year's production at 190.316 million metric tons (excluding 2.168 million metric tons of LPG production from natural gas).

Source: Basic Statistics on Indian Petroleum and Natural Gas 2011-12, Ministry of Petroleum and Natural Gas, Government of India, New Delhi (Economic Division)

On the other hand the import of crude oil and gas continued to increase at gradual pace. "In 2012, India's consumption of oil has increased from 3488 thousand barrels daily (2011) to 3652 thousand barrels daily, which is 5% gradual increase in consumption, which 4.2% of the share of total consumption in the world. Whereas India's consumption of Gas has decreased from 55.0 Million tonnes oil equivalent in 2011 to 49.1 Million tonnes oil equivalent, which is -11.0% decreases in consumption. Over all India shares 1.6% of the global share to total consumption in the world."

The safety of this crude import falls on the wellbeing of sea lines of communication from all the possible threats in the region. The continuous flow of crude oil, industrial goods and various other types of goods makes these sea lines of communication the major bloodlines of Indian economy. Therefore, it needs to be under the surveillance from any non-state actors or rogue state.

Thus any illegal activity in Indian EEZ is a direct violation of India's law of the land and such violation need to be deal with serious nature. The threat to these installations can't be ignored as some of these installations are in close proximity with some countries as well as in close proximity with big cities in India, which has attracted influx of populations. 26/11 terror attack in Mumbai is the classic example.

Culprits had managed to snoop into Indian Territory and made their route through busy streets and carried out the attack. It was merely luck that they did not have lost in crowd or else it would have been major debacle for India's national security.

2) Piracy in Indian Ocean

The immediate non-conventional maritime threat to India's maritime security in Indian Ocean is in the form of maritime piracy, robbery or violence at sea. The act of piracy particularly in Somalian water has grown at alarming proportions and has its spillover effects in Indian Exclusive Economic Zone. Their presence in Indian Exclusive Economic Zone has highlighted yet another loophole in Indian maritime security post 26/11. The continuous threats and spread of piracy from the coast of Somalia has also highlighted major security threats to India's sea line of communication and safety of its cargos and container ship, which are destined to India.

The following table titles: Piracy in the Indian Ocean region: Actual and Attempted attacks till 2010 would help to draw an attention of the growing menace of piracy.

Table 3: Piracy in the Indian Ocean region: Actual and Attempted attacks

	South – East of Asia							
	2003	2004	2005	2006	2007	2008	2009	2010
Indonesia	121	94	79	50	43	28	15	40
Malacca strait	28	38	12	11	7	2	2	2
Malaysia	5	9	3	10	9	10	16	18
Myanmar		1				1	1	
Singapore	2	8	7	5	3	6	9	3
Thailand	2	4	1	1	2		1	2
	Indian Subcontinent							
Bangladesh	58	17	21	47	15	12	17	23
India	27	15	15	5	11	10	12	5
Sri lanka	2			1	4	1		

Africa								
Egypt					2			2
Eritrea		1			1			
Kenya	1	1			4	2	1	
Madagascar		1	1		1			
Mozambique	1				3	2		
South Africa	1							
Tanzania	5	2	7	9	11	14	5	1
Horns of Africa								
Gulf of Aden*	18	8	10	10	13	92	116	53
Red Sea*							15	25
Somalia	3	2	35	10	31	19	80	139
Rest of the Indian ocean								
Arabian Sea*		2	2	2	4		1	2
Arabian Gulf	1							
Gulf of Oman							1	
Other Indian Ocean*			1				1	
Iran	2			2	2			
Iraq		1	10	2	2			2
Oman*					3		4	
Saudi Arabia				1				
Seychelles						1		
UAE		2						
Year total	277	206	222	166	171	200	297	311

*The attacks in the Gulf of Aden, Red Sea, Arabian Sea, Indian Ocean and Oman are all attributed to Somali pirates.

Source : "Maritime security in the Indian Ocean: strategic setting and features", Institute for Security Studies paper, August, 2012 No. 236 . http://www.issafrica.org/uploads/Paper236.pdf

The above table highlights the shift of piracy from the coast of Somalia to the international water is noticeable with range of area and scope they operate in. The presence of US task force and multinational naval cooperation itself is the evident of the vitality but still this operation has failed to combat the menace of piracy. From Indian perspective it become more visible as India has maritime installation in Arabian Sea, and entire sea lines of crude oil at its stakes. The recent arrest of pirates off the Coast of Lakshadweep Island has alarmed more as they have links to terrorist organisation such as Al-Shabab and Al-Quida.

With all understanding of the nature of piracy, its causes and the environment in which they operates, it has developed a serious challenge to the entire mercantile world. "This recrudescence of piracy is a serious threat to freedom of movement and security of supplies in an area with nearly 2500 sailing vessels per year (70 to 80 ships per day)." Certainly piracy in the Indian Ocean has taken its toll on the mercantile world because of the three reasons. First, the area falls in between the busy shipping lanes which go across the Red sea and Arabian Sea. Secondly, prominently the ideal reason for piracy to snoop in deep Indian Ocean region is because of its ideal location. As the region has attracted more capital and investment, pirates have simply followed the money. Thirdly the failed states and rogue state has all created an environment to bread piracy. Beside this the nexus between the piracy and terrorist outfits will lead to asymmetric warfare in the region. Targeting more lucrative cargo or container ships and the ransom, which later get diverted to fund the terrorist activities in the region.

Moreover the effect of maritime piracy off the coast of Somalia has undeniably rampaged international economy by great extent. According to the One Earth Future Foundation, "piracy extracts costs to the international economy of $7 to $12 billion per year." It is very clear that piracy has storm the international economy and its trade. Lawless Somalia and its coast have become more challenging. Even though the UNCLOS has given authority for states to act in its own capability, it continues to remain unchanged. Whatever the international community intend to do at sea, it remains unmovable. Therefore, the solution of piracy lies behind the coast – on interior stability of Somalia.

It's hard to accept that Somalia will give up the piracy, as there is no formally instituted institution which would look out for other avenues.

Today piracy has grown full time business with very lucrative earning of large amount of ransom, which gets channelized to found some of the terrorist organisation like Al- Shabab. The lawless state of Somalia needs political solution and as they operate and control vast areas, it looks like they are here to dominate their deterrence for a long time. Their deterrence will continue till terrorist organisation support the business with weapons.

Hypothetically, the growing nexus between piracy and terrorist organisation may lead to unconventional terror attack on naval ship as well as on container ships. The advancement of technology and its easy availability to non-states actors has emerged as a new challenge. India cannot negate the growing piracy and its snooping act in the Indian water merely as a small incident. It is a threat to India's maritime policy in the region and it's requires a strong vision to strengthen India's space and position in the Indian Ocean. Every action of India to curb down piracy or its role of assistance to escort the ship in and around piracy affected area 'horns of Africa' indeed will give India an edge and frontier posture to its Maritime Policy.

Conclusion

With all challenges and threats perception, Indian maritime security policy has evolved in an age of globalisation. It's preparedness to deal with maritime threats has come to a mature. Its deployment of forces in piracy affected area since 2008 has earned world wild accreditation. By merely understanding the various maritime threats post 26/11 will not help, but it need a system and an institution in place to manage India's maritime security post 26/11. Need an integrated institution and infrastructure, which would monitor the development in and around India's maritime domain.

Certainly, India has a wide maritime ground, which needs to be covered. It must match up with the need of the hour and to picture itself as dominant maritime power in the contemporary world. To achieve this objective, it is vital to maximise cooperation between the maritime authorities, institutions, stakeholders and private industries in order to create enhanced maritime domain awareness.

Therefore, India must develop a mechanism, wherein it takes all the agents and players into consideration which share the same understanding and its commitment to the maritime world, resources and environment.

The security of India's maritime frontiers is challenged by non-states actor as well as rogue states. Primarily it is the task of armed forces to protect the integrity and sovereignty of India. Simultaneously it is equally the responsibility of the other stakes holders to share the information and security measures to build strong maritime policy.

References

Marine Mineral Resources : Scientific Advances and Economic Perspectives, A Joint Publication by the United Nations Division for Ocean Affairs and the Law of the Sea, Office of Legal Affairs, and the International Seabed Authority, United Nations 2004.

David Michel and Russell Sticklor (Ed) "Indian Ocean Rising: Maritime Security and Policy Challenges", Stimson, Washington, JULY 2012.

Richard Cronin and Amit Pandya(Ed), "Exploiting Natural Resources, Growth, Instability, and Conflict in the Middle East and Asia", The Henry L. Stimson Center, Washington, 2009.

Marine Pollution: Causes and Consequences, Marine Ecosystem: EMCBTAP-ENVIS Newsletter, Department of Geology, University of Kerala, Kariavattom - 695 581 Vol. 1, No. 2, 2003.

Dr. Hari Saran and Dr. Harsh K. Sinha, "India's Maritime Stakes and Challenges in

Indian Ocean" , Centre for Defence Sciences research and development, Vol. 2, No. 1, January-June 2011, 01-12

David Brewster, "An Indian Sphere of Influence in the Indian Ocean? , Security Challenges", Vol. 6, No. 3 (Spring 2010)

"Migration Amendment (Unauthorised Maritime Arrivals and Other Measures) Bill 2012", Senate Committee on Legal and Constitutional Affairs, Law council of Australia, 17 December 2012.

C. Uday Bhaskar and Geoffrey Kemp, "Maritime Security Challenges in the Indian Ocean Region", A Workshop Report February India International Centre , New Delhi, India, 23-24, 2011

G.S. Khurana, "Maritime Security in the Indian Ocean: Convergence Plus Cooperation Equals Resonance", Strategic Analysis, Institute for Defence Studies and Analyses, Vol. 28, No.3, Jul-Sep 2004

Vice Admiral P.S. Das, "India's Maritime Concerns and Strategies", Journal of the United service Institution of India, Delhi, Vol. Cxxxvi, No-565, July-September, 2006.

Dr. Eric Grove, "Maritime Dimensions of a new world order", New Delhi, 2007, p.1.

Rahul Roy Choudhury, "Indias maritime security", 2000, p.63.

John F. Frittelli, "Port and maritime Security: Background and Issues", USI Digest, Delhi, Vol. IX, No. 17, 2006.

Vijay Sakhuja , " Indian ocean and the Strategy of Sea Lines of communication", Strategic Analysis, New Delhi, 2001.

Anil Singh, "Effects of Globalisation : Robust growth in India's container volumes", Cargotalk , South Asia's Leading Cargo Monthly, Vol XI No. 9, DDP Publication, August , 2011.

Ratan Kr Paul, " Cargo traffic from Indian ports: Need for speed in capacity building", Cargotalk , South Asia's Leading Cargo Monthly, Vol XI No. 9, DDP Publication, August, 2011.

"Marine Ecosystem: EMCBTAP-ENVIS Newsletter, Department of Geology, University of Kerala, Kariavattom - 695 581 Vol. 1, No. 2, 2003. http://www.dgukenvis.nic.in/newsletters/Newsletter2.pdf

Marie Leòntine Razanadrasoa, "Global and Regional Approaches: Madagascar Perspective", (Ed).Bimal N Patel and Hitesh Thakar, " Maritime Security and Piracy: Global Issues, Challenges and Solution", Eastern Book Company, New Delhi-2012.

"Marine Mineral Resources" http://www.isa.org.jm/files/documents/EN/Brochures/ENG6.pdf

"Marine Nation 2025: Marine Science to Support Australia's Blue Economy, Oceans Policy Science Advisory Group", March 2013

http://www.aims.gov.au/documents/30301/550211/Marine+Nation+2025_web.pdf/bd99cf13-84ae-4dbd-96ca-f1a330062cdf

"Maritime security, disarmament forum, United Nations Institute for Disarmament Research" , 2010. http://www.unidir.org/files/publications/pdfs/maritime-security-en-319.pdf

Chris Trelawny, "IMO maritime security policy : Background paper"

http://www.imo.org/blast/blastDataHelper.asp?data_id=18937&filename=IMOmaritimesecuroitypolicy.pdf

"Maritime Security Sector reform" http://www.marad.dot.gov/documents/Maritime_Security_Sector_Reform.pdf

M.N. Murty and Surender Kumar, "Water Pollution in India An Economic Appraisal, India Infrastructure - Report 2011", .http://www.idfc.com/pdf/report/2011/Chp-19-Water-Pollution-in-India-An-Economic-Appraisal.pdf

"Costal and Marine pollution", National Institute of Oceanography Dona Paula, Goa, India March,2008 http://saarc- sdmc.nic.in/pdf/workshops/goa/india/COASTAL%20AND%20MARINE%20POLLUTION.pdf

M J Varkey, "Pollution of Coastal Seas", http://www.ias.ac.in/resonance/Jan1999/pdf/Jan1999p36-44.pdf

"Container-security-initiative-(csi)", US customs and border protection. http://www.sanmina.com/pdf/partners/security/container-security-initiative-(csi).pdf

"Container-security-initiative-(csi)", US customs and border protection, 2011. http://www.cbp.gov/linkhandler/cgov/trade/cargo_security/csi/csi_brochure_2011.ctt/csi_brochure_2011.pdf

"Container security: Major Initiatives and Related International Developments",

Report by the UNCTAD secretariat, United nations conference on Trade and Development http://unctad.org/en/Docs/sdtetlb20041_en.pdf

"The Indian Ship building Industry", International business development, April 2012

http://di.dk/SiteCollectionDocuments/DIBD/The%20Indian%20Shipbuilding%20Industry%202012.pdf

"Maritime security in the Indian Ocean: strategic setting and features", Institute for Security Studies paper, August, 2012 No. 236 . http://www.issafrica.org/uploads/Paper236.pdf

Vice Admiral Premvir Das (Retd), "Maritime Power: Key to India's Security Interests", Aspen Institute India, January 2011. http://www.aspenindia.org/pdf/martime.pdf

Cdr. P K Ghosh, "Maritime Security Challenges in South Asia and the Indian Ocean: Response Strategies", A paper prepared for the Center for Strategic and International Studies – American-Pacific Sea lanes Security Institute conference on Maritime Security in Asia. January 18-20, 2004, Honolulu, Hawaii.

http://community.middlebury.edu/~scs/docs/ghosh,%20maritime%20

security%20challenges%20in%20SAsia%20&%20Indian%20Ocean.pdf

Amal Jayawardane, "Terrorism at Sea: Maritime Security Challenges in South Asia". http://www.rsis-ntsasia.org/activities/conventions/2009-singapore/Amal%20Jayawardane.pdf

Dr. N.V.Vinithkumar, "Maritime Pollution – A Perspective , monitoring and control in india", http://www.niot.res.in/m5/mbic/me/data/me.pdf

Rajesh M. Basrur and Friedrich Steinhäusler, "Nuclear and Radiological Terrorism threats for India: Risk Potential and Countermeasures,". http://jps.anl.gov/vol1_iss1/3-Threats_for_India.pdf

"Basic Statistics on Indian Petroleum and Natural Gas 2011-12" , Ministry of Petroleum and Natural Gas, Government of India , New Delhi (Economic Division) http://petroleum.nic.in/petstat.pdf

"BP Statistical Review of World Energy, June 2013". bp.com/statisticalreview

"Somali Piracy's Impact on the Global Economy Nears $7 Billion in 2011". One Earth Future Foundation, 9-11-2011. http://oceansbeyondpiracy.org/sites/default/files/ecop_press_release_feb_8_2012.pdf

"Department of Commerce", Government of India. http://commerce.nic.in/

"Maritime Terrorism: An Indian Perspective" see: http://www.southasiaanalysis.org/paper12/paper1154.html

"India's Naval Acquisitions I: Defence Ship-building in India" , Thought Leadership Series, December, 2011. http://www.aviotech.com/pdf/Aviotech_Thought_Leadership_Series_Naval_Shipbuilding_December_2011.pdf

http://www.marinebuzz.com/2009/01/26/major-and-minor-ports-in-india/

http://www.niot.res.in/m5/mbic/me/data/me.pdf

http://articles.timesofindia.indiatimes.com/2011-08-07/india/29860993_1_mv-wisdom-ship-breakers-association-crew-members

http://worldoceanreview.com/en/wor-1/energy/marine-minerals/

http://www.cbp.gov/xp/cgov/trade/cargo_security/csi/csi_in_brief.xml

http://www.maritimeterrorism.com/definitions/

http://www.cfr.org/homeland-security/targets-terrorism-nuclear-facilities/p10213

http://jps.anl.gov/vol1_iss1/3-Threats_for_India.pdf

http://di.dk/SiteCollectionDocuments/DIBD/The%20Indian%20 Shipbuilding%20Industry%202012.pdf

http://www.bpc.gov.au/site/page5777.asp

http://worldoceanreview.com/en/wor-1/energy/marine-minerals/

13 | Post 26/11 Terrorist Threats In India – Is National Counter Terrorism Centre Alone the Solution

Unnikrishnan G

Abstract

The 26/11 terrorist attacks in Mumbai had more impact on public consciousness and state policy of India than any preceding incident or cluster of incidents in the past. It even forced the then Home Minister Shivaraj Patil to resign and P. Chidambaram assumed as the new Home Minster of India. As the Home Minister Chidambaram had taken a lot of initiatives to curb terrorism and the notable among them was the proposed National Counter Terrorism centre. It is a federal anti- terror agency modelled on the National Counter Terrorism centre of the USA and it has intelligence, investigative and operational functions. But the crucial question is whether it is the only solution for countering terrorism in India. The answer to this question lies the fact that in India it is not the lack of institutional arrangement for countering terrorism is the problem but the system wide deficiencies in skills and capabilities. Moreover we focus more and more on meta- institutional reform and the creation of new institutions to monitor coordinate and oversee the largely dysfunctional apparatus.

Introduction

Terrorism means the policy of striking terror in the minds of the people by violent methods to achieve some ends. People who are disgruntled and who are unable to get their desires fulfilled by normal and accepted methods in society are resorting to terrorism. Terrorism is not confined to any area or activity and now it has become an international phenomenon. There are terrorists in developed and advanced countries as well as in developing countries like India. Governments all over the world are doing their best to put an end to terrorism. There are also a few who encourage and support terrorism in other countries to meet their own political ends.

Terrorism in India

Terrorism in India is not new, but it has increased very rapidly in the last few years. Terrorism in India must be looked upon as an integral part of our colonial legacy. The British followed the policy of 'divide and rule' and ultimately divided the subcontinent into two nations, which later grew into three after the independence of Bangladesh. This partition on the basis of religion, faith and community has sown seeds of hatred, violence, terrorism, separatism and communal divide. The rise of extremism and terrorism in our northeastern states of Nagaland, Mizoram, Tripura, Manipur and Assam etc is also a part of our colonial legacy. The long colonial rule never attempted to bring the tribals of these states into the mainstream of the nation. Rather, a feeling of hatred, alienation and disharmony was created in their hearts. Consequently, they felt neglected after independence and also misled by a false sense of losing their ethnic identity and independence and decided to take terrorism and violence. The emergence of terrorism in north-eastern states also reflects the lack of will and proper efforts on the part of our political leaders and the government to bring these groups of tribals into the national mainstream and the democratic process.

Besides socio-political and economic aspects, psychological, emotional and religious aspects are also involved in the problem of terrorism. The unprecedented spate of terrorism in the recent past in Punjab and Jammu and Kashmir can be understood only in this background. Both got much support from Pakistan by way of supply of arms and ammunition, training and finance. Poverty, unemployment and lack of education, etc among these people also further worsen the situation.

26/11 Mumbai attack

The 26/11 terrorists attacks in Mumbai[1] had more impact on public consciousness and state policy than any preceding incident or cluster of incidents in the past. Although the Mumbai attacks of November 2008 attracted the most global attention,[2] they were merely the most recent and dramatic in a series of bloody terrorist incidents throughout urban India. It revealed to the world India's anemic internal security infrastructure and serious loopholes that exist in our system of national security. Moreover public anger against the state reached its all time high and it even forced the then Home Minister Shivaraj Patil to resign and Chidambaram assumed as the new Home Minister. As the new Home Minister Chidambaram had taken a lot of initiatives to curb terrorism and vast allocations were made to revamp the internal security system. Notable among this was National Investigation Agency, NSG hubs, Multi Agency Centre, National Intelligence Grid and Nation Counter Terrorism Centre. Among these institutions the yet to materialise National Counter Terrorism centre assumed the central focus, concern and an arena for heated debate and discussions. It is considered as the 'brain child' of Chidambaram, and the one and only solution for terrorist problems in India.

What is NCTC

The National Counter Terrorism Centre is a proposed Federal anti-terror agency modelled on the National Counter Terrorism Centre of the USA.[3] The National Counter Terrorism Centre will derive its powers from the Unlawful Activities Prevention Act, (UAPA) 1967, in respect of 'searches' and the issue of arrest warrants throughout India to prevent terrorist attacks. The proposed NCTC will have access to counter-terrorism intelligence generated by India's covert services, as well as authority over the National Security Guard and the National Intelligence Agency. It is envisaged as an apex body, a single and effective point of control for all counter terrorism measures. It will also execute counter-terror operations and collect, collate and disseminate data on terrorism. Moreover it also has the power to conduct searches and arrests in any part of India. In short, it has intelligence, investigative and operational functions.

Justification for NCTC

The Union Government justified the proposed NCTC on the ground that, it is unavoidable because, at present, the Union Government cannot deploy its military and para-military forces suo motu to deal with internal security problems in the states. Moreover the states are unwilling to accept these Central Forces due to dubious political compulsions. This has occurred when large-scale communal riots occurred in 1993 (post Babri Masjid) and 2002 (post Godhra). Secondly, the need for NCTC is justified because the states lack the political will to fight determinedly against terrorism. Often the states have not deployed their police and state armed forces to deal firmly with law and order situations in a timely manner. Moreover they have also used their state forces to serve their own political ends. Thirdly,

India is a Union of States and not a Federation, which necessitates the centre to play a crucial role in all activities concerned with the welfare of people. NCTC is a need of the hour and rather than looking at narrow concerns of infringement of state rights (which can be resolved by a consensus and also showing some trust in centre) a more important concern of counter terrorism must be addressed.

Functions of NCTC

The NCTC would function under the Intelligence Bureau (IB), it would analyze the intelligence pertaining to terrorism and associated criminality. It would maintain relevant data bases, develop appropriate responses, and undertake threat assessments for dissemination to the Union and state governments.

Oppositions to NCTC

NCTC received opposition from many State governments (particularly non Congress states). Their main cause of dispute is the section 43(a) of the NCTC act which empowers it "to arrest and detain any person if the body feels that the subject is associated with a terror act." This provision has been widely criticized by non Congress states alleging it as a central domination on state powers and authority. To them, law and order is a state subject and an all-powerful Central Agency will violate the autonomy of state governments. Secondly, the NCTC will be directed solely at the behest of Home Ministry without taking the consent of the state concerned. So, there will be political mileage to be generated in respect of searches and arrests against opponents. Moreover the clear cut consent or concurrence of the state concerned for launching probe in the event of a terrorist attack has not been spelt out, and also whether the NCTC is bound to inform the state concerned of the stages or progress of investigation is not specifically stated.

Thirdly, critics pointed out that vesting investigative, intelligence and operational powers on NCTC are not only extraordinary but also too much for a single body to handle effectively. Intelligence should be the only prerogative of NCTC and the rest should be handled by the already existing setups of police and central agencies. Finally, NCTC is considered as 'draconian' in nature, a POTA with a different name. In addition to this, the mode of appointment of the investigating officers and the nature of accountability of the officers in the NCTC are not specified.

The Indian and American NCTC's: A Comparison

The American NCTC is part of its Directorate of National Intelligence, which is manned by officials from the Pentagon, FBI, CIA and related agencies who can access their databases. The American NCTC analyzes and collates terrorism related information to plan and support counter-terrorism operations. Its charter visualizes its providing this information to the intelligence agencies for responding to terrorist incidents within the US, and also brief policy makers. In short, the American NCTC, collect, collates and assess terrorism-related information but not conduct intelligence operations. It has no powers to investigate or arrest. The Indian NCTC has the power to investigate and arrest, hence it differs radically from its American counterpart. Moreover, placing the NCTC within the Intelligence Bureau (IB) (as in the Indian case) would convert the Bureau into an operational body, which would be disastrous for the general polity.

Is it alone the solution

The following points will analyze is National Counter Terrorism Centre alone is the solution for terrorist problems in India.

(1) No Institutional response to terrorism in India is likely to be effective, unless it is supported by an effective police infrastructure. The failure to perform essential police functions is the crux of the problem and where the riot lies even today.[4] The Maharashtra governments official enquiry on 26/11 terrorist attacks in Mumbai, led by Former Intelligence Officer Ram Pradhan,[5] noted that the intelligence services had issued at least 17 alerts on Lashkar attacks on the city starting from August 7, 2006. To him, the Mumbai police officials took the warnings seriously but lacked the resources to mount on effective response. Thus the key problem is ineffective police infrastructure, as they are the first responders in a crisis and the first contact of community intelligence. But till today there is no agreed national road map on how these needs will actually be met and when.

(2) The joint efforts of the Centre and State Governments to fight the demon of terrorism is the another need of the hour. Moreover the state governments must strengthen their own intelligence and operational capabilities to address the menace of terrorism.[6] Their need for financial assistance should be considered sympathetically

by New Delhi and in addition to this the additional forces needed must be raised, training institutions must be upgraded, police stations authorized must be physically established, arms and ammunition sanctioned must be centrally purchased and supplied.

(3) The placing of NCTC within the intelligence Bureau (IB) would convert the Bureau into an operational body which would be disastrous for the general polity. It is an open secret that the IB assiduously gathers 'political intelligence' on behalf of the political party in power about rival factions within the party and about the opposition parties. Moreover, the NCTC would also get embroiled in IB's running battle with the Research and Analysis Wing (RAW), which is responsible for external intelligence. In short the investigative, intelligence and operational powers of the NCTC will overburden it. So it must fully concentrate on its sole objective of integrated intelligence gathered from across the nation, rather than creating confusion with other bodies on matters of investigative and operational jurisdiction. Moreover the NCTC, along with National Information Grid (NAT GRID), National Threat Reduction Organization (NTRO) should be placed under a new ministry of Internal Security.[7]

(4) The close relationship or joint working between Police and Security service is the another need of the hour. In USA and UK, such a mechanism is existing[8] and both were equipped and trained to deal with terrorism. But in India, such a process is only just beginning and at a pace which would put a tortoise to shame.

(5) Adequate arrangements are required to ensure a continuing validation of the professional abilities of the Union and State forces employed in the anti-terrorism and counter-insurgency role.[9] An independent inspectorate can be established for this purpose that would function like an Ombudsman to evaluate the capability of these forces to undertake the challenging tasks confronting them. The need for this outside evaluation is all more necessary since the intelligence agencies and their activities are not subject to parliamentary oversight.

(6) The excessive emphasis on the role of the centre in all internal security issues is the other major problem. The monolithic national

internal security architecture must be replaced by a decentralized response capabilities and decision-making system. It will also to a large extent ameliorate the concerns of the state governments.

(7) Finally, the underlying governance issues must be tackled to strengthen the anti-terrorism strategy. This include establishment of special courts to try terrorism related offences, credible programs to ensure witness protection and to ensure the anonymity of whistle-blowers, the prosecution of politicians and bureaucrats linked to such activities, an effective rotational postings policy for executive officers in the government, implementation of social services and development programs especially those relating to education and public health etc.

The Home Ministry under the Narendra Modi led NDA government is now pitching for a National Counter Terrorism Centre. A new policy is being drawn up for sharing of intelligence and action in terrorism cases as well as strengthening the role of the Multi Agency Centre (MAC) of the Intelligence Bureau. The draft policy named "Publicity and Sharing of Intelligence in Terrorism Cases" is under consideration of the Union Home Ministry. It aims at streamlining the flow of intelligence information between various agencies and also puts down a mechanism in black and white on who will coordinate action on such information. In short now there is a greater realisation at the Home Ministry that a streamlined system of intelligence sharing and counter terrorism action is required in some form, though it would not be in the name or exact shape of NCTC.

Conclusion

Thus the key problem is not the lack of institutional arrangement for the management of India's Counter terrorism responses, but system-wide deficiencies in skills and capabilities. But we focus more on meta-institutional reform and the creation of new institutions to monitor, coordinate and oversee this largely dysfunctional apparatus. Moreover the imperative need to coordinate the anti-terrorism intelligence gathering and joint operational efforts of the Union and State governments needs no emphasis.

Notes

1. The 2008 Mumbai attacks were twelve coordinated shooting and bombing attacks across Mumbai, India's largest city by members of Lashkar-e-Taiba. Eight of the attacks occurred in South Mumbai: at Chhatrapati Shivaji Terminus, the Oberoi Trident, the Taj Mahal Palace and Tower, Leopold Café, Cama Hospital, the Nariman House Jewish Community Centre, the Metro Cinema, and a lane behind the Times of India building and St. Xavier's College. There was also an explosion at Mazagaon, in Mumbai's port area, and in a taxi at Vile Parle. By the early morning of 28 November, all sites except for the Taj hotel had been secured by Mumbai police and security forces. On 29 November, India's National Security Guards (NSG) conducted '*Operation Black Tornado*' to flush out the remaining attackers; it resulted in the deaths of the last remaining attackers at the Taj hotel and ending all fighting in the attacks.

2. The attacks are sometimes referred to as 26/11, after the date in 2008 that the attacks began, in similar style to the 9/11 attacks in the United States, the 3/11 attacks in Madrid, Spain and the 7/7 bombings in London, United Kingdom.

3. The American National Counter Terrorism Centre was established by the Intelligence Reform Act of 2004. The American NCTC was intended to close the gaps in intelligence-sharing that allowed a number of September 11, 2001 hijackers to enter the US.

4. Chidambaram as Home Minister had himself admitted this fact in an interstate Council meeting in 2009. In his speech he pointed out the desperate need for better police infrastructure and training. To him for the effective performance of the police functions, the states would have to hire at least 400,000 police constables in the next two years.

5. Ram Pradhan in his report pointed out that police constables were getting practice of firing only once a year because of the lack of ammunition. They were carrying guns more like 'lathis.' Bullet proof jackets were not really bullet proof.

6. A look at the state and status of 'Force One' is useful in this context. It was the tactical counter-terrorism (CT) response unit set up by the Mumbai Police to tackle another 26/11 type attack. Its sanctioned strength was 350 personnel, but 'suitable and willing' personnel have been hard to find, and the current strength is 250 men. Of these, only a fraction has both bullet proof jackets and helmets. Indeed, the Mumbai Police has not been able to purchase a single bullet proof jacket since 26/11 and was eventually prevailed upon to accept a gift of 100 jackets from private sector companies eager to improve the 'police-public interface' and ensure a better counter-terrorism response. Further, 'force one' has no hands-free radios, no night sights for weapons, no stun grenades, no dedicated trainers, no specialized eyewear to provide protection against explosions, not even a fully equipped training facility.

7. In India the establishment of a separate Ministry of Internal security conceived several years back, but continues to languish. The US established its Department of Homeland security after 9/11.

8. Peter Clarke, head of the Scotland Yard's Counter-terrorism command, said in 2007: "the most important change in counter-terrorism in the UK has been the development of the relationship between the police and the security service (MIS), the joint working between the police and the MIS has become recognized as a beacon of good practice." That was possible because both MIS and the police were extensively equipped and trained to deal with terrorism.

9. Five years after 26/11, India's intelligence services are still functioning with staffing deficits of up to 40 percent. The Research and Analysis Wing (RAW) also faces endemic shortages of personnel both with specialist language and area skills, and technology experts critical to modern espionage. The Intelligence Bureau (IB), in turn has been unable to expand its counter-terrorism efforts, despite mounting threats.

References

1. Kumar, Updesh and Mandal, Manas (2010) Countering Terrorism – Psychosocial Strategies, New Delhi: Sage Publications.

2. Stohl, Michael (2005). The Politics of Terrorism, New York: Marcel Dekker.

3. Tama, Jordan (2011). Terrorism and National Security Reform, New York: Cambridge.

4. Mahapatra, Chintamani and Tripathy, Amulya (2008). Transnational Terrorism – Perspective on Motives, Measures and Impacts, New Delhi: Reference Press.

5. Swami, Praveen, "Why UPA's NCTC is the most Stupid National Security Idea ever," The Hindu (Chennai) 5 June 2013.

6. Swami, Praveen, "Five years after 26/11 India Faces Intelligence Famine," The Hindu (Chennai) 27 February 2013.

7. "India does not need NCTC," The Pioneer (New Delhi) 2 May 2012.

8. "NCTC emerges a tooth less wonder," The New Indian Express (Kochi) 5 June 2013.

9. "The alphabet soup of Internal Security", The Hindu (Chennai) 11 January 2010.

PART – IV

HUMAN SECURITY IN INDIA; THE CHALLENGES AND POLICY OPTIONS

14 | India's Security Challenges And Policy Options: A Human Security Perspective

Suresh R.

Abstract

Human security or people's security focuses on the basic units of nation states, that is, the individual. People centred development would help to solve the problems of the individuals in a better way than the state centred development. In a state centered development paradigm the basic issues of individuals get less attention. Nation states were the creation of people who desired to protect and promote their security. It was one of the means to achieve people's security at a particular stage of human civilization when the threat to security of the people emanates mainly from external sources, that is, from other states. Security, therefore in the ultimate analysis means human security. In the post-cold war period the external threat perception has been diminished or even eliminated and new threat to security of nation states as well as people are evolved. These nontraditional threats to security of nations including terrorism, global economic slowdown and global climate change can be addressed only with multilateral effort. Again it is widely accepted that even if nations are secure people may not be secure. People are not secure in their daily life as long as poverty, illiteracy and hunger remains. Moreover unless the social economic and political rights of the people living in all nation states are not secured and protected there is no human security, national security and international security. Thus the blurred boundary between human security and national security on the one hand and national security and international security on the other hand again emphasis the significance of human security. The modern states are welfare states and the welfare state concept envisages a minimum standard of living to all individuals. Though India is celebrating the 68th anniversary of its independence nearly one third of its population lives in poverty and nearly forty per cent of the population are illiterate, the gap between rich and poor is alarmingly growing. The political equality was ensured with one man one vote, however social, economic and educational inequality is looming large in the Indian society. In a welfare state it is the responsibility of the government to ensure minimum standard of living to all. The failure on the part of the government to ensure people's security is gross violation of the constitution. Thus the threat to security emanates not only from external aggression but also from poor management of the scarce resources to ensure human security. It appears that the best option before India is to focus more on human security issues than pure military security. Since the threat to security of the nation emanates mostly from non-state actors with the support of some nation states the cooperation of other actors in the international system are required to address these issues. In the long run armament and arm race in the region is particularly detrimental to India both in terms of scarce resource use and also instability of the political system in the immediate neighbourhood having nuclear weapon power. In the present context it appears that India should focus more on addressing the human security concerns than on accelerating military built up in the region. This would enable India to solve most of the internal security issues by undertaking the various welfare measures to alleviate poverty and other human security issues. However, the British colonial system entrenched strong bureaucratic and defence structure in India could easily resist any attempt to restructure the existing security policy by the political executive which is weakened through the compulsions of coalition politics and deeply drenched in corruption charges.

I. Introduction

In the post Second World War period independent India played a major role in the formation of NAM (Nonaligned Movement) at the international level. Though the military power dominated cold war period was not conducive to the growth of such an international movement, which was not based on power equations, it provided the newly independent developing nation a forum to articulate their particular as well as common grievances. The super power rivalry and competitions had posed many challenges to the nascent NAM. Though NAM was not very effective to meet the challenges of power politics it acted as an international pressure group to reduce the negative impact of power rivalry and competitions. However, the cold war has ended without the outbreak of a world war or any pressure exerted by the NAM towards that objective.

In the post-cold war period the end of ideological confrontation has given place to the process of integration of domestic economy with global economy. The perception regarding security of nation states also underwent a marked change. During the cold war period the developed and developing nations focused mainly on arms built-up to ensure the security of nation from the threat posed by potential rival nation states. The general belief was that if the nations are secure from external threat posed by other nation states the people living in that nation are also secure. Therefore during the cold war period national security was purely based on military security and nation states paid maximum attention to enhance their military power. Concomitantly military alliances, armament and arms race were the natural corollaries of such a state of affair. (Karl Deutsch, 1989: 182) However in the post-cold war situation the capacity of non-state actors to harm human and material resources manifested that no nation whatsoever powerful can single handedly meet the threat posed by them to their security. (Suresh, 2010: 103) Similarly the global economic meltdown and global climate change demand concerted action by the developed and developing nations.

Again the development in field of Information and Communication Technology (ICT) has united the people across the world transcending the manmade territorial boundaries of nations. The international non-governmental agencies act as an agency to aggregate and articulate problems confronted by ordinary people in their daily life across the world. These problems include poverty, denial of basic human rights, child labour and many other predicaments in the realm of protection and promotion social, economic and political rights. Most of these matters can be considered as human security issues. This paper is an attempt to examine the human security concerns before India and policy options available in the changed international context.

II. Dimensions of Security

With the end of the cold war, the concept of security has increasingly come under scrutiny from scholars of international relations and other discipline. In the classical formulation, security is about how nation states use force to manage threats to their territorial integrity, their autonomy, and their domestic political order, primarily from other nation states. This classical national security formulation has been criticized on various grounds. A nation may be secure but does not mean that all people living in that nation are secure. The social economic and political orders prevalent in that nation have an implication on the security of the people. (Suresh R, 2011: 125)

The debates on security is centered on the presuppositions about what security is, what is being secured, the causes of insecurity, and how best to address insecurity. (Kanti Bajpai, 2003: 195) International relations theorists and policy experts have varying perspectives on these questions, which have evolved and have had changing levels of acceptance over time. Realists and neo-realists emphasise the nation state as the central referent of security, both as the lens through which security is understood, as well as the tool by which security is best maintained or restored. (Hans J Morgenthau, 1983, 23; Kenneth Waltz, 1979: 31) Liberal theorists recognize a wider set of values embedded in the concept of the state and state security, in the methods and means to address insecurity, and the actors involved. [1] The critical constructivist scholars understand that the interests and identities of nation states are themselves constructed by the distribution of ideas and interests within the state-based system and this shapes a state's security interests and how these are conceived, and in turn impacts upon the actions necessary to ensure security. [2] Thus there are divergent views with regard to concept of security, whose security, that is whether the security of the nation or people, the causes of insecurity, and how to ensure security.

The Westphalia state system had made nation states as the basic unit in the international system. And nation states are sovereign and independent. Each nation decides their internal and external policies. The prime responsibility of a nation state is to promote its national interests. [3] The national interests of nation states are mainly to ensure peace, security and prosperity. However they differ with regard to the means adopted to achieve these national interests. Some nations employ aggressive means and some peaceful methods. [4] And foreign policy of a nation is the means to achieve their respective national interests. Therefore, though the national interests are similar nations frame divergent foreign policy, which in turn is conditioned by the interplay of internal and external factors. Thus, the foreign policy changes in accordance with the transformations in the internal and external conditions. [5]

III. India's Security Concerns

Independent India took the initiative to a nonaligned foreign policy rooted on the Indian tradition of faith in nonviolence. However the cold war politics of super power rivalry and competitions along with an unfriendly atmosphere in the South Asian region prompted India to fell in the lines of power politics propounded by the realist. [6] The ensuing armament, arms race and competitions prompted India to keep its nuclear weapon option open and also involve in a 'civilian cum military alliances' with the former Soviet Union. [7] At that period the international politics was purely based on power politics and India and likeminded nations had only limited policy options to ensure security of the nation from external threat.

However, the end of cold war and the ongoing globalization process along with the proliferation of nontraditional threat to security of the nations led to multilateralism in international relations. (Suresh R 2010: 50) Though the great powers are not ready to accept the new developments, the post-cold war events such as threat from non-state actors to the security of nation, the global economic slowdown, and global climate change compelled even the most militarily powerful nation to seek multilateral approach to address these menaces. [8]

The ideological confrontations during the cold war led to armament, arms race between the capitalist bloc and communist bloc nations. During the cold war period military security was the dominant security concern of nation states as the threat to security of nations emanates solely from rival nation states. However in the changed context of international power structure and the advent of nontraditional threat to the security of nations along with the ongoing economic integration at the global level and greater interaction of people across the world transcending artificial territorial boundaries compelled the nation states to evolve a common strategy to address emerging security concerns.

The global movements towards democratization and protection and promotion of human rights supported by ICT once again brought individuals rights and security into focal point. It appears that even if nations are secure people living there may not be secure. The civil wars taken place in some nation states to protect the rights of multiethnic groups or the demand for right to self-determinations of people are examples of such a situation. In this context security means people's security and international efforts are required to ensure people's security from any threat emanates from within or outside the nation states. Thus human security assumes great significance in the post-cold war era of profoundly interdependent global system.

IV.   Human Security

Though the idea of human security in its rudimentary form may be traced in 1960s, it was the Independent Commission on International Development Issues in its North-South Report of 1980 highlighted the changing thinking on development and security. The chairman of the commission Willy Brandit observed "Our Report is based on what appears to be the simplest common interest that mankind wants to survive, and one might even add has the moral obligation to survive. This not only raises traditional questions of peace and war, but also how to overcome world hunger, mass misery and alarming disparities between the living conditions of the rich and poor."[9]

Another notable development in the idea of human security was the Common Security Report of the Independent Commission on Disarmament and Security Issues chaired by Olaf Palm. It acknowledges that Third world security was also threatened by poverty and deprivation by economic inequality. The report noted "common security requires that people live in dignity and peace, that they have enough to eat and are able to find work and live in a world without poverty and destitution."[10]

With the end of superpower rivalry the call for new thinking in security matters gained momentum. In 1991 the Stockholm Institute on Global Security and Governance issued a call for " Common Responsibility in the 1990s ",which maintained a" wider concept of security ,which deals with threats that stem from failures in development, environmental degradation, excessive population growth and movement, and lack of progress towards democracy." Again in 1995, the Commission on Global Governance's report, Our *Global Neighbourhood*, stated that "The concept of global security must be broadened from the traditional focus on the security of states to include the security of people and the security of the planet."[11]

The above commission reports may be considered as precursors to human security thinking. However, a human security perspective was developed by the UNDP (United Nations Development Programme) in the Human Development Report of 1994. This report contains a section on 'Redefining Security: The Human Dimension'.[12] It proposes an alternative to traditional security and a necessary supplement to human development. The report discusses in details the question of security for whom by reference to traditional notion of security. These were concerned with security of territory from external aggression, or as protection of national interest in foreign policy or as global security from the threat of nuclear holocaust. It has been related more to nation state than to people. What this conception overlooked was the "legitimate concern of ordinary people who sought security in their daily lives".[13] Human security, on the other hand, is people centered.

The Human Development Report maintains that Human security means protecting vital freedom of the individuals. It means protecting people from critical and pervasive threats and situations, building on their strengths and aspirations. It also means creating systems that give people the building blocks of survival, dignity and livelihood. Human security connects different types of freedoms - freedom from want, freedom from fear and freedom to take action on one's own behalf. To do this, it offers two general strategies: protection and empowerment. Protection shields people from dangers. It requires concerted effort to develop norms, processes and institutions that systematically address insecurities. Empowerment enables people to develop their potential and become full participants in decision-making. Protection and empowerment are mutually reinforcing, and both are required in most situations. Human security complements state security, furthers human development and enhances human rights. It complements state security by being people-centered and addressing insecurities that have not been considered as state security threats. By looking at "downside risks", it broadens the human development focus beyond "growth with equity". Respecting human rights are at the core of protecting human security.[14]

Thus, human security focuses on the basic units of nation states, that is the individuals. People centred development would help to solve the problems of the individuals in a better way than the state centred development. In a state centered development paradigm the basic issues of individuals get less attention. Nation states were the creation of people who desired to protect and promote their security. It was one of the means to achieve people's security at a particular stage of human civilization when the threat to security of the people emanates mainly from external sources that is from other states. Security, therefore in the ultimate analysis means people's security. In the post-cold war period the external threat perception has been diminished or even eliminated and new threat to security of nation states as well as people are evolved. These nontraditional threats to security of nation states including terrorism, global economic slowdown and global climate change can be addressed only with multilateral effort. Again it is widely accepted that even if nations are secure people may not be secure. People are not secure in their daily life as long as poverty, illiteracy and hunger remains. Moreover unless the social economic and political rights of the people are not secured and protected there is no human security, national security and international security. Thus the blurred boundary between human security and national security on the one hand and national security and international security on the other hand again emphasis the significance of human security.

V. India and Human Security Issues

In the age of globalization protection of the vulnerable groups in the society, who are affected by development based displacement or by loss of job and income, assumes great significance. India had taken several steps to ensure human security or the security of the people. Being the largest democratic system in the world it has a strong democratic structure to implement human security measures at the national level. Though the political foundations of India are strongly based on a parliamentary system in the economic and social fields it confronted with many challenges. It includes poverty, unemployment, illiteracy, social inequality communalism, casteism, the economic disparity between haves and have-nots. All these factors have an implication on human security in India. For instance, a quick glance into the economic condition in India shows that it is moving from bad to worse.

The official statistics of the government of India maintains that the economy has grown at an average annual rate of about 8 per cent for the last 3 years, reducing poverty by 10 per cent. However, 40 per cent of the world's poor still live in India, and 27 per cent of the country's population continues to live below the poverty line. More than one third live on less than a dollar a day, and 80 per cent live on less than two dollars a day. India's recent economic growth has been attributed to the service industry, but 60 per cent of the workforce remains in agriculture. [15]

For the poor, lack of basic health, education and training opportunities mean that not only are they in a miserable condition today, there is not much hope for the future either. The official statistics below further support this statement.

1. 27.5 per cent of Indians live below the national income poverty line.
2. More than 60 per cent of women are chronically poor, as are 43 per cent of Scheduled Tribes and 36 per cent of Scheduled Caste groups.
3. More than 90 per cent of the overall workforce is employed in the informal economy; 96 per cent of women are in the informal economy.
4. 48.6 per cent of farmer households are in debt, and only 27 per cent have access to formal credit.
5. 296 million people are illiterate and 233 million are undernourished.
6. 254 per 100,000 live births is the maternal mortality rate and is an indicator not only of the quality of maternal health care services but also of the level of empowerment of women.[16]

Estimates shows that millions of people in India live in a state of abject poverty, without food, shelter, employment, health care and education. According to UNDP Report of 2010, Indian society is a highly inequitable society where the richest 10 percent consume 33.5 per cent of resources and the poorest 10 per cent get only 3.5 per cent of resources. Around 233 million people are chronically hungry. Around 51 per cent of the population does not have sustainable access to affordable essential drugs. Infant Mortality rate is 68 per 1000; under 5 child mortality rate is 93 per 1000; 26 per cent children are underweight; and 24 per cent of the population is undernourished. Maternal mortality ratio is 440 per 1,00,000 and 72 per cent of the population does not have access to improved sanitation.[17] It is a paradox to note that, India is the largest importer of arms[18] and spent Rs 193000 corers annually for defence.[19] The huge defence spending of India not only has an adverse effect on the scarce resource of India but also affect the military spending of other South Asian countries.

The Union Parliament adopted 86th Constitutional Amendment

whereby elementary education has been made fundamental right in the Constitution.[20] Despite the 86th Constitutional Amendment; around 35 per cent of the population is still illiterate. About 50 million children are out of school. Even where enrolment is high, the dropout rate is over 50 per cent by the time the students move over to high school. Gender Parity Index is 0.82. It means for every 1000 boys enrolled, there are 820 girls seeking admissions. The problem related to education and health would further aggravate with the gradual withdrawal of state from the education and health sector due to the compulsions of economic structural adjustment programme initiated as part of liberalisation, privatisation and globalisation process. (Suresh, 2009: 30)

In a democratic system human security assumes great significance. Since the support of the people is required for the government formation no political party can ignore human security issues. Again India is confronted by several internal security issues which are rooted in lack of development in certain regions and also lack of inclusive growth. The globalization process has also contributed towards the inclusion of human security issues in the national and international agenda. The awareness of the people regarding their own basic problems and the increased interaction among people across the manmade territorial borders as a result of the development in ICT, has also promoted the importance of human security in the security debates and action plan.

VI. India's Security: Policy Options

The prime responsibility of a nation state is to ensure security to its people and their property. Since each nation state is sovereign nations they have every right to decide about the means to be pursued to ensure security. The method or means followed by nations to ensure security often based on the domestic situations, especially its economic power. Generally economic powerful nations invest more on developing a superior defence force not only to ensure its security but also to extend security cover to its allies. The world history shows ample examples about this proposition.

Though the scientific and technological developments resulted in revolutionary changes in human life situations there is less change in the approach towards security. In international politics there are various approaches towards peace and security. Broadly these approaches can be classified as coercive means to ensure peace and security and non-coercive means. While the realist and neo realist theorist focuses on coercive methods others focus on mainly on non-coercive methods.

A quick glance into the history of international politics shows that there were various methods adopted by nation states to protect and promote their national interests. During the 19th century and early 20th century it was the policy of imperialism and colonialism. However with the end of Second World War and the establishment of the United Nations Organization marked the end to the policy of colonialism as a means to promote national interests. The cold war period witnessed the dominance of power politics in international politics. In fact international politics had become synonym with military power and its predominance. However without the use of military power, either conventional or nuclear weapons, the cold war has ended. The unexpected disappearance of discipline enforced by the super power rivalry and competitions on nation sates prompted at least one incident of violation of sovereignty and territorial integrity of a nation in the international system. The enthusiasm shown by the international community of nations under the collective security principle to nip in the very bud the revival of use of force to endanger the sovereignty and territorial integrity of nation was also a warning to all decision makers of nation states, especially the dictators who adopt war as an instrument of foreign policy.

Further the end of cold war marked the beginning of accelerated pace of globalization. The post-cold war period also witness some major alterations in the national security threat perception of nation states. The nontraditional threat to the security of nation states have become more grave, numerous and imminent than the traditional threat that emanates solely from other nation states. Among these threats international terrorism, global economic slowdown and global climate change are the serious and looming. A viable solution to these tribulations can be found only through collective efforts of all developed and developing, militarily strong and weak nations.

The modern states are welfare states and the welfare state concept envisages a minimum standard of living to all individuals. Though India is celebrating the 68th anniversary of its independence nearly one third of its population still lives in poverty and nearly forty per cent of the population are illiterate, the gap between rich and poor is alarmingly growing. The political equality was ensured with one man one vote, however social, economic and educational inequality is looming large in the Indian society. In a welfare state it is the responsibility of the government to ensure minimum standard of living to all. The failure on the part of the government to ensure people's security is gross violation of the constitution. Thus the threat to security emanates not only from external aggression but also from poor management of the scarce resources to ensure people's security or human security.

It is the responsibility of the government to frame policies to ensure people's security. While framing the policies both domestic and external, the security of the people should be the sole criterion. It is very difficult for the decision makers to take new course of action based on drastic amendments in the existing policies. India has to revisit its external policy under the changed international situation. Commensurate with changes in the international situation the defence policy also need reorientation. The futility of arms race and competitions are well reflected towards the end of cold war. Moreover the vertical and horizontal nuclear weapon proliferation makes the conventional arms built up as a means for the survival of international arms business establishments. In the post-cold war deeply interdependent world war as an instrument of foreign policy has lost its relevance. However a minimal force is required to wage limited war and to deter any military adventure from state or non-state actors across the land or maritime borders.

India's traditional security concerns were revolved round the threat from Pakistan, China and the US presence in the Indian Ocean. However, in the post-cold war period a major threat from Pakistan have only remote chance because of two major developments in the region. Pakistan's decision makers both military and civilian are well aware of the fact that they may not get any support which they had received in 1971 war, from their cold war defence ally, the US. Secondly since Pakistan becomes a nuclear weapon power, no major players at the international level or the UN would allow the outbreak of a nuclear war in South Asia. With regard to the threat from China, though there is an unresolved border problem, China may not initiate a 1962 type war with nuclear India due to nuclear deterrence. Here again the global players and the UN would not allow a nuclear war in Asia. And India's defence collaboration with the US especially with the signing of Indo US civilian nuclear agreement marked a sea change in Indo US relations. Thus in the post-cold war period India's traditional security concerns have undergone a discernible transformation, though the defence establishments in India pay least attention to these developments.

It appears that the best option before India is to focus more on human security issues than pure military security. Since the threat to security of the nation emanates mostly from non-state actors with the support of some nation states the cooperation of other actors in international system are required to address these issues. In the long run armament and arm race in the region is particularly detrimental to India both in terms of scarce resource use and also instability of the political system in the immediate neighbourhood having nuclear weapon power. In the present context it appears that India should focus more on addressing the human security concerns than on accelerating military built up in the region. This would enable India to solve most of the internal security issues by undertaking the various welfare measures to alleviate poverty and other human security issues. However the British colonial system entrenched strong bureaucratic and defence structure in India could easily resist any attempt to restructure the existing security policy by the political executive.

Notes

1. Liberal theory believes in global integration and the strategy towards integration, unlike the coercive means of realist is democratization; conflict resolution; and rule of law.
2. Critical constructivist school on security believes that security is a social construction. They emphasize the importance of social, cultural and historical factors, which leads to different actors construing similar events differently.
3. National Interests according to Hans J Morgenthau is defined in terms of national power.
4. Generally developed nations spent more on defence compared to the developing countries.
5. For a detailed analysis of foreign policy determinants see Suresh R *Foreign Policy and Human Rights: An Indian Perspective*. Madhav Books, Gurgaon, 2009
6. Realists argue that moral principles cannot be applied in the actions of the state.
7. The Indo Soviet Peace and Friendship Treaty of 1971 though not a defence treaty some provisions, especially article 9 are termed as components of a

defence treaty. Suresh R *Peace in the Indian Ocean: A South Asian Perspective*, Serials Publications, New Delhi 2012 p 46

8. In the post-cold war international order though the US is the sole super power, on all international issues such as international terrorism, economic meltdown, and environmental degradation the support of other nations are required for effective solution.

9. The Independent Commission on International Development Issues, North-South A Programme for survival, Cambridge,1980 p-9

10. The Independent Commission on Disarmament and Security Issues, Common Security A Blueprint for Survival 1982

11. The Commission on global Governance, Our Global Neighbourhood, Oxford University Press, New York, 1995 p 306

12. UNDP Report 1994, Oxford University Press, New York, 1994

13. Ibid.

14. Ibid.

15. UNDP Country Programme for India (2008-2012) page 2

16. **Ibid**

17. Ibid.

18. "India's imports of major weapons increased by 38 percent between 2002-2006 and 2007-11," **Stockholm International Peace Research Institute** (SIPRI) said **Asia tops other regions when it comes to weapon imports, according to a study released by the SIPRI** India is the world's largest recipient of arms while South Korea is second and Pakistan and China are tied in third place, says the Stockholm International Peace Research Institute (SIPRI) in a study on international arms transfers.

19. The Defence Minister of India stated that India's annual expenditure for Defence is Rupees 1,93,000 Crores see www.indiannavt.nic.in 21 Aug 2012

20. The 86th Constitution Amendment act came into force on 12/12/2002

References

1. Karl W Deutsch, (1989).*The Analysis of International Relations*, McGraw Hill, New Delhi

2. Suresh R (2011) India and Peace in the Indian Ocean: Imperatives for Human Security Approach in the Post Cold War Period, *Holistic Thought*, Vol X No 1&2, pp 124- 135

3. Suresh R (2009) *Foreign Policy and Human Rights: An Indian Perspective.* Madhav Books, Gurgaon,

4. Suresh R (2010) *India and the Present Global Order: A Security Perspective*, in Mohanan B Pillai (Ed.) *Foreign Policy of India Continuity and Change*, New Century Publications New Delhi

5. Kanti Bajpai (2003) The Idea of Human Security *International Studies* Vol. 40, pp 195- 228.

6. Kenneth Waltz (1979) *Theory of International Politics.* McGraw Hill. New York:

15 | The Changing Dimensions of Security and Emerging Nontraditional Threats in South Asia: A Human Security Perspective

Rakhee Viswambharan

Abstract

One of the major functions of nation states is to ensure security to its people from external threats. Modern nation states maintain a large defence force to deter any threat from other nation states. However, in the post cold war period the threat to the security of nation states also emanates from nontraditional sources. The nontraditional security issues includes the challenges to the survival and well-being of peoples and states that arise primarily out of nonmilitary sources, such as climate change, cross border environmental degradation and resource depletion, infectious diseases, natural disasters, irregular migration, food shortages, people smuggling, drug trafficking, and other forms of transnational crime. The South Asian countries need to develop multilateral responses to mitigate the challenges of nontraditional security issues through the regional mechanism of the SAARC. Though a good beginning has been made in certain areas like disaster management, yet geopolitical competition and lack of trust are obstructing the adoption of a multilateral approach to such nontraditional security challenges as transnational crime, drug trafficking, illegal migration, money-laundering and gun-running, and terrorism. The nontraditional security challenges also include climate change, cross border environmental degradation and resource depletion, and infectious diseases. The water security is another area where some instances of cooperation exist in the South Asian region. As in the global level, in the South Asian region also most of the nontraditional issues to security are transnational and therefore require a multilateral approach. In short, the existence of human security related nontraditional security issues pose a challenge as well as opportunity to the South Asian countries.

The challenge is to tackle these common transnational problems through multilateral approach. And the opportunity is to evolve a common strategy to address these problems. This paper is an attempt to examine the non-traditional security issues in South Asian region and the imperatives of regional cooperation to address these security issues especially in the context of changing dimensions of security.

I Security - The Changing Dimensions

It appears that in the post-cold war period the perception regarding security of nation states underwent a marked change. During the cold war period the developed and developing nations focused mainly on arms built-up to ensure the security of nation from the threat posed by potential rival nation states. The general belief was that if the nations are secure from external threat posed by other nation states the people living in that nation are also secure. Therefore during the cold war period national security was purely based on military security and nation states paid maximum attention to enhance their military power. Concomitantly military alliances, armament and arms race were the natural corollaries of such a state of affair. (Karl Deutsch, 1989: 182)

The end of cold war marked the beginning of new thinking on the concept of security. In the classical formulation, security is about how nation states use force to manage threats to their territorial integrity, their autonomy, and their domestic political order, primarily from other nation states. This classical national security formulation has been criticized on various grounds. A nation may be secure from the external military threat but that does not mean all people living in that nation are secure. The social economic and political orders prevalent in that nation have an implication on the security of the people. (Suresh R, 2011: 125) Thus the source of threat to the security of the people is not solely from other nations defence forces but also from within the nation. The system of government prevalent, the standard of living, the rights enjoyed by the people have a bearing on the security of people as well as security of nations. Thus the main referent of security includes not only the nation states but also the people living in the state.

The debates on security in the post-cold war period is centered mainly on the presuppositions about what security is, what is being secured, the causes of insecurity, and how best to address insecurity. (Kanti Bajpai,

2003: 195) International relations theorists and policy experts have varying perspectives on these questions, which have evolved and have had changing levels of acceptance over time. Realists and neo-realists emphasise the nation state as the central referent of security, both as the lens through which security is understood, as well as the tool by which security is best maintained or restored. (Hans J Morgenthau, 1983, 23; Kenneth Waltz, 1979: 31) Liberal theorists recognize a wider set of values embedded in the concept of the state and state security, in the methods and means to address insecurity, and the actors involved. The critical constructivist scholars understand that the interests and identities of nation states are themselves constructed by the distribution of ideas and interests within the state-based system and this shapes a state's security interests and how these are conceived, and in turn impacts upon the actions necessary to ensure security. Thus there are divergent views with regard to concept of security, whose security, that is whether the security of the nation or people, the causes of insecurity, and how to ensure security.

The Westphalia state system had made nation states as the basic unit in the international system. And nation states are sovereign and independent. Each nation decides their internal and external policies. The prime responsibility of a nation state is to promote its national interests.[1] The national interests of nation states are mainly to ensure peace, security and prosperity. However, they differ with regard to the means adopted to achieve these national interests. Some nations employ aggressive means and some peaceful methods.[2] And foreign policy of a nation is the means to achieve their respective national interests. Therefore, though the national interests of nation states are similar nations frame divergent foreign policy, which in turn is conditioned by the interplay of internal and external factors. Thus, the foreign policy changes in accordance with the transformations in the internal and external conditions. [3] Concomitantly the security policy of nations also changes.

It appears that in the post-cold war global system threat to security of peoples and nation states emanates largely from nontraditional sources. In this context the classical security paradigm which is based solely on military security fails to address the nontraditional security issues. This again demands a new approach to security in order to address the nontraditional threats which are not purely military in nature. Again since most of the nontraditional threats to security are transnational in nature they demand a multilateral effort form nation states.

The conceptual shift that has occurred after the end of the cold war is that security can be dealt with through cooperation rather than confrontation. Since the threat to the security of nations are not mainly from the threat posed by the military of other nation, and also the existence of nontraditional threats along with the transnational nature of these threats have necessitated cooperation of nation states on security matters. At present no nation, whatsoever powerful is in a position to resolve these security problems singlehandedly. All these factors point to need for cooperation of nations on security related issues.

However, the cooperation in security matters depends upon mutual trust, transparency, acceptance of global norms and relinquishing cold war based military power dominance and zero-sum approach to security. It requires a broader look at the concept of national interests. In order to address nontraditional security threats, dialogue, transparency, information sharing, capacity building, and confidence building measures are significant means. Again track II diplomacy assumes great significance in information sharing in the age of information and communication technology. Along with the government, the civil society organizations are also need to play a dominant role in international relations.

Another notable feature with regard to security is that since the cold war, the concept of security has become more and more institutionalized. At the national level each nation possesses military power to meet any threat to its national security from other nation states. Similarly at the international level the United Nations Security Council is mandated to maintain international peace and security even by adopting coercive means. The international mechanism established to meet the challenges to world peace in the aftermath of Second World War has become defunct to address the 21st century global problems. This is not only because of the changes in the nature of security threats but also due to the lack of representations to nations with high quantity of human resources in the global governance. It is essential to initiate democratic governance at the international level.

The existing international institutions are less capable of mitigating the global challenges posed by climate change, water, food, and energy security. Similarly the growing significance of non-state actors which are more powerful than the nation states in terms of resources and area of operation also demand new international regulatory mechanism. The domestic and international institutions need to further evolve and develop mechanisms to engage each other more adequately, in order to be better equipped to deal with these global challenges.

Thus in the 21st century the states are confronted with a number of new security challenges which necessitates a change in the way the states approached these challenges. As a result of the impact of globalization and consequently more interconnectedness of the world, any change in one part of the world affects the other. State failures are increasing as a result of ongoing globalization process which also poses a threat to the security of the nation as well as people. In this context it is necessary to define what constitutes a security issue today. Scholars have found that classical frameworks are not easily adapted to the contemporary security landscape since there exists a blurred boundary between human security and national security on the one hand and the national security and international security on the other. (Suresh R; 2012; 196)

II Nontraditional Security

Since the beginning of civilization, social or political unrest and destabilization has been considered in the context of physical threats. This perception is duly supported by a number of historical evidences. But some inevitable phenomena such as climate change establishes that security of any geographical boundary is not prone to traditional security threats only, but also the nontraditional security threats; that are not limited to any geographical demarcation.

The IPCC in 2007 listed different aspects of human life such as availability of water, food, health, and the fragile ecosystems as being potentially impacted by climate change. The scarcity and demand for water in the above mentioned areas, is likely to exacerbate the nontraditional security threat. The IPCC also stated that most of the disasters will be water related.[4] In order to understand the factual picture of nontraditional security threats, we can consider the example of hurricane Katrina in New Orleans, 2005, where thousands of people were displaced and around 1,800 died; and caused huge monetary losses. These nontraditional security threats in the form of disasters have been witnessed in the most populous geographical regions such as East Asia that was hit by Tsunami in 2004;

and, Florida that was hit by four hurricanes in one year. Moreover, heat waves in Europe killed 38,000 people in 2003 and almost 3 million North Koreans died between 1995 and 1997 due to famine. [5]

The concept of nontraditional security issues is still evolving and not defined precisely. However, there is a general agreement among scholars that the traditional concept of security, which focuses on inter-state relations, conflict and military issues, is too narrow to fully describe the security challenges of today. One of the common feature of the nontraditional security threats is that they are transnational and thus wider international cooperation are required to tackle these threats.

Traditional, Nontraditional, and Human Security

Type of Security	Referent Object	Responsibility to Protect	Possible Threats
Traditional Security	The State	The territorial Integrity and sovereignty of the State	Interstate War, Nuclear Proliferation
Nontraditional Security	• The State • Regional Organizations • International Organizations	The integrity of State and regions and whole world	• Climate change security • Water security • Natural disaster • Transnational terrorism • Energy security • Food security
Human Security	The Individual	The security of the Individual	Poverty, Disease, Natural Disaster, Violence, Landmines, Human Rights violations

The security discourse is dominated by the traditional state-centric paradigm which privileges the territorial defence of a country against armed attack from foreign countries. However most people in Asia a continent that counts for more than half of the world's population the greatest threats to security come from disease, hunger, environmental contamination, crime and localized violence. For some, a still greater threat may come from their own government itself, rather than from an 'external' adversary. The citizens of states that are 'secure' according to the concept of traditional security can be perilously insecure in terms of their everyday reality.

The nontraditional security issues has been defined as "Challenges to the survival and well-being of peoples and states that arise primarily out of nonmilitary sources, such as climate change, cross border environmental degradation and resource depletion, infectious diseases, natural disasters, irregular migration, food shortages, people smuggling, drug trafficking, and other forms of transnational crime". [6] Thus unlike traditional security threats which arise mainly from the defence forces of other nations, the nontraditional security threats arises from nonmilitary sources and demand a transnational approach to resolve it. Since the nontraditional threats are emerging more in number a new approach is to be evolved to address these security threats on a priority basis.

III Nontraditional Security issues in South Asia

From the nontraditional security perspective, the South Asian region faces challenges from water security, energy security and more importantly climate change security. It also includes infectious diseases natural disasters irregular migration people smuggling drug trafficking and transnational crime. The nature of nontraditional security challenges faced by South Asia may offer opportunities to change the existing security agenda, perhaps even subsuming traditional security concerns in the region. (Vinod Anand 2011: 31)

One of the notable features of nontraditional threat is that many of the challenges which have grown up understanding as nontraditional security challenges have now migrated and are being termed as traditional security threats, and it is difficult divide traditional and nontraditional security issues. Similarly the nontraditional security threats of tomorrow could themselves become sources of future traditional conflict if they are not effectively addressed today. Therefore it is important to address the nontraditional threat to security on a priority basis through multilateral approach.

Again many of the nontraditional threats facing the region are transnational in nature. For instance, it appears that the glacial melt in the Himalayas affects water supply throughout the region. Those cross-border issues merit a cross-border response. Similarly the problems such as transnational crimes and irregular migrations need to be tackled at the multilateral level.

IV Regional cooperation in South Asia

South Asia has numerous, long standing conflicts left over from history. In the last few years several other issues have been added to the portfolio of security issues. Economic development in South Asia is being threatened by burgeoning human security issues. Many security issues such as demography, economic security, environmental security, terrorism, etc., are issues requiring cooperation among countries of the region. Most states in South Asia are vulnerable to nontraditional security threats. South Asia lacks capabilities and mechanisms to deal with these issues.

So far as the human security is concerned, protections from crime, hunger, environmental hazards, disease, and economic security are very important. However, by absorbing nontraditional security threats into traditional threats reduces the value and coherence. Human security is very comprehensive which covers many aspects of security. However, a concept as broad as this can be used by policy makers with policy prioritization.

South Asian countries are routinely ravaged by floods, famines, hurricanes, pandemics and many other forms of natural and man-made disasters that take a heavy human toll. Floods in Pakistan in 2010, earthquake in India in 2011, Tsunami in India, Sri Lanka and Maldives in 2004, Hurricane Sidr in Bangladesh and Myanmar took thousands of lives. Yet, South Asian countries do not have a mechanism for dealing with natural disasters and human relief. They lack cooperative mechanisms to deal with these problems.

One of the major hurdles towards cooperation in South Asia is the India – Pakistan conflict embedded in the history of the two countries. It appears that the problem of military's stronghold and religious fundamentalism in Pakistan, forces Pakistan government to develop cold feet in wholeheartedly reciprocating India's offer of peace and friendship. This strengthens hardliners within India and complicates the process of normalization of relations between the two estranged neighbours, though geography, history and societal linkages bind them. The British colonial power created bureaucracy and defence establishments in the two countries never allow the political executive to resolve the existing bilateral issues amicably and devote their scarce resources for the welfare of people instead of arms buildup. [7]

South Asia, despite its high population and common culture is one of the most poorly connected regions in the world. This is because mutual mistrust has prevented countries of the region from giving priority to build multiple connectivity. Intra-regional trade and tourism is at a low level. Building this connectivity will go a long way in mitigating some of the human security challenges in South Asia.

The countries of the region can also cooperate in tackling the challenges of food, water and energy security. South Asia faces the huge challenge of feeding its billions over the next decades. Agriculture, fishing and forestry are the mainstays of food security. South Asian countries are suffering from energy deficits and the picture is becoming increasingly grim day by day. Climate change poses a major threat to South Asia. Yet, there is no mechanism among the countries of the region to come up with coordinated actions.

The South Asian countries need to develop multilateral responses to mitigate the challenges of nontraditional security issues through the regional mechanism of the SAARC. Though a good beginning has been made in certain areas like disaster management, yet geopolitical competition and lack of trust are obstructing the adoption of a multilateral approach to address such nontraditional security challenges as transnational crime, drug trafficking, illegal migration, money-laundering and gun-running, and terrorism. The nontraditional security challenges also include climate change, cross border environmental degradation and resource depletion, and infectious diseases. The water security is another area where some instances of cooperation exist in the South Asian region.

In short, the existence of human security related nontraditional security issues pose a challenge as well as opportunity to the South Asian countries. The challenge is to tackle these common transnational problems through multilateral approach by strengthening the existing regional organization. And the opportunity is to evolve a common strategy to address these human security related problems on a priority basis. It was well known during the cold war period that focus on state-centric military-based security had led to double insecurity: more state insecurity and jeopardized human security.

SAARC – An Institution for Regional Cooperation on Human Security issues

The SAARC provides a forum for discussing the human security and nontraditional security problems. Indeed many of these problems have been discussed in the SAARC forum. However no credible action plan exists. Institution building is important for the success of the cooperative security approach. Institutional platforms are required at the national, regional and international levels. At the same time, broad participation of governmental, non-governmental and civil society stakeholders in these institutions is important. The track-II dialogues serve a useful purpose in addressing the nontraditional threats to security.

If the human security related nontraditional issues go unattended for a long time and remain as a deficit of human security it would morphed into a situation of national security deficit. The security thinking should go beyond the political and planning horizon. It must begin to encompass the government, private enterprises, and civil society organizations. In short there must be a horizontal progression of things especially within the government.

The 17th SAARC summit, held in Addu, Maldives in November 2011, came up with some significant initiatives which might potentially address the human security challenges of the region by strengthening regional cooperation in critical areas. The SAARC summit declaration emphasised the importance of bridging differences and strengthening the institutions of regional cooperation. The event was notable because concurrently with the summit, the first summit of SAARC Forum was also held. This opens up the opportunity in the future to discuss some sensitive issues which might not be discussed at the formal summits. The summit directed the South Asia Forum to continue to work towards the development of the "Vision Statement" for South Asia on the goal and elements of a South Asian Economic Union. [8]

Conclusions

The nontraditional security issues includes the challenges to the survival and well-being of peoples and states that arise primarily out of nonmilitary sources, such as climate change, cross border environmental degradation and resource depletion, infectious diseases, natural disasters, irregular migration, food shortages, human trafficking, drug trafficking, and other forms of transnational crime. [9]

The South Asian countries need to develop multilateral responses to mitigate the challenges of nontraditional security issues through the regional mechanism of the SAARC. Though a good beginning has been made in certain areas like disaster management, yet geopolitical competition and lack of trust are obstructing the adoption of a multilateral approach to such nontraditional security challenges as transnational crime, drug trafficking, illegal migration, money-laundering and gun-running, and terrorism. The nontraditional security challenges also include climate change, cross border environmental degradation and resource depletion, and infectious diseases. The water security is another area where some instances of cooperation exist in the South Asian region. As in the global level, in the South Asian region also most of the nontraditional issues to security are transnational and therefore require a multilateral approach.

In short, the existence of human security related nontraditional security issues pose a challenge as well as opportunity to the South Asian countries. The challenge is to tackle these common transnational problems through multilateral approach. And the opportunity is to evolve a common strategy to address these problems. It appears that focus on state-centric military-based security may lead to double insecurity: more state insecurity and jeopardizing human security. One of the major hurdles towards cooperation in South Asia is the India – Pakistan conflict embedded in the history of the two countries. The British colonial power based bureaucracy and defence establishments in the two countries never allow the political executive to resolve the existing bilateral issues amicably and devote their scarce resources for the welfare of people instead of arms buildup. [10] Even the initiative taken by the new government towards better neighbourly relation with all South Asian countries including Pakistan was also thwarted by the defence establishment in Pakistan.

The cooperation in security matters depends upon mutual trust, transparency, acceptance of global norms and relinquishing cold war based military power dominance and zero-sum approach to security. It requires a broader look at the concept of national interests. In order to address nontraditional security threats dialogue, transparency, information sharing, capacity building, and confidence building measures are significant means. Again track II diplomacy assumes great significance in information sharing in the age of information and communication technology. Along with the government, the civil society organizations are also need to play a dominant role in international relations.

Notes

1. National Interests according to Hans J Morgenthau is defined in terms of national power.

2. Generally developed nations spent more on defence compared to the developing countries.

3. For a detailed analysis of foreign policy determinants see Suresh R *Foreign Policy and Human Rights: An Indian Perspective*. Madhav Books, Gurgaon, 2009

4. Report of Intergovernmental Panel on Climate Change, IPCC 2007

5. Ibid.

6. Caballero-Anthony, Mely: Non-traditional Security and Multilateralism in Asia: Reshaping the Contours of Regional Security Architecture? The Stanley Foundation Policy Analysis Brief, June 2007.

7. India's imports of major weapons increased by 38 percent between 2002-2006 and 2007-11, Stockholm International Peace Research Institute (SIPRI) said Asia tops other regions when it comes to weapon imports, according to a study released by the SIPRI India is the world's largest recipient of arms.

8. The Hindu dated 2 Nov 2011

9. The Defence Minister of India while addressing the Unified Commanders Conference in New Delhi on 30 April 2013 stated that the contemporary concept of security encompasses not merely military threats but also cyber-attacks, insurgencies, organized trans-border crimes, pandemics and natural disasters. The Hindu dated 01 May 2013.

10. The Defence Minister of India stated that India's annual expenditure for Defence is Rupees 1,93,000 Crores see www.indiannavy.nic.in 21 Aug2011.

References

Karl W Deutsch, (1989). *The Analysis of International Relations*, McGraw Hill, New Delhi

Suresh R (2011) India and Peace in the Indian Ocean: Imperatives for Human Security Approach in the Post Cold War Period, *Holistic Thought*, Vol. X No 1&2

Suresh R (2009) *Foreign Policy and Human Rights: An Indian Perspective*. Madhav Books, Gurgaon,

Suresh R(2010) *India and the Present Global Order: A Security Perspective*, in Mohanan B Pillai (Ed.) *Foreign Policy of India Continuity and Change*, New Century Publications New Delhi

Kanti Bajpai (2003) The Idea of Human Security *International Studies* Vol. 40,

Hans J Morgenthau (1983) Politics among Nations: The Struggle for Power and Peace, McGraw Hill. New York. Kenneth Waltz (1979) Theory of International Politics. McGraw Hill. New York.

Suresh R (2012) Human Security in India: Problems and Policy Options, *International Journal of South Asian Studies*, Vol 5 No.2

Vinod Anand (2011) Non-traditional Threats: An Analytical Perspective from South Asia in Klaus Lange (ed.) The Future of Security, Hanns-Seidel-Stiftung E.V., Munich.

Index

A

A B Vajpayee 33

Afghanistan 8, 16, 31, 41, 94, 104, 107, 115, 120, 145, 154-168, 171, 215

Aircraft Carrier 16, 168, 171

  INS Arihant 16, 171

  INS Vikramaditya 171

Aksai Chin 73

Al-Qaeda 155, 167

Al-Shabab 223

Andaman and Nicobar 188, 192, 193, 213, 214

Antarctica 9, 42

Anthropocene 8, 42

Anti Piracy Measures 179

A.Q. Khan 100, 104

Arthashastra 28, 58, 146

B

Bajarang Dal 62

Balkanisation 47

Balkanize India Theory 13, 66, 67

Bandung Conference 148

Batang La 72

Best Management Practices 180

Bhabha Atomic Research Centre 129, 187, 215

Biological Perspective 5, 40

Biological warfare 9, 43

Brahmaputra 73

Brasstacks Crisis 108, 111

B Vivekanandan v, vii, 13

C

Caliphates 44

Capitalist bloc 2, 245

Cavalry battle 46

Central Intelligence Agency 129

Chabahar 157

Chernobyl 10, 48

China Institute of International Strategic Studies (CIISS) 71

China Pakistan Economic Corridor 177

Chumbi Valley 72

Civil Nuclear Cooperation 137, 142

Coastal security 3, 187, 203-205, 209

Coast Guard Act 203

Cold War 37, 53, 64, 78, 117, 120, 122, 125, 254, 268

Communist bloc 2, 245

Comprehensive Test Ban Treaty 85, 130, 143

Condoleezza Rice 33

Confidence Building Measures 77

Contain China Theory 13, 66-68

Council for Security Cooperation in the Asia Pacific 206

Credible Minimum Deterrence 132

Credible nuclear deterrent 30

C. Vinodan v, vii, 90

D

Dalai Lama 26, 58, 71, 73, 74, 148

Defence Research and Development Organisation 129, 190

Deng Xiaoping 69, 70

Department of Atomic Energy 128, 129, 135, 142, 215

Destabilize India Theory 13, 66, 67

Devender Sharma vi, vii, 15, 144

Durand Line 155, 159

E

Economic security 6, 8, 41, 263

European Union 201

Exclusive Economic Zone 173, 175, 176, 180, 184, 193, 197, 199, 213, 218, 219, 220, 221

F

Federal Administrated Tribal Areas 155, 159, 160

Feroz Haisan Khan 98

Fissile Material Control Treaty 130, 132

Food security 5, 6, 8, 11, 38, 40-41, 63, 261, 264

Fukushima 10, 48

G

Galle conference 181

Gandhian 28, 29

Genghis Khan 46

Global climate change 2, 6, 8, 19, 46, 241, 243, 245, 248, 251

Gujral Doctrine 30, 32

Gulf of Kutch 196

Gwadar 76

H

Hainan Island 75

Haiti 8, 41

Hambantota port 76

Haqqani group 155

Harish K. Thakur v, vii

Hiroshima 10, 48, 84

Hobbesian state 53, 161

Homo sapiens 9, 42

Hu Jintao 70, 73, 74

Human security 3, 18, 19, 20, 21, 241, 242-243, 246-248, 250, 252, 253, 256, 260, 263-266

Hurricane Katrina 11, 48, 49

Index

Hyde Act 136

I

Indian Ocean Region 182, 184, 225

India's Nuclear Doctrine 131, 138, 141

   India's Credible Minimum Deterrence 132

   No First Use 133, 142

India's Nuclear Policy v, 14, 122, 123, 141

   Historical Context 123

India's Three stage nuclear program 126

India-US relations 37

Indira Doctrine 30, 32

Indira Gandhi 32-34, 36-37, 86-87, 122, 126-128

Indo-pacific 37

Indo-Sino relations 76

Indo-US nuclear agreement 99

Indo-US Nuclear Deal v, 14, 134, 139

Industrial Revolution 10, 48

International Atomic Energy Agency 15, 104, 106, 128, 134-136, 138

International Maritime Organisation 179

Irish Potato Famine 45

Iron Curtain Theory 13, 66, 67

J

Jawaharlal Nehru vii, 60, 83-85, 89, 122, 124, 210

Jiang Jiamin 70

Jiang Zemin 70

Jihadi ideology 4, 36, 38

K

Kanti Bajpai 85, 96, 114, 244, 255, 257, 268

Kargil conflict 109, 202

Kargil Review Committee 204

Kargil War 103

Kautilya 28, 58, 146

Khyber Pass 202

Kosovo 47

L

Lakshadweep Island 192, 223

Lashkar-e-Toiba 95

Lippmann 54

LTTE 94, 176, 196, 204

M

Madrassas 26

Magna Carta 44

Malacca Straits 174

Manmohan Singh 32-36, 61, 135, 136, 140

Maoist 25, 36, 94

Maoists 17, 186

Marine commandos 204

Maritime domain awareness 18, 190, 224

Maritime security 3, 16-17, 21, 171, 189, 190, 195, 198, 201, 204, 205-207, 214, 216, 218, 221, 224, 226

Maritime Silk Route 177

Maritime Terror 186

Maritime Terrorism 205, 228

McMahon Line 69, 72-73, 77, 84, 147

Military Operations Other Than War 175

Missile Technology Control Regime 134, 138

Modi Doctrine 30, 39

Mohanan Bhaskaran Pillai vii, 4, 25

Morarji Desai 86-87, 128

Mujahidins 17, 186

Mukund Narvekar vi, viii, 17, 192

Multiethnic groups 3, 245

N

Nagasaki 10, 48

Nanda Kishor M S v, vii, 50

Narasimha Rao 32-35, 61

Narendra Modi 33-35, 62, 155, 164, 191, 236

National Counter Terrorism Centre 18, 230, 232, 233, 234, 235, 236, 237, 238

National Oil Spill Disaster Contingency Plan 174

National security 1, 3, 4, 11, 12, 19, 25, 28-31, 36, 50, 54–64, 97-98, 109, 126, 132, 182, 190, 197, 214, 218, 221, 231, 241, 243, 244, 248, 251, 257, 259, 260, 265

NATO 16, 74, 154, 155, 156, 157, 158, 159, 160, 162, 165

Nawaz Sharif 105, 156, 158, 159, 165

Naxalites 17, 94, 186

NEFA 73

Nehruvian 28-29, 31-32, 34-35, 59-60, 124

Neo-liberalism 32-33, 35, 38

Neo-realists 1, 244, 258

No First Use 133, 142

Non-Proliferation Treaty 84, 85, 112, 130, 135, 136

Non State Actors 2, 11, 14, 18-19, 63, 90, 94, 106, 107, 172, 193, 208, 212, 216, 218, 219, 220, 225, 242-243, 245, 252-253, 259

North Waziristan 26, 157, 159

Nuclear bombs 9, 43

Nuclear Damage Act 15, 138

Nuclear Non-Proliferation Act 136, 137

Nuclear Suppliers Group 15, 40, 134, 135, 136, 137, 138, 142, 143, 152, 232, 237

Nuclear terrorism 105, 106, 107

O

Oil and Natural Gas Corporation 198

One China Theory 13, 66, 67

Operation Enduring Freedom 155, 160, 162

Index

Operation Pawan 204

Operation Swan 204

Operation Tasha 204

Operation Vijay 58

Osama bin Laden 158

Osirak nuclear plant 98

Ottomans 47

P

Pakhtunistan 16, 154, 155

Panchsheel 31, 69, 148

Peter R. Laroy 98

Poison gas 9, 43

Pokhran II 114, 125, 150

Port of Sudan 75

Pyrenees 9, 43

R

Rajesh Kuniyil v, vii, 14, 122

Rakhee Viswambharan vi, viii, 20, 256

Rann of Kutch 193

Realists 1, 244, 253, 258

Research and Analysis Wing 187, 235

R S Vasan vi, viii, 16, 171

S

SAARC 20, 30, 33, 58, 156, 182, 256, 264, 265, 266

Sarajevo 47

Sea Lines of Communication 172, 173, 208

Shimla Conference 77

Simla Conference 69

Sir Creek 193

Social security 5, 6, 8, 40, 41, 54

Somalia 8, 41, 76, 175, 179, 221, 222, 223, 224

South China Sea 74, 75, 76, 78, 178, 181, 185, 189, 203

S. Sathis Chandran v, vii, 5

Stephen Cohen 85

Stephen Kappes 156

Stockholm International Peace Research Institute 151, 254, 267

Straits of Hormuz 172, 175, 187

Straits of Malacca 172

Strategic autonomy 5, 28, 29, 30, 31, 34, 35, 36, 38, 130

Strategic culture 28

  Gandhian 28, 29

  Nehruvian 28-29, 31-32, 34-35, 59-60, 124

Strategic Petroleum reserve 174

Strategic Thinking v, 4, 25, 139

String of Pearls Theory 13, 66, 67

Sudhir Singh vi, vii, 16, 154

Sumdorong Chu 73

Sunni radicalism 25, 26, 36

Suresh R vi, viii

T

Taliban 16, 26, 94, 154-156, 158-160, 162-167

Tawang 73, 74

Thar Desert 110

The String of Pearls 75-76

Transnational Jihadi terrorism 206

U

Uighurs 163

Ullman 55, 65

Unnikrishnan G vi, viii, 18, 230

Utopianism 59

V

Ved Prakash Sharma vi, vii, 15, 144

Vibhuti Singh Shekhawat vi, viii, 17, 186

Viloent Non State Actors 172

W

Wahabi 26

Westphalia 2, 244, 258

WMD proliferation 135

Wolfers 54, 55, 56, 59, 65

World Customs Organization 201

X

Xinjiang 69, 94, 163

Z

Zhou En Lai 69, 70

Zia-ul-Haq 86

www.ingramcontent.com/pod-product-compliance
Lightning Source LLC
Chambersburg PA
CBHW071358160426
42811CB00111B/2235/J